# Evaluating Sex Trafficking Victim's Lifespan

Elmer S. Putnam

This research is an original approach that applies industrial engineering and operations research tools to the sociological problem of sex trafficking victimization. Such an approach enables quantitative evaluation of the impacts on an individual's lifetime by anti-trafficking efforts and public policies.

A fully interconnected, lifetime model for the experience of sex trafficking victimization is defined as the result of a comprehensive review of literature. Beginning with victimization risk, the defined model is an anticipatory tool to understand the incidences and consequences to individuals during their lifetime. This research develops the model further into a Discrete-Time Markov Chain (DTMC) with definitions of variable-form calculations, as well as demonstration of calculation and sensitivity analysis on a published case study dataset. Open-source Decision Support Systems (DSSs) are also presented to aid with dataset evaluation.

Several theoretical and applied results were achieved through this work. Parameters evaluated included: expected time in each state, life expectancy, probability of transition to defined states, as well as maximum likelihood of presence in a state. Of particular significance in the sensitivity analysis results is the importance of initial victimization risk and the likelihood of intervention for magnitude of impact on the lifetime experiences.

The model, DTMC definition, DSSs, and overall approach to analysis supports ongoing considerations towards resource allocation and public policy. Guidelines for future research are presented.

© Copyright

# TABLE OF CONTENTS

**LIST OF TABLES** ..................................................................................................................

**LIST OF FIGURES** ................................................................................................................

**LIST OF ACRONYMS** ..........................................................................................................

**CHAPTER 1** ..........................................................................................................................1

**INTRODUCTION** ..................................................................................................................1

    1.1 Trafficking Prevalence ..................................................................................................1

    1.2 Human Lifetime Experience ..........................................................................................2

    1.3 Sex Trafficking Victimization Experience ....................................................................4

    1.4 Research Objectives .......................................................................................................4

    1.5 Research Organization ...................................................................................................4

**CHAPTER 2** ..........................................................................................................................6

**LITERATURE REVIEW** ......................................................................................................6

    2.1 Research Pillars ..............................................................................................................6

        2.1.1    Markov Chains and Criminal Activity ............................................................13

        2.1.2    Markov Chains and Human Trafficking ..........................................................15

        2.1.3    Markov Chains and Sex Trafficking ................................................................15

        2.1.4    Operations Research and Sex Trafficking .......................................................15

        2.1.5    Markov Chains and Lifetime Experience ........................................................19

        2.1.6    Markov Chains, Lifetime Experience and Criminal Activity .........................21

        2.1.7    Markov Chains, Lifetime Experience and Human Trafficking ......................23

        2.1.8    Markov Chains, Lifetime Experience and Sex Trafficking ............................23

Table of Contents—continued

2.1.9 Operations Research, Lifetime Experience and Sex Trafficking ............23

2.1.10 Lifetime Experience and Sex Trafficking ............26

2.1.11 Operations Research and Lifetime Experience ............30

2.1.12 Operations Research, Lifetime Experience and Criminal Activity ............31

2.1.13 Operations Research, Lifetime Experience and Human Trafficking ............33

2.1.14 Lifetime Experience and Human Trafficking ............34

2.1.15 Lifetime Experience and Criminal Activity ............35

2.1.16 Lifetime Experience ............35

2.1.17 Research Pillars Summary ............38

2.2 Victimization Stages ............40

2.2.1 The General Lifetime Experience Model ............40

2.2.2 Macro Victimization Stages ............41

2.2.3 Identifying Micro Stages within Macro Victimization Literature ............47

2.2.4 Micro Victimization Stages ............48

2.2.5 Flow Among States ............52

2.3 Anti-trafficking Approaches ............53

2.3.1 '4P Paradigm' ............54

2.3.2 'Nordic' Model (a.k.a. Swedish Model) ............54

2.3.3 Research Contributions towards Policy ............55

2.4 Research Significance ............55

2.5 Research Assumptions ............56

2.6 Literature Review Summary ............58

Table of Contents—continued

**CHAPTER 3** .................................................................................................................... 63

**METHODOLOGY** ........................................................................................................... 63

    3.1 Lifetime Model of the Sex Trafficking Victimization Experience ....................... 64

    3.2 Modelling Entity ................................................................................................... 65

    3.3 Model Validation .................................................................................................. 65

        3.3.1    Survivor Case Studies ............................................................................ 65

        3.3.2    Expert Validation ................................................................................... 67

    3.4 Preparing the Markov Model ............................................................................... 67

        3.4.1    States and Transitions ............................................................................ 70

        3.4.2    Probability Transition Matrix ............................................................... 71

        3.4.3    The User .................................................................................................. 73

    3.5 Markov Model Calculations ................................................................................ 74

        3.5.1    Expected Time in Each State Before Absorption ............................... 74

        3.5.2    Probability of Transition in n-Steps Calculations ............................... 75

        3.5.3    Expected Number of Steps Before Absorption ................................... 76

        3.5.4    Calculation Variations with Probability of Transition in n-Steps ..... 76

        3.5.5    Probability Victimization Begins Between Ages $a_i$ and $a_{ii}$ ............ 77

        3.5.6    Probability of Visiting State j before State k ....................................... 77

        3.5.7    Sensitivity Analysis ................................................................................ 78

    3.6 Case Study ............................................................................................................ 82

    3.7 Microsoft Excel® Tool ......................................................................................... 82

    3.8 Policies for Impact ................................................................................................ 87

Table of Contents—continued

3.8 Methodology Summary ........................................................................................................ 89

**CHAPTER 4** .................................................................................................................................. 90

**RESULTS, ANALYSIS, AND DISCUSSION** ............................................................................ 90

    4.1 Case Study Background ...................................................................................................... 90

    4.2 Assumptions ........................................................................................................................ 91

        4.2.1    Step Size ................................................................................................................ 91

        4.2.2    Life Expectancy ..................................................................................................... 91

        4.2.3    Monthly risk of death ............................................................................................ 92

        4.2.4    Transition Probabilities D, F, and K ..................................................................... 93

    4.3 DTMC Transition Probabilities .......................................................................................... 93

    4.4 Initial Testing Framework .................................................................................................. 95

        4.4.1    Initial Results – Expected Duration in Each State, Life Expectancy ................... 96

        4.4.2    Initial Results – Probability of Transition in n-Steps ........................................... 96

    4.6 Sensitivity Analysis for Base Case: Scenario 1 - $S_{Liz}$(Low,Low) ....................................... 104

        4.6.1    Sensitivity Analysis Organization ....................................................................... 104

        4.6.2    Sensitivity Analysis – Approach 1 (Increments of 20%) .................................... 107

        4.6.3    Sensitivity Analysis – Approach 2 (Increments of 0.0002) ................................ 131

        4.6.4    Monte Carlo Simulation Background ................................................................. 148

        4.6.5    Sensitivity Analysis – Approach 3 (±60% Variability) ...................................... 151

        4.6.6    Sensitivity Analysis – Approach 4 (±0.0006 Variability) ................................... 162

    4.7 Implications of Analysis for Anti-Trafficking Interests ................................................... 173

    4.8 Decision Support System (DSS) ....................................................................................... 175

Table of Contents—continued

    4.8.1    Background .................................................................................................... 175

    4.8.2    Research DSS ................................................................................................ 176

    4.8.3    Research User Guide ..................................................................................... 178

**CHAPTER 5 ................................................................................................................................ 179**

**CONCLUSIONS AND FUTURE RESEARCH .......................................................................... 179**

    5.1 Conclusions for Objective 1 ................................................................................... 179

    5.2 Conclusions for Objective 2 ................................................................................... 180

    5.3 Conclusions for Objective 3 ................................................................................... 183

    5.4 Conclusions for Anti-Trafficking & Policy-Making Communities ........................ 183

    5.5 Future Work ............................................................................................................ 184

# LIST OF TABLES

1: Definitions of Operations Research, Social, and Problem (Merriam-Webster, 2020) ............................................. 1

2: Definitions of "Lifetime" and "Experience" (Merriam-Webster, 2020) ................................................................. 3

3: Experience 'Type' Illustrations ................................................................................................................................. 3

4: Term Definitions for Literature Review .................................................................................................................. 9

5: Numerical Notations of Research Components ..................................................................................................... 11

6: Review of Research Pillar References ................................................................................................................... 11

7: Markov Methods used by Category 1 Researchers ............................................................................................... 15

8: Markov Methods used by Category 5 Researchers ............................................................................................... 20

9: Markov Methods used by Category 6 Researchers ............................................................................................... 22

10: Definitions of the "4Ps" (Konrad et al., 2017) ..................................................................................................... 54

11: Selected Case Studies in terms of Framework, Validation of Framework ......................................................... 66

12: State Identification ............................................................................................................................................... 71

13: Transition Definitions .......................................................................................................................................... 71

14: Select Transition Probabilities for Sensitivity Analysis, Anti-Trafficking Perspective .................................... 79

15: Impact of Factored Select Transition Probability Changes ................................................................................ 82

16: A Validated Account of Ms. Liz Williamson's Lived Sex Trafficking Experiences ......................................... 91

17: Initial Testing Framework and Naming Convention, Base Case ....................................................................... 95

18: Initial Results for Expected Duration in Each State, Life Expectancy (months) .............................................. 96

19: Maximum Probabilities of Transition in n-Steps for State 3, State 5 ................................................................ 96

20: Probability of Transition to each State in n-Steps starting in General Population, Month-by-Month ............ 98

21: Rate of Change in n-Step Probability of Transition from General Population, Month-by-Month ................ 101

22: Significant n-Step Probability Calculations Starting in General Population, Month-by-Month ................... 103

23: Summary of Maintaining Sum of Departing Transition Probability Requirement ......................................... 104

24: Structure for Sensitivity Analysis, 3-Tier Organization ................................................................................... 106

25: Sensitivity Analysis Output – B at 20% ............................................................................................................ 107

26: Sensitivity Analysis Output – F at 20% ............................................................................................................ 110

27: Sensitivity Analysis Output – I at 20% ............................................................................................................. 113

List of Tables—continued

28: Sensitivity Analysis Output – L at 20% .................................................................................................. 116

29: Sensitivity Analysis Output – M at 20% ................................................................................................. 119

30: Summary of Comparative BFILM Sensitivity Analysis, 20% Increment ........................................... 131

31: Sensitivity Analysis Output – B at 0.0002 .............................................................................................. 132

32: Sensitivity Analysis Output – F at 0.0002 .............................................................................................. 134

33: Sensitivity Analysis Output – I at 0.0002 ............................................................................................... 136

34: Sensitivity Analysis Output – L at 0.0002 .............................................................................................. 137

35: Sensitivity Analysis Output – M at 0.0002 ............................................................................................. 138

36: Summary of Comparative BFILM Sensitivity Analysis, 0.0002 Increment ....................................... 148

37: Summary of Figure 56 through Figure 62 Sensitivity Results (BFILM ± 60%) ................................ 162

38: Summary of Figure 71 through Figure 77 Sensitivity Results (BFILM ± 0.0006) ............................ 173

39: General policy-related observations from current research ............................................................... 174

40: Case Study Base Case Results for Expected Time, Maximum Probability, and n-Step Transition Probabilities 182

# LIST OF FIGURES

1: Research Pillars ..................................................................................................................7

2: Stochastic Process Flow Chart (Mubayi et al., 2019) ........................................................8

3: Literature Review Map .....................................................................................................10

4: Graph of Cited Literature Counts (derived from results of Table 6) ................................13

5: General Lifetime Experience Model ................................................................................40

6: Sex Trafficking Victimization Lifetime Experience Model – Macro ...............................41

7: "Potential influences throughout the lifespan of adverse childhood experiences" (Felitti et al., 1998) ...............42

8: Components of Macro Victimization Stages ....................................................................47

9: Lifetime Experience Model of Sex Trafficking Victimization .........................................64

10(a-b): Development of the Lifetime Experience of Sex Trafficking Victimization Model ...................68

11(a-b): Development of the Lifetime Experience of Sex Trafficking Victimization Model ...................69

12(a-b): Development of the Lifetime Experience of Sex Trafficking Victimization Model ...................70

13: Sex Trafficking Victimization Experience Model (model previously defined) ..............80

14: Microsoft Excel® Tool – Inputs .....................................................................................84

15: Microsoft Excel® Tool – Outputs (Expected Time) ......................................................85

16: Microsoft Excel® Tool – Outputs (Probability of Transition) ......................................86

17: Sex Trafficking Victimization Experience Model (previously defined) ........................88

18: U.S.A. Female Annual Risk of Death (SSA.gov, 2019) .................................................92

19: Division of Victimization versus Non-victimization Duration During Individual's Lifetime, Transition Probability B Sensitivity Analysis (20%) ....................................109

20: Division of Victimization versus Non-victimization Duration During Individual's Lifetime, Transition Probability F Sensitivity Analysis (20%) ....................................111

21: Division of Victimization versus Non-victimization Duration During Individual's Lifetime, Transition Probability I Sensitivity Analysis (20%) .....................................114

22: Division of Victimization versus Non-victimization Duration During Individual's Lifetime, Transition Probability L Sensitivity Analysis (20%) ....................................117

23: Division of Victimization versus Non-victimization Duration During Individual's Lifetime, Transition Probability M Sensitivity Analysis (20%) ...................................120

## List of Figures—continued

24: Impact of BFILM changes on Expected Time in State 1, 20% Increments ..................................................... 121

25: Impact of BFILM changes on Expected Time in State 2, 20% Increments ..................................................... 122

26: Impact of BFILM changes on Expected Time in State 3, 20% Increments ..................................................... 123

27: Impact of BFILM changes on Expected Time in State 4, 20% Increments ..................................................... 124

28: Impact of BFILM changes on Expected Time in State 5, 20% Increments ..................................................... 125

29: Impact of BFILM changes on Maximum Probability of Being in State 3, 20% Increments .................................. 126

30: Impact of BFILM changes on Maximum Probability of Being in State 5, 20% Increments .................................. 127

31: Impact of BFILM changes on Expected Lifespan, 20% Increments ............................................................... 128

32: Impact of BFILM changes on Maximum Likelihood of Transition, 20% Increments ........................................ 130

33: Division of Victimization versus Non-victimization Duration During Individual's Lifetime, Transition Probability B Sensitivity Analysis (0.0002) ..................................................................................................... 133

34: Division of Victimization versus Non-victimization Duration During Individual's Lifetime, Transition Probability F Sensitivity Analysis (0.0002) ..................................................................................................... 135

35: Division of Victimization versus Non-victimization Duration During Individual's Lifetime, Transition Probability I Sensitivity Analysis (0.0002) ....................................................................................................... 136

36: Division of Victimization versus Non-victimization Duration During Individual's Lifetime, Transition Probability L Sensitivity Analysis (0.0002) ..................................................................................................... 138

37: Division of Victimization versus Non-victimization Duration During Individual's Lifetime, Transition Probability M Sensitivity Analysis (0.0002) .................................................................................................... 139

38: Impact of BFILM changes on Expected Time in State 1, 0.0002 Increments ................................................. 140

39: Impact of BFILM changes on Expected Time in State 2, 0.0002 Increments ................................................. 141

40: Impact of BFILM changes on Expected Time in State 3, 0.0002 Increments ................................................. 142

41: Impact of BFILM changes on Expected Time in State 4, 0.0002 Increments ................................................. 142

42: Impact of BFILM changes on Expected Time in State 5, 0.0002 Increments ................................................. 143

43: Impact of BFILM changes on Maximum Probability of Being in State 3, 0.0002 Increments ......................... 144

44: Impact of BFILM changes on Maximum Probability of Being in State 5, 0.0002 Increments ......................... 144

45: Impact of BFILM changes on Expected Lifespan, 0.0002 Increments ........................................................... 145

46: Impact of BFILM changes on Maximum Likelihood of Transition, 0.0002 Increments .................................. 147

## List of Figures—continued

47: Preparation for Monte Carlo Simulation and Sensitivity Analysis ................................................... 150

48: Collection of Crystal Ball output for Expected Time in State 1 (BFILM ± 60%) ............................. 152

49: Collection of Crystal Ball output for Expected Time in State 2 (BFILM ± 60%) ............................. 153

50: Collection of Crystal Ball output for Expected Time in State 3 (BFILM ± 60%) ............................. 154

51: Collection of Crystal Ball output for Expected Time in State 4 (BFILM ± 60%) ............................. 155

52: Collection of Crystal Ball output for Expected Time in State 5 (BFILM ± 60%) ............................. 156

53: Stacked Bar Chart of Results for Expected Time in States 1, 3, and 5 (BFILM ± 60%) ................... 157

54: Collection of Crystal Ball output for Maximum Probability being in State 3 (BFILM ± 60%) ......... 158

55: Collection of Crystal Ball output for Maximum Probability being in State 5 (BFILM ± 60%) ......... 159

56: Crystal Ball sensitivity output for Expected Time in State 1 (BFILM ± 60%) .................................. 160

57: Crystal Ball sensitivity output for Expected Time in State 2 (BFILM ± 60%) .................................. 160

58: Crystal Ball sensitivity output for Expected Time in State 3 (BFILM ± 60%) .................................. 160

59: Crystal Ball sensitivity output for Expected Time in State 4 (BFILM ± 60%) .................................. 161

60: Crystal Ball sensitivity output for Expected Time in State 5 (BFILM ± 60%) .................................. 161

61: Crystal Ball sensitivity output for Maximum Probability of being in State 3 (BFILM ± 60%) ......... 161

62: Crystal Ball sensitivity output for Maximum Probability of being in State 5 (BFILM ± 60%) ......... 161

63: Collection of Crystal Ball output for Expected Time in State 1 (BFILM ± 0.0006) ......................... 163

64: Collection of Crystal Ball output for Expected Time in State 2 (BFILM ± 0.0006) ......................... 164

65: Collection of Crystal Ball output for Expected Time in State 3 (BFILM ± 0.0006) ......................... 165

66: Collection of Crystal Ball output for Expected Time in State 4 (BFILM ± 0.0006) ......................... 166

67: Collection of Crystal Ball output for Expected Time in State 5 (BFILM ± 0.0006) ......................... 167

68: Stacked Bar Chart of Results for Expected Time in States 1, 3, and 5 (BFILM ± 0.0006) ............... 168

69: Collection of Crystal Ball output for Maximum Probability being in State 3 (BFILM ± 0.0006) ..... 169

70: Collection of Crystal Ball output for Maximum Probability being in State 5 (BFILM ± 0.0006) ..... 170

71: Crystal Ball sensitivity output for Expected Time in State 1 (BFILM ± 0.0006) ............................. 171

72: Crystal Ball sensitivity output for Expected Time in State 2 (BFILM ± 0.0006) ............................. 171

## List of Figures—continued

73: Crystal Ball sensitivity output for Expected Time in State 3 (BFILM ± 0.0006) ............... 171

74: Crystal Ball sensitivity output for Expected Time in State 4 (BFILM ± 0.0006) ............... 172

75: Crystal Ball sensitivity output for Expected Time in State 5 (BFILM ± 0.0006) ............... 172

76: Crystal Ball sensitivity output for Maximum Probability of being in State 3 (BFILM ± 0.0006) ............... 172

77: Crystal Ball sensitivity output for Maximum Probability of being in State 5 (BFILM ± 0.0006) ............... 173

78: Screenshot of Website Input Page (http://siddharthc30.pythonanywhere.com/) ............... 176

79: Screenshot of Website Input Page (http://siddharthc30.pythonanywhere.com/) ............... 177

80: Screenshot of Website Output Page (http://siddharthc30.pythonanywhere.com/) ............... 178

# LIST OF ACRONYMS

| | |
|---|---|
| 4Ps | Prevention, Protection, Prosecution, Partnership |
| AIDS | Acquired Immunodeficiency Syndrome |
| CSE | Commercial Sexual Exploitation |
| CST | Child Sex Trafficking |
| Dec-POMDP | Decentralized Partially Observable Markov Decision Process |
| DMST | Domestic Minor Sex Trafficking |
| DSS | Decision Support System |
| DTMC | Discrete Time Markov Chain |
| ECRE | European Council on Refugees and Exiles |
| HIV | Human Immunodeficiency Virus |
| IMBs | Illicit Massage Businesses |
| LDL | Low-Density Lipoprotein |
| MC | Markov Chain |
| MCMC | Markov Chain Monte Carlo |
| MDP | Markov Decision Process |
| PTSD | Post-Traumatic Stress Disorder |
| SAARC | South Asian Association for Regional Cooperation |
| UN.GIFT | United Nations Global Initiative to Fight Human Trafficking |
| UNODC | United Nations Office on Drugs and Crime |

# CHAPTER 1

# INTRODUCTION

The fundamental goal of this research is to develop methodologies towards solutions to a social problem using operations research techniques. Table 1 displays the Merriam-Webster (2020) definitions required to understand the dynamics of this research goal. Altogether, operations research techniques are positioned to integrate existing knowledge and techniques of different disciplines to serve beneficial solutions related to the complex system of many interacting individual persons. The social problem considered in this research is that of sex trafficking victimization, as it is experienced during an individual's lifetime.

*Table 1: Definitions of Operations Research, Social, and Problem (Merriam-Webster, 2020)*

| Term | Definition |
| --- | --- |
| Operations Research (noun) | "the application of scientific and especially mathematical methods to the study and analysis of problems involving complex systems" |
| Social (adjective) | "of or relating to human society, the interaction of the individual and the group, or the welfare of human beings as members of society." |
| Problem (noun) | "an intricate unsettled question.". |

## 1.1 Trafficking Prevalence

The Human Trafficking industry, and the sub-industry of Sex Trafficking, remains hidden and discrete (UNODC, 2018). As a result, assessment and measurement of the industry is formidable. Nonetheless, organizations such as the United Nations have collected and reported estimates for the grim reality of trafficking prevalence domestically and internationally.

In the most recent United Nations Office on Drugs and Crime (UNODC) Global Report on Trafficking in Persons, the global total of number of detected victims in 2016 was nearly 25,000 individuals (UNODC, 2018). Including all reports of human trafficking, an estimated 72% of trafficked persons are female, 28% male. Among trafficked persons, 83% of women and 72% of girls are trafficked for sexual exploitation, while the same is true for 10% of men and

27% of boys. Internationally, the main profiles of exploitation are sexual exploitation and forced labor.

Throughout the Americas, the main profile of trafficking is sexual exploitation of women and girls (UNODC, 2018). In North America, 71% of detected trafficking cases were in the form of sexual exploitation, while 24% of detected cases were forced labor and 5% were equally sexual exploitation and forced labor or other forms of trafficking. The most recent estimate for the number of detected victims in the Americas was between 1.2 and 1.4 persons per 100,000 population. The report cites literature suggesting a 4 to 5 multiplier for the number of actual trafficking victims to those detected. The 2015 human trafficking victimization rate (out of every 100,000 population) was estimated to be around 3 in Ireland, 6 in Romania, 12 in Serbia, and 37 in the Netherlands.

While UNODC reports focus on detected trafficked persons, the United Nations Global Initiative to Fight Human Trafficking (UN.GIFT) offers aggregate estimates of trafficking totals. A global summary suggested 2.5 million trafficked persons annually, 1.2 million of which are children (UN.GIFT, 2008).

Though complete data is lacking for the hidden industry of trafficking, known trafficking cases offer a glimpse into a successfully operating industry that thrives on victimizing humans. This research aims to offer analytic support to anti-trafficking initiatives as well as policy-making considerations. Further, the developed model of this research is positioned to support testing and verification of data reasonableness.

### 1.2 Human Lifetime Experience

Within the span of time between birth and death, humans encounter and process through various life experiences. Table 2 defines both the dictionary form of "lifetime", as well as "experience." This research specifically focuses on the individual lifetime experience of sex trafficking victimization.

*Table 2: Definitions of "Lifetime" and "Experience" (Merriam-Webster, 2020)*

| Term | Definition |
|---|---|
| Lifetime (noun) | "the duration of the existence of a living being" "an amount accumulated or experienced in a lifetime" |
| Experience (noun) | "the fact or state of having been affected by or gained knowledge through direct observation or participation." "something personally encountered, undergone, or lived through." "the conscious events that make up an individual life." |

Table 3 presents an illustration of different 'types' of lifetime experiences found in the literature an individual may participate and cycle among during their lifetime. Important considerations for each 'type' are:

- The beginning status in a lifetime is noted with *italics*.
- Structure of flow among the experience status classifications is 'type'-dependent.
- An individual may observe some or all the different classifications during their lifetime.
- In addition to the listed classifications within each experience 'type', Deceased is a universal ending node of the human lifetime.

*Table 3: Experience 'Type' Illustrations*

| Experience 'Type' | Individual Status Classifications |
|---|---|
| Marriage (Duffin, 2019) | *Never Married*, Married, Divorced, Widowed |
| U.S. Citizenship Immigration Process (Mejer, 2015) | *Non-U.S. Citizen*, U.S. Citizen, U.S. Resident, Non-Immigrants, Undocumented |
| Employment ("How the Government Measures Unemployment", 2015) | Employed, Unemployed, *Not in the Labor Force* (e.g. Student, Retired, Domestic, Discouraged Workers) |

This table information is conceptual and a small sample of all potential individual lifetime experiences. Only a few illustrations are needed to demonstrate the vast range of applicability for analytical research into the individual lifetime experience through a designated 'type' lens. There exists a combination of social and theoretic value in better understanding individual lifetime experiences. This research takes specific focus on the victimization experience within sex trafficking, a form of human trafficking. There are no limitations for extending and applying the model methodology to other 'types' of individual experiences during their lifetime.

## 1.3 Sex Trafficking Victimization Experience

A fundamental scheme of the sex trafficking victim's experience emerges from literature (Zimmerman, Hossain, and Watts, 2011; Kleemans and Smit, 2014; Mancuso, 2014; Baarda, 2016; Konrad et al., 2017). Traffickers use a variety of tactics to *recruit* a victim. Once a victim is successfully recruited, the trafficker exercises various methods of control to *traffic* and *exploit* the victim. The state-transitions during victimization led to the consideration of the potential value of stochastic modelling methodologies. How this three-stage process relates to the individual's lifetime is explored in detail throughout the remainder of this research.

## 1.4 Research Objectives

The three research objectives of this work are:

1. To determine a method for analyzing the impact of the sex trafficking victimization experience during a human lifetime.
2. To analyze the impact of general, variable-form policy changes on the Sex Trafficking Victim's individual lifetime experiences.
3. To develop an open-source tool to support anti-trafficking activities and initiatives.

## 1.5 Research Organization

Stochastic modeling for social applications is an established pairing (Billard, 2015). The lifetime model for sex trafficking victimization developed and evaluated with stochastic techniques is one of the significant, original contribution of this research. There is primary and secondary significance to this research. Of first significance, by understanding the victimization experience, insights may be extracted for supporting individual victims, as well as the greater community of those who are at-risk of experiencing, are experiencing, and have experienced victimization. Of second significance, the approach of research is directly applicable to other human lifetime experience structures, which meet the model's assumptions.

The next section presents existing literature, as well as identifies relevant literature gaps. Following the literature review, the research methodology is presented inclusive of both theoretical and applied approaches. The research methodology is fully executed on a case study dataset in the results, analysis, and discussion chapter. Conclusions are stated to identify the key findings of this work. Finally, guidance for model use and related future work is presented.

# CHAPTER 2

# LITERATURE REVIEW

The nature of human trafficking operations is secretive, and the data required to complete related numerical research is sparse, missing, and/or inaccurate (Gerassi, Edmond, and Nichols, 2017; Konrad et al., 2017). Comparable to illegal weapons and drugs trades, human trafficking is a phenomenon based on business transactions to satisfy demand. Unlike weapons and drugs trades, human trafficking has a unique appeal to the traffickers because victims are essentially 'renewable commodities' that generally may be sold more than once.

Analytic literature in human trafficking is in its infancy. Konrad et al. (2017) organized a dense review focused on the opportunities for operations research application in anti-human trafficking initiatives. The use of stochastic processes is one opportunity of operations research application to model aspects of trafficking systems over time.

## 2.1 Research Pillars

The contributions of this research begin with a systematic aggregation of literature among a breadth of disciplines. The following review will discuss existing literature, as well as acknowledge substantial literature gaps, at the convergence of three pillar topics (see Figure 1Figure 1: Research Pillars): namely Stochastic Processes, Sex Trafficking, and Lifetime Experiences.

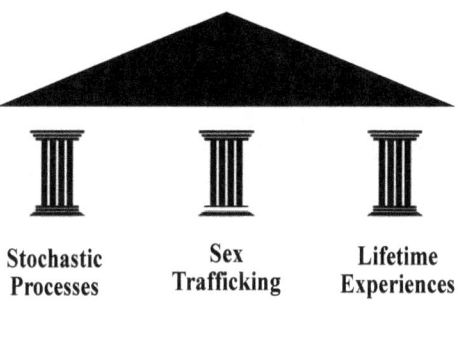

*Figure 1: Research Pillars*

The first research pillar, Stochastic Processes, is a dense and broad topic. Ross (1996) defined that,

> "A *stochastic process* $\underline{X} = \{X(t), t \in T\}$ is a collection of random variables. That is, for each $t$ in the *index set* $T$, $X(t)$ is a random variable. We often interpret $t$ as time and call $X(t)$ the state of the process at time $t$. If the index set $T$ is a countable set, we call $\underline{X}$ a discrete-time stochastic process... Any realization of $\underline{X}$ is called a sample path."

With this definition of Stochastic Process, consideration is required towards a more specific focus on type of stochastic process that would apply to evaluating aspects related to the second and third research pillars (i.e., the lifetime experience of sex trafficking victimization). Figure 2 shows Mubayi et al. (2019) tree diagram of all that is encompassed by the term 'stochastic processes.' It becomes imperative to focus on the type of stochastic process that is suitable for research context.

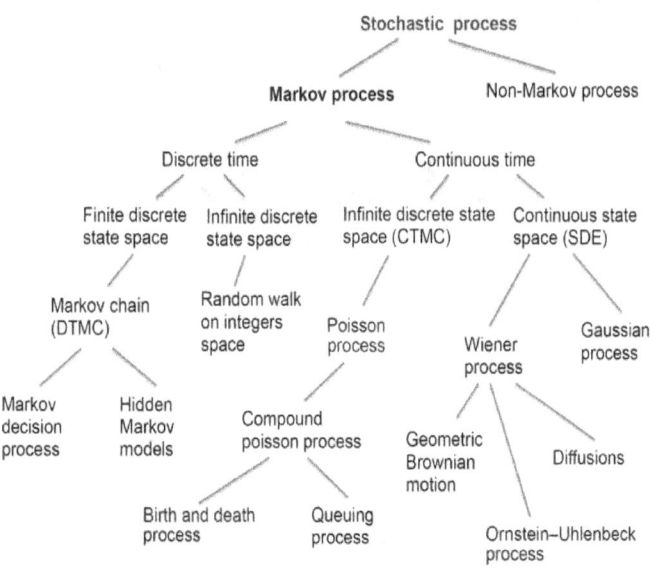

*Figure 2: Stochastic Process Flow Chart (Mubayi et al., 2019)*

To choose the specific stochastics modelling structure to approach this research, the characteristics of sex trafficking victimization needs considered. The lacking detail of trafficking industry data suggests non-continuous time to reduce data input requirements. Discrete time, as opposed to continuous time, allows analysis in equivalent time increments through the evaluation period. Discrete time situations do not require the added input of distributions of time between transitions. The pursuit to define specific stages of experiences during a lifetime, with specific start at birth and end at death, suggests finite state space. Finite state space results from specific state definitions for the modeled entity throughout the evaluation period. Collectively, efforts are therefore directed towards Markov Chain, specifically Discrete-Time Markov Chain (DTMC), methodologies which are appropriate for modeling processes in discrete time-finite state space. The process modelled in this research is the lifetime experiences of sex trafficking victimization.

Having defined the specific modeling approach for this work, additional definitions and categories are required to outline a successful literature review. Already introduced, Markov

Chain modeling is a common technique used in Operations Research. Operations Research, previously defined, is a diverse and dense discipline that provides many toolsets to solve complex problems. Sex Trafficking, a form of Human Trafficking, is among all types of the general category of Criminal Activity. Finally, this research classifies the Lifetime Experience as a perspective to evaluating the individual's progression among state classifications throughout their lifetime. Each of these terms, as evaluated in this research, are defined in Table 4.

*Table 4: Term Definitions for Literature Review*

| Term | Definition |
|---|---|
| Markov Chain | "A stochastic model describing a sequence of possible events in which the probability of each event depends only on the state attained in the previous event." (Oxford, 2020) |
| Criminal Activity | The act of committing a crime, defined by Oxford (2020) as, "An action or omission which constitutes an offence and is punishable by law." |
| Human Trafficking | The incidence of force, fraud, and/or coercion used for the purposes of exploitation. (United Nations, 2000) |
| Sex Trafficking | The incidence of force, fraud, and/or coercion used for the purposes of sexual exploitation. Note any sexual exploitation of a minor (<18 years old) is considered Sex Trafficking. (United Nations, 2000) |
| Lifetime Experience | Specifically related to humans; an **over time, state transition** among types of experiences. Oxford (2020) defines experience as, "Practical contact with or observation of facts or events." |

These terms and their respective definitions were imperative in developing the search criteria and completing the literature review. The literature review process was completed:

- Using subscribed access to the Western Michigan University Library Database; late 2018 into 2023.
- With specific search terms. The search keywords/phrases were recorded in Appendix H.
- For specifically *Human* lifetime experiences (i.e., not for other biological or ecological entities).
- For non-English articles by requesting an English version from the corresponding author.
- Excluding subjective and argument-based research from this review.

While the final categorization of existing literature may be subjective, the relevance of literature to this research topic was not subjective.

A visual representation of the initial literature review is provided in Figure 3. The corresponding interpretations of the sixteen evaluated figured components are defined in Table 5. For literature to be included in this section of the review, literature from search results must be directly related to one of the sixteen components labelled in Table 5.

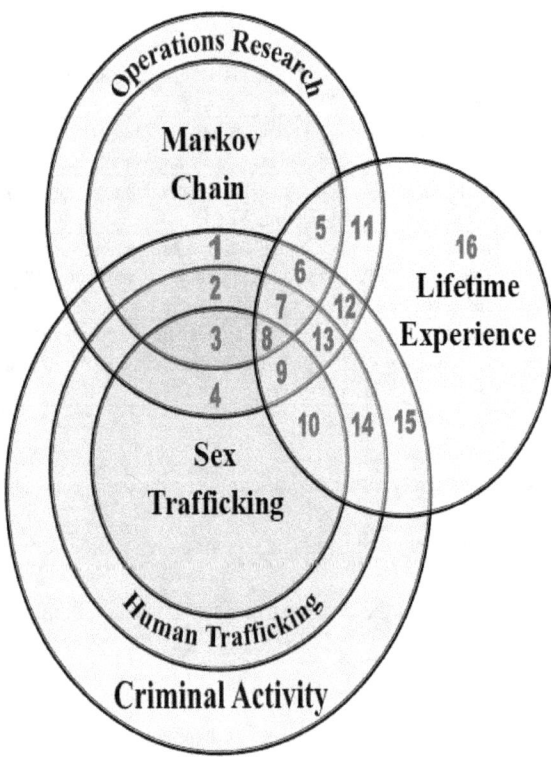

*Figure 3: Literature Review Map*

*Table 5: Numerical Notations of Research Components (\* Contribution of this Research)*

| Figure 2 Coding | Interpretation |
|---|---|
| 1 | Markov Chains & Criminal Activity |
| 2 | Markov Chains & Human Trafficking |
| 3 | Markov Chains & Sex Trafficking |
| 4 | Operations Research & Sex Trafficking |
| 5 | Markov Chains & Lifetime Experience |
| 6 | Markov Chains & Lifetime Experience & Criminal Activity |
| 7 | Markov Chains & Lifetime Experience & Human Trafficking |
| 8* | Markov Chains & Lifetime Experience & Sex Trafficking |
| 9 | Operations Research & Lifetime Experience & Sex Trafficking |
| 10 | Lifetime Experience & Sex Trafficking |
| 11 | Operations Research & Lifetime Experience |
| 12 | Operations Research & Lifetime Experience & Criminal Activity |
| 13 | Operations Research & Lifetime Experience & Human Trafficking |
| 14 | Lifetime Experience & Human Trafficking |
| 15 | Lifetime Experience & Criminal Activity |
| 16 | Lifetime Experience |

In summary of the categorical findings, Table 6 and Figure 4 are defined to summarize and support fellow researchers interested in related future work. Note, the final column of Table 6 is the input data for Figure 4.

*Table 6: Review of Research Pillar References*

| | Section | References | Number of References |
|---|---|---|---|
| 1 | Markov Chains & Criminal Activity | Batabyal and DeAngelo, 2012; Baycik, Sharkey, and Rainwater, 2019; Britt et al., 2005; Buta and Doss, 2011; Chen and Lee, 2016; Cohen et al., 1998; Kim and In, 2008; Kim et al., 2016; Kolokoltsov, 2015; Rey, Mack, and Koschinsky, 2012; Yu and Brooks, 2017; Zhang et al., 2016; Zhou and Raskutti, 2018 | 13 |
| 2 | Markov Chains & Human Trafficking | No relevant research found, literature gap. | 0 |
| 3 | Markov Chains & Sex Trafficking | No relevant research found, literature gap. | 0 |
| 4 | Operations Research & Sex Trafficking | Ahn et al., 2013; Bedford et al., 2017; Brewster et al., 2014; Cockbain, Brayley, and Laycock, 2011; Crane, 2013; Crotty and Bouché, 2018; Fedorschak et al., 2014; Fong and Cardoso, 2010; Gibbs et al., 2015; Granata, Steeger, and Rebennack, 2013; Greenbaum, 2014; Hansen et al., 2018; Jani and Felke, 2017; Kaltiso et al., 2018; Konrad et al., 2017; Konstantopoulos et al., 2013; Kővári and Pruyt, 2014; Lamb-Susca and Clements, 2018; Matheson and Finkel, 2012; Macy and Graham, 2012; Nami and Keiko, 2009; Tepelus, 2008 | 22 |

Table 6 - continued

| | | | |
|---|---|---|---|
| 5 | Markov Chains & Lifetime Experience | Apenteng and Ismail, 2015; Ayer, Alagoz, and Stout, 2012; Constant and Zimmermann, 2012; Frühwirth-Schnatter et al., 2012; Kaplan, 2008; Rueff-Lopes et al., 2015; Shauly et al., 2011 | 7 |
| 6 | Markov Chains & Lifetime Experience & Criminal Activity | Andersson, 1990; Bijleveld and Mooijaart, 2003; Goldstick et al., 2019; Holland and McGarvey, 1984; Jones et al., 2010; Leal-Enríquez, 2018; Pettiway, Dolinsky, and Grigoryan, 1994; Rey et al., 2014; Stander et al., 1989 | 9 |
| 7 | Markov Chains & Lifetime Experience & Human Trafficking | No relevant research found, literature gap. | 0 |
| 8* | Markov Chains & Lifetime Experience & Sex Trafficking | No relevant research found, literature gap. | 0 |
| 9 | Operations Research & Lifetime Experience & Sex Trafficking | Hickle and Roe-Sepowitz, 2017; Jung, 2017; Moore et al., 2019; Muraya and Fry, 2016; O'Brien et al., 2017; Thomson et al., 2011 | 6 |
| 10 | Lifetime Experience & Sex Trafficking | Merry, 1974; O'Brien, 2018; O'Brien, White, and Rizo, 2017; Palmer and Foley, 2017; Reid, 2012; Rothman, Bazzi, and Bair-Merritt, 2015; Sprang and Cole, 2018; Staiger, 2005; Williamson and Cluse-Tolar, 2002 | 9 |
| 11 | Operations Research & Lifetime Experience | Atkins et al., 2012; Kim, 2010; Lee, Fagan, and Chen, 2012; Ma, Shen, and Nguyen, 2016; Noonan et al., 2012; Polachek, 2017; Xiong et al., 2010 | 7 |
| 12 | Operations Research & Lifetime Experience & Criminal Activity | Arocho and Dush, 2016; Bersani, Loughran, and Piquero, 2014; Constantine et al., 2013; Kang and Lynch, 2014; Wright et al., 2014; | 5 |
| 13 | Operations Research & Lifetime Experience & Human Trafficking | Bhaumik, Roy, and Weber, 2019; Egyud et al., 2017; Paraskevas and Brookes, 2018; Zimmerman, Hossain, and Watts, 2011; | 4 |
| 14 | Lifetime Experience & Human Trafficking | Hurtado, Iranzo Dosdad, and Gómez Hernández, 2018; Kaye, Winterdyk, and Quarterman, 2014; Keo et al., 2014; | 3 |
| 15 | Lifetime Experience & Criminal Activity | Esbec and Echeburúa, 2016 | 1 |
| 16 | Lifetime Experience | Agronin, 2014; Jacoby, 2015; Kompanichenko, 1994; 5emuri et al., 2018 | 4 |

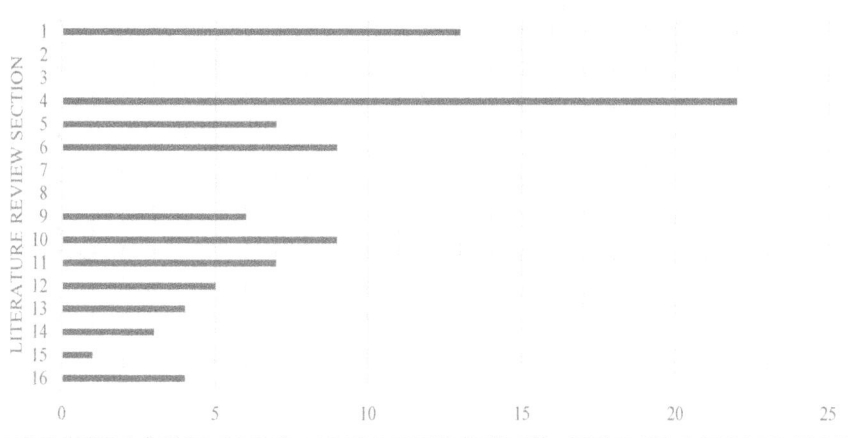

*Figure 4: Graph of Cited Literature Counts (derived from results of Table 6)*

From Table 6 and Figure 4, the reader may observe certain areas of relevant research to this work are more densely present in the literature. The same demonstrates that there are several areas lacking literature, namely:

- Section 2: Markov Chains and Human Trafficking
- Section 3: Markov Chains and Sex Trafficking
- Section 7: Markov Chains, Lifetime Experience, and Human Trafficking
- Section 8: Markov Chains, Lifetime Experience, and Sex Trafficking

These key gaps in the literature identify the opportunity for contributions through this current research work. This research specifically addresses one key literature gap; *Section 8: Markov Chains, Lifetime Experience, and Sex Trafficking*.

### 2.1.1 Markov Chains and Criminal Activity

Markov Chain methods have been an active tool in research around criminal activity. With regards to physical crime:

- Rey, Mack, and Koschinsky (2012) implemented a conditional spatial Markov Chain approach, among other methods, to assess a location's likelihood of a future residential burglary.
- Batabyal and DeAngelo (2012) modelled a theoretical economics scenario of a commodity's demand being much greater than supply was approached with a Discrete Time Markov Chain (DTMC) to determine the likelihood of violence based on queue length and the number of unsupplied individuals.
- Kolokoltsov (2015) evaluated the theoretical structure of conflict interactions with Markov decision models. The research discussion focused on targeted pressure on crime rates in an area.
- Kim et al. (2016) took focus on crime prevention and prediction by generating optimal routes for police officers by a two-folded approach with Markov chains and risk mapping to a geographical area.
- In combatting drug trafficking at the city-level, Baycik, Sharkey, and Rainwater (2019) proposed a decision-support methodology that includes a Markov Decision Process (MDP) to maximize the value of impact of law enforcement activities in the scenario of having intelligence regarding multiple criminals.

Markov Chain research approaches to cyber-criminal activities include:

- Kim and In (2008) addressed digital forensic challenges of identifying a digital criminal activity by proposing a combined approach of Markov Chain and noise page elimination algorithm (NPEA).

- Yu and Brooks (2017) studied the use of a Decentralized Partially Observable Markov Decision Process (DEC-POMDP) towards promoting network security that balances performance with cost.

Criminal activity research that applied Markov Chain methods as a sub-tool included both primary modeling approaches in Bayesian solution form (Cohen et al., 1998; Britt et al., 2005; Buta and Doss, 2011; Chen and Lee, 2016; Zhang et al., 2016) and non-parametric networks (Zhou and Raskutti, 2018).

Table 7 summarizes the previous discussion, noting the literature cited with the Markov method employed. The literature that featured Markov methods as a non-primary methodology are not included in the tabular summary.

*Table 7: Markov Methods used by Category 1 Researchers*

| Researcher(s) | Year | Markov Method* |
|---|---|---|
| Rey, Mack, and Koschinsky | 2012 | Conditional Spatial MC |
| Batabyal and DeAngelo | 2012 | DTMC |
| Kolokoltsov | 2015 | MDP |
| Kim et al. | 2016 | MC |
| Baycik, Sharkey, and Rainwater | 2019 | MDP |
| Kim and In | 2008 | MC |
| Yu and Brooks | 2017 | Dec-POMDP |

*See List of Acronyms*

*2.1.2 Markov Chains and Human Trafficking*

No relevant research found, literature gap.

*2.1.3 Markov Chains and Sex Trafficking*

No relevant research found, literature gap.

*2.1.4 Operations Research and Sex Trafficking*

One of the most relevant pieces of literature was done by Konrad et al. (2017) who enlightened the operations research community with a comprehensive review of research and analytic opportunities for combatting human trafficking. Literature exists at the intersection of Operations Research and Sex Trafficking. In terms of combatting sex trafficking:

- Cockbain, Brayley, and Laycock (2011) used existing resources available to UK police to apply social network analysis (SNA) to gather intelligence on child sex trafficking (CST) network structure, powerful individuals, victim networks, and offender networks.
- Granata, Steeger, and Rebennack (2013) made theoretical operations research contributions to further support anti-sex trafficking initiatives.
- Fedorschak et al. (2014) prototyped a human trafficking database through a three-step analysis of news articles, Truckers Against Trafficking call data, and US government spending on anti-trafficking agencies.
- Kővári and Pruyt (2014) simulated the interactions of prostitution and sex trafficking supply and demand within the Dutch population to assess policy options on 'industry' economics, money flow, and anti-crime objectives. Victims were modeled through an 'enslavement ratio' for individuals providing sexual services against their free will.
- Brewster et al. (2014) and Bedford et al. (2017) employed such strategies as text analytics and semantic analysis to support law enforcement, along with building awareness and understanding of human trafficking.
- Crotty and Bouché (2018) completed geographic analysis which revealed illicit massage businesses (IMBs), home to substantial sex trafficking activities within the United States, locate in neighborhoods and commercial landscapes with specific characteristics.

While combatting sex trafficking is imperative to the anti-trafficking efforts, so is the considerations for the needs of existing victims.

- Fong and Cardoso (2010) reviewed the specific needs and characteristics of child sex trafficking victims, as it applies to programs and policies of child welfare. The broader term of child sexual abuse and the connection to child welfare services were discussed.
- Gibbs et al. (2015) combined data with discussion around the articulated needs of domestic minor sex trafficking (DMST) victims.

Research efforts observed in literature have demonstrated the value of applying Operations Research within the anti-trafficking community.

Operations research employs analytic approaches to achieve solutions to complex problems, such as sex trafficking. Attaining these solutions require an understanding of how systems, especially those of society(ies) in the case of sex trafficking, are structured and function. On a societal level:

- In Japan, the perception of sex trafficking and demand for sexual service differs among genders and occupations of the Japanese people (Nami and Keiko, 2009).
- Crane (2013) applied a management perspective to present and detail a *Theory of Modern Slavery* framework, wherein the conditions enabling slavery, exploiting and insulating capabilities, and sustaining and shaping capabilities are compared and discussed.
- Jani and Felke (2017) focused on the role gender inequality can take in driving female susceptibility for sex trafficking victimization.

More narrowly, on an industry level:

- Tourism is a dense, global system with existing best practices and ongoing innovation in policies geared towards anti-trafficking objectives (Tepelus, 2008). However, stakeholders in the tourism industry disagree as to the impact of mega sporting events on the prevalence of sex trafficking activity within the host locale (Matheson and Finkel, 2012)

- The healthcare industry is another system that may potentially interact with sex trafficking victims and provide means for potential intervention. Macy and Graham (2012) took an aggregate review of 20 service provider documents to define an identification questionnaire for sex trafficking victims during interactions with human services. Ahn et al. (2013) reviewed educational systems designed for informing healthcare providers about different topics within human trafficking, including victim identification and response methods. Konstantopoulos et al. (2013) took a surveyed approach to evaluating public health system limitations in understanding and addressing the presence of sex trafficking among eight international cities. Greenbaum (2014) presented a direct review of child sex trafficking for the purpose of informing medical providers how to identify, treat and intervene victims, appropriately. The research discussion is organized according to earlier research which outlined the five stages of human trafficking as:

    1. Pre-departure stage
    2. Travel and transit stage
    3. Destination stage
    4. Detention, deportation, and criminal evidence stage
    5. Integration and reintegration stage.

Hansen et al. (2018) targeted building awareness, knowledge, and confidence among healthcare professionals of child sex trafficking through an online training program. On the front-end of interaction with potential victims of child sex trafficking in an emergency room setting, Kaltiso et al. (2018) concluded positively on the impact of a basic verbal screening tool to identify victims. Lamb-Susca and Clements (2018) directed emergency room nurses to use the commonly held trust of patients in nurses to provide non-judgmental interactions with, and treatment to, potential victims. Further, the research proposed that assessment and treatment should address comprehensive care for all health complications related to the victim's trafficking experience.

Collectively, societal systems enable and/or challenge sex trafficking existence.

### 2.1.5 *Markov Chains and Lifetime Experience*

A diversity of literature exists for applying Markov methodologies to human experiences, over time.

- A comparative analysis of different Markov modeling techniques was applied to adolescent reading development progression through four sequential sampling periods, between 'nonmastery' and 'mastery' states (Kaplan, 2008).
- A multi-model approach, including a Markov Chain model, was developed to better understand the mortality of individuals treated for dyslipidemia (Shauly et al., 2011).
- The developed transition probability matrix was organized by four distinct age range groups to respect the statistical significance of the relationship between age of disease detection and the associated mortality hazard. A six-state, partially observable Markov decision process is modeled for the lifetime experience and subsequent mortality from developing breast cancer to design a customized mammogram screening schedule for individual patients (Ayer, Alagoz, and Stout, 2012).
- Markov Chain clustering and sampling were among the methodologies implemented to assess Austrian male career patterns, finding a strong effect of initial market conditions

on the individual's career pattern type: 'upward', 'downward', 'static', or 'mobile' (Frühwirth-Schnatter et al., 2012).

- Migration patterns between 'host' and 'home' were modeled with a discrete-time discrete-space (i.e., two state) Markov Chain to better understand repetitious immigration flow during an individual's life to the 'host' country; analysis organized by numerous influencing factors such as gender, age, and language proficiency (Constant and Zimmermann, 2012).

- Apenteng and Ismail (2015) designed and assessed a Markov Chain Monte Carlo model of the dynamics of AIDS development among HIV-infected individuals during their lifetimes.

- The flow among 'Positive', 'Neutral', and 'Negative' vocal interaction states, as experienced between call center employee and customer, was modeled with a Markov Chain to better understand the patterns of vocal mimicry (Rueff-Lopes et al., 2015).

Table 8 summarizes this section in terms of researcher, the Markov method applied to which experience, and the state structure for the model.

*Table 8: Markov Methods used by Category 5 Researchers*

| Researcher(s) | Year | Markov Method* | Experience | States* |
|---|---|---|---|---|
| Kaplan | 2008 | Various | Reading Development | Nonmastery Mastery |
| Shauly et al. | 2011 | DTMC | Treated Dyslipidemia Mortality | 6 combinations total of: Consuming statins, Not consuming statins LDL $\leq$ 100, LDL > 100, No lipidogram<br><br>Death was the seventh state. |
| Ayer, Alagoz, and Stout | 2012 | Partially Observable MDP | Customized Mammogram Screening Schedules | No cancer<br>In situ cancer<br>Invasive cancer<br>In situ post-cancer<br>Invasive post-cancer<br>Death |

20

Table 8 – continued

| | | | | |
|---|---|---|---|---|
| Frühwirth-Schnatter et al. | 2012 | MC clustering & sampling | Austrian Male Career Patterns | Upward<br>Downward<br>Static<br>Mobile |
| Constant and Zimmermann | 2012 | DTMC | Migration Flow of Immigrants | Host<br>Home |
| Apenteng and Ismail | 2015 | MCMC | AIDS Development from HIV | Susceptible<br>Infected<br>Pre-AIDS after HIV<br>AIDS after HIV |
| Rueff-Lopes et al. | 2015 | MC | Vocal Mimicry | Positive<br>Neutral<br>Negative |

*See List of Acronyms*

### 2.1.6 Markov Chains, Lifetime Experience and Criminal Activity

As with the previous section, application of Markov modeling to a criminal's individual life experience is also ongoing in literature. Such literature analyzes the criminal's experiences within pre-criminal, criminal, recidivism, and/or post-criminal activities.

- Holland and McGarvey (1984) modeled the individual pattern for criminal offences among violent and nonviolent crimes using an MDP.

- Stander et al. (1989) used a Markov model to test the hypothesis of specialization within individual male criminal careers, identifying past criminal behavior as predictive of future types of criminal offenses; a contradictory finding to a first-order assumption.

- Andersson (1990) studied the risk of recidivism, concluding similarly for male criminals, finding past criminal activity was predictive for future criminal activity. A first-order model, however, was suited for modeling female criminal activities.

- Pettiway, Dolinsky, and Grigoryan (1994) designed a first-order Markov model for the routine of daily ritual activities by criminals.

- Bijleveld and Mooijaart (2003) contributed to recidivism research by developing a latent Markov model and analyzing delinquent criminal careers between the ages 13 and 16.
- Rey et al. (2014) completed post-crime analysis with Markov chains to model the changes in sex offender residences among restricted and unrestricted locations.
- Goldstick et al. (2019) employed Markov Chain modeling for better understanding the shifts of an individual's firearm assault behavior, over time.

Markov modeling for criminal careers is well-established and ongoing.

A focus on application of Markov modeling to domestic violence criminal experiences is also present.

- Jones et al. (2010) developed a Hidden Markov Model for violent and abusive behavior over time, through the perspective of the victimizer in a domestic violence situation.
- Leal-Enríquez (2018) modeled and simulated the intimate partner, domestic violence perpetrator's state of self-control over time, through a two-state (i.e., 'self-control' and 'loss of control') Markov model. The 'loss of control' state was adapted with a proportional factor to represent the proportion of control lost, in addition to modeling parameters for the severity and frequency of violent acts.

Using Markov modeling for lifetime experiences within and around criminal activities is founded. That too as it relates to crimes dealing with the interaction of two individuals; domestic violence. Table 9 summarizes this sixth category in terms of the Markov method used and the states composing the model design.

*Table 9: Markov Methods used by Category 6 Researchers*

| Researcher(s) | Year | Markov Method* | States |
|---|---|---|---|
| Holland and McGarvey | 1984 | MDP | Distal and proximal offense sequences were evaluated. Number of offenses modeled ranged from 3 to 8 offenses. The transitions between Violent and Nonviolent crimes were recorded within each count of offenses. |

Table 9 – continued

| | | | |
|---|---|---|---|
| Stander et al. | 1989 | MC | Non-index<br>Injury<br>Theft<br>Damage<br>Combination |
| Andersson | 1990 | MC | Not convicted<br>Not serious<br>Serious<br>Research reviewed age range 15-30, for both genders. |
| Pettiway, Dolinsky, and Grigoryan | 1994 | MC | Crime-related activities<br>Drug-related activities<br>Financial/human service/welfare/job-related activities<br>Household/personal/shopping activities<br>Entertainment/recreation/sport activities<br>Relaxation/resting activities<br>Legal issues/medical/school/transportation activities |
| Bijleveld and Mooijaart | 2003 | Latent Markov model | No contact<br>Violent crime<br>Property crime<br>Vandalism |
| Rey et al. | 2014 | MC | Unrestricted<br>Restricted |
| Goldstick et al. | 2019 | MC | Firearm assault<br>No firearm assault |
| Jones et al. | 2010 | HMM | 4 states, ranging from least violent/controlling to most violent/controlling |
| Leal-Enríquez | 2018 | DTMC | Self-control<br>Loss of control |

*See List of Acronyms*

### 2.1.7 Markov Chains, Lifetime Experience and Human Trafficking

No relevant research found, literature gap.

### 2.1.8 Markov Chains, Lifetime Experience and Sex Trafficking

No relevant research found, literature gap. Focus of this research.

### 2.1.9 Operations Research, Lifetime Experience and Sex Trafficking

The grand term of "sex trafficking" is all-encompassing for a variety of forms of sexual exploitation which results in the diversity of experiences faced by victims. While not every victim or victim-experience is identical, there is an important observation in literature that victim experiences often start before exploitation, include exploitation, and continue thereafter into a period post-exploitation.

Hickle and Roe-Sepowitz (2017) investigated the incidence of sexual exploitation, and therefore sex trafficking, upon entry into the sex trade industry. The researchers emphasized that an individual can both have autonomy in joining the sex trade industry and have also experienced sexual exploitation (i.e., sex trafficking), making them a victim (though they may not recognize their own sex trafficking victimization). The results of research identified one third of surveyed participants (i.e., women arrested for prostitution in a prostitution diversion program) reported sex trafficking victimization experiences. These same participants did not observe that their experiences were forms of sex trafficking. Women having experienced sex trafficking victimization also had significantly more negative childhood experiences and had significantly more diverse sex work experiences as compared to those not having experienced sex trafficking victimization.

The sex trafficking victimization experience of adolescent males is less prevalent in the literature to date. Yet, in a study of 800 justice-involved juvenile males, 10.4% self-reported past sex trafficking victimization (O'Brien et al., 2017). The researchers believed the actual exploited subset of the sampled group to be even greater due to underreporting concerns. Further, this research found a strong positive association of sexual abuse, as well as substance misuse and lower levels of sexual discomfort, with elevated risks of sex trafficking victimization.

Among the diverse experiences faced by sex trafficking victims is compromised health.

- Jung (2017) analyzed survey data of female sex workers in South Korea pre- and post-prohibition of sex trafficking policy implementation. Positively, the study found a significant reduction in the rate of sexually transmitted infections among female sex workers after the prohibition policy took effect, as well as a reduction in the number of female sex workers. Negatively, the study identified a younger population in the latter survey, suggesting an increase proportionally in previously unseen, younger female sex workers.

- Moore et al. (2019) organized an analysis comparing 'suspected' and 'confirmed' victims of domestic child sex trafficking, 67 patients in total, as presented to a children's hospital for medical services. The findings suggest an indifference between the two victim categories in terms of demographic, psychosocial, medical, and psychiatric parameters. The medical conditions reviewed related to the ongoing lifetime experience of victims prior to, during, and following victimization.

Impact on health throughout a lifetime is a notable result of victimization.

Following the direct victimization experiences of sexual exploitation, post-victimization can be an involved element of the victim's lifetime experience.

- Thomson et al. (2011) provided a case study review of a residential treatment center for sexually exploited female children. The center was transformed for improved patient benefit through a renovated approach to provision of care. Reflections on the changes made within the program with subsequent observed outcome improvement (i.e., rate of completed treatment goals), as well as more generally structured suggestions for successful residential treatment programs, are among the research results.

- Muraya and Fry (2016) composed a detailed review of policies and procedures, internationally, for serving the victim after their victimization experience. The research defined three stages of aftercare required to adequately serve the victim: rescuing, recovery, as well as reintegration and repatriation.

Collectively the research in this literature review category defines that lifetime experiences as it relates to sex trafficking can include certain pre-victimization, victimization, and post-victimization considerations.

### 2.1.10 Lifetime Experience and Sex Trafficking

Though memoirs are subjective reflections of one's experiences, the value of their content remains a just point of discussion. Palmer and Foley (2017) reviewed three memoirs of female child sex trafficking survivors, with the objective to identify the factors contributing to positive outcomes for recovering victims of child sex trafficking. In the initial *Grooming* phase, the researchers found that social isolation and compromised relationships with parents were instrumental leading into victimization. The victims would be treated with, "flattery, friendship, gifts, and [significant amounts of] alcohol and drugs." Alcohol and drugs served many purposes in the grooming phase (e.g., relaxation, perceived social value, dulling memories, and confusing 'choice' and 'consent'). During their individual timeframes of exploitation, survivors recollected purposefully misbehaving in public to gain help from others in escaping exploitation. The research concluded that rather than survivors of child sexual exploitation recovering from their experiences, they instead adapt to their new life situations. The most important factor in recovery is being believed by family, service providers, and members of the judicial system.

Reid (2012) composed a dense literature review and analysis of victim vulnerabilities to sex trafficking exploitation in the United States. Literature is categorized and reviewed according to the victim's origin and route (i.e., domestic, or international), gender, and age. The research also presents a collection of vulnerability factors and attributes increasing victimization risk by sex trafficking exploitation.

Semi-structured interviews with female sex trafficking survivors revealed several characteristics of individuals trafficked by dating partners (Rothman, Bazzi, and Bair-Merritt, 2015).

- "Insecurity about physical attractiveness; lack of self-worth"
- "No experience with healthy dating relationships"
- "Sexual assault and rape survivors may feel "broken" and hopeless"
- "Early dating phase includes flattery and romantic gestures that facilitate girls' emotional attachment and fuel fantasies of a committed relationship"
- "Girls may be attracted to acquaintances with higher social status in their peer group or community; these acquaintances then exploit the girls"
- "Initial involvement in sex work may temporarily convey a (false) sense of power or control for some girls; outearning other sex workers or feeling sought after can boost self-confidence in the short-term"

The same research also introduced a framework for susceptibility of victimization by a dating partner throughout the evolution of their "relationship". The framework is summarized sequentially through three stages of:

- Prior to dating
- Early phase dating
- Late phase dating

Each phase further perpetuating the vicious cycle of exploitation and abuse.

Literature demonstrates the role significance of persons relating to at-risk and victimized individuals.

- O'Brien (2018) interviewed thirteen survivors of DMST, finding three themes among the individuals for their experience, as it relates to interpersonal relationships. These themes were: "interpersonal relationship as a risk factor", "interpersonal relationship as a protective factor", and "interpersonal relationship fostering resiliency". The findings demonstrated the positive and negative potential of interpersonal relationships (i.e., "parents, siblings, mentors, religious leaders, and peers") to the risk of sex trafficking victimization.

- As compared with non-victims of DMST, substance use, PTSD and other mental illnesses, externalizing behavior (e.g., aggressive, runaway, and absentee behaviors, as well as vandalism), and involvement with child welfare systems is more prevalent in DMST survivors (O'Brien, White, and Rizo, 2017). This study also found equal prevalence of DMST reporting between genders.

- In a study of 31 minors involved with the child welfare system who were primarily trafficked by family members, 64.5% were trafficked by their mother, 32.3% were trafficked by their father, and 3.2% by another family member (Sprang and Cole, 2018). Participants ranged from 6 to 17 years old, averaging 11.96 years, and were from families with potentially multiple children sexually exploited (average 2.1 children per family; the study only considered one child from each family). 86.3% were prostituted, 50% were recorded in pornography, and 18% were placed in strip clubs. 81.8% of these minors were trafficked for a payment in the form of illicit drugs. Beyond the use of threats, intimidation, and authority to control the victim, 29% were further controlled with drugs. More than half of participants had attempted suicide in their lifetime.

External individuals to at-risk persons and victims can have positive and negative impacts on individual lifetime experiences as it relates to sex trafficking.

Sex trafficking can take different forms; *prostitution* is one potential form. It is particularly important to note a differentiation within the general term: *prostitution*. "Pimp-controlled prostitution" is another term for sex trafficking, as the pimp (i.e., trafficker) exploits the prostitute (i.e., victim) for the benefits received (e.g., money) of commercial sex activities (Williamson and Cluse-Tolar, 2002). "Pimp-controlled prostitution" is different from, "independent entrepreneurial prostitution." In "pimp-controlled prostitution", the victim may experience different forms of emotional and/or physical violence, threats, and intimidation. Love, violence, threats, and intimidation may all be prohibiting factors for the victim to leave the pimp's control. Williamson and Cluse-Tolar (2002) define a *Pimp* as, "one who controls the actions and lives off the proceeds of one or more women who work the streets." The pimp may be just one of a collection of individuals involved in the supplying of the victim to sex trafficking activities.

This research is focused on the lifetime experiences related to sex trafficking victimization. However, there are also the lifetime experiences of the traffickers (i.e., suppliers and consumers). Merry (1974) reviewed two texts, *Black Players: The Secret World of Black Pimps* and *Gentleman of Leisure: A Year in the Life of a Pimp*, which articulate details of the pimp's (i.e., supplying trafficker) individual experiences. A notable point of the texts is the pursuit by pimps to achieve and demonstrate their manhood by controlling women, arguing this to be the natural relationship between man and woman. To control women, pimps threaten, intimidate, and are emotionally and physically violent (Williamson and Cluse-Tolar, 2002). Staiger (2005) presents an observational review of 'pimping' culture as it is perceived, and such types of activities experienced and discussed, among a specific high school student body. A striking takeaway of the interviews presented were the valuation of relationships among students in terms of money or monetary value of products gained, as well as valuation of significant others on the metric of appearances.

*2.1.11 Operations Research and Lifetime Experience*

The realm of analytic applications to lifetime experiences is quite diverse. To begin, with regards to Public Health:

- Xiong et al. (2010) simulated the spread of HIV/AIDS throughout mainland China among injecting drug users. The simulation was based on an individual model, having the states of Health; Injecting drug user; HIV infected injecting drug user; HIV infected, Non-injecting drug user; AIDS diagnosed; Dead. The individual state was implemented into a model of disease spread throughout the region.

- A system-wide approach to spinal-cord injury health care provision in Canada is addressed, with further consideration to secondary complications, for patient outcomes and costs across the "care continuum" for individual patients (Noonan et al., 2012; Atkins et al., 2012). The "care continuum" entails the span from time of injury through Pre-Hospital, Acute Care, Rehabilitation Care phases, terminating with the individual's (i.e., patient's) return home.

- Ma, Shen, and Nguyen (2016) reported on a research-developed simulation to inform policymakers and city-planners of upcoming elderly Japanese society demands for daycare services. The individual's lifetime stages modeled in the daycare planning simulation flow sequentially through Be a baby; Grow up; Get married; Get old; Pass away. The 'Get married' stage was the source of the birth rate, while the 'Pass away' stage was the source of the death rate.

Economics of lifetime experiences is yet another analytic approach.

- Kim (2010) assessed earnings residuals through the scope of human capital theory by modeling with stochastic rental rates throughout a lifetime and categorizing resulting variances.

- Polachek (2017) applied the lifecycle human capital model to better understand how employee ability and information impact negotiation of wages among employees and employers.

The individual lifetime experiences of fatherhood was another investigated topic in this literature review category.

- Lee, Fagan, and Chen (2012) addressed the prevalence of depressive symptoms among fathers, with a child between the ages of three and five, who were in Late adolescence, Emerging adulthood, and Adulthood. Other factors were also considered in depressive symptom analysis.

Altogether, the use of Operations Research to assess various lifetime experiences is established in literature.

*2.1.12 Operations Research, Lifetime Experience and Criminal Activity*

An individual's lifetime experience with crime can be from the victim's or criminal's perspectives. From the victim's perspective in criminal activity:

- Victims of family-based domestic violence have varying willingness to report victimization events to authorities (Kang and Lynch, 2014). The willingness significantly depends on the relationship between victim and offender (e.g., child, spouse, etc.), but not significantly on the victim's age. The life-stages assessed included three classifications: Young adult (18-47 years old), Adult (48-54 years old), Older adult (55 or older). Victim education and employment status did not impact the likelihood to report violence. Prior victimization did increase the likelihood of victims reporting of violent events.

From the criminal's perspective, research has been done to better understand the criminal's life experiences, over time.

- A five-class arrest trajectory scheme was used to evaluate adolescents with and without emotional disturbances (Constantine et al., 2013). Emotional disturbances, including psychotic and behavioral disorders, biased an individual's arrest likelihood towards the highest trajectory. The researchers also conclude an importance for proper health services, especially mental health, to support youth towards less crime activity as they transition into adulthood.

- Wright et al. (2014) evaluated the impact of residence neighborhood conditions on serious criminal individuals reoffending between the ages of 18 and 22.

- A large-sampled comparative assessment of the criminal activity patterns between first and second generational immigrants, over the course of 84 months (starting in the 14-17 age range), who were previously court-involved for serious crime, revealed comparable criminal activity between the two generational immigrant groups over the aging period from adolescence into adulthood (Bersani, Loughran, and Piquero, 2014).

- "Now think about five years from now. What is the percent chance that you will be married?" This question was used by Arocho and Dush (2016) to measure marital expectations by youth. The results were analyzed for a connection between marital expectation and criminal activity, finding an expectation of marriage was associated with less criminal activity after one year. However, the opposite case of lower expectation of marriage leading to increased criminal activity was unfound.

Experiences of victims and criminals can be analyzed through various perspectives and throughout different stages of individual lifetimes.

*2.1.13 Operations Research, Lifetime Experience and Human Trafficking*

As with criminal activity, an individual's lifetime experience in and with human trafficking can be from the victim or trafficker (i.e., supplier or consumer) perspectives. From the victim perspective:

- Zimmerman, Hossain, and Watts (2011) presented a loosely connected model of the human trafficking process, and the associated health risks to the victim at each stage. The stages of this process were Recruitment, Travel and Transit, Exploitation, which were potentially followed by Detention, Integration or Re-integration, and Re-trafficking in some cases. The researchers identified various health concerns at every stage in the trafficking process, including pre-exploitation, exploitation, and post-exploitation concerns. Along the trafficking process, individuals may experience an accumulation of health consequences: mental health, physical health, sexual and reproductive health, substance use and misuse, social health, financial, legal and security, and occupational injuries and disease.

- Egyud et al. (2017) developed, implemented, and trained emergency department personnel on a tool for identifying and treating human trafficking victims. The tool included a risk-assessment component linked to the victim's health record and a process for silent notification. The research demonstrated success of tool and training through the identification of one human trafficking victim. Victims of other types of abuse were also identified.

- Paraskevas and Brookes (2018) employed a mapping approach to identify the stages ("nodes") and potential individuals for intervention ("guardians") during a hotel stay by a victim. The researchers emphasized the collective importance of having appropriate policies and procedures in place, staff training and awareness to warning signs, and an authority with the staff member to intervene and disrupt human trafficking activities. Though the research is mapped specifically for a hotel-based experience, the authors suggest the opportunity for other members of the tourism industry, as well tourism destinations, to employ a similar approach towards trafficking disruption opportunities.

From the trafficker perspective:

- A specific mathematical approach developed the Prisoner Dilemma model for two affiliated people, arrested for their involvement with human trafficking (Bhaumik, Roy, and Weber, 2019). In their research model scenario, no clear evidence exists for the suspects' human trafficking involvement, and there are four agencies, with increasing weights of punishment, who may interrogate the suspects. The researchers conclude, "that a clue to get more information about trafficking and other related phenomena, can be easily obtained by making a situation of betrayal between traffickers."

Operations Research literature has addressed various victim and trafficker experiences in human trafficking.

*2.1.14 Lifetime Experience and Human Trafficking*

Literature presents information for human trafficking involved persons, and their experiences, as well as for anti-trafficking members.

Keo et al. (2014) outlined data and related laws for arrested human traffickers in Cambodia. Research considered trafficker motivation, methodology, financial outcome, and their court proceedings. Hurtado, Iranzo Dosdad, and Gómez Hernández (2018) addressed a complex issue of the overlapped presence of human trafficking among children recruited into direct- and indirect-wartime activities. The authors identify an unfulfilled need of protection for trafficked victims beyond current, if any, protections for war-recruited children who will often view their affiliation as being a 'war criminal' and not as a 'victim'.

Kaye, Winterdyk, and Quarterman (2014) qualitatively approached the Canadian system definitions within human trafficking, anti-trafficking initiatives, and assessed trafficking presence, as perceived by members of social service systems. The research called for further anti-trafficking partnership, in the form of cross-sector collaboration to increase service effectiveness for trafficking victims.

*2.1.15 Lifetime Experience and Criminal Activity*

Esbec and Echeburúa (2016) considered the co-presence of differing intensities of drug use and criminal activity in cases handled by an international court system. The criminal's experiences are related to the level of drug addiction, criminal activity done, the legal conclusion of criminal responsibility, rehabilitation mandated, and subsequent consequences including imprisonment. The sequence and observation of certain experiences was related to the individual's drug-influenced state at the time crime was committed.

*2.1.16 Lifetime Experience*

Literature pertaining to the human lifetime experience is diverse and stages are organized through different application perspectives. The perspectives can be that of an individual lifetime, or collection of lifetimes. With regards to individual lifetimes:

- Agronin (2014) aggregated a historical to present review of the human lifetime, aging process viewpoints from different developmental theoreticians. The review discussed Erik H. Erikson's eight stages of the human lifetime, namely: Infancy, Early childhood, Play age, School age, Adolescence, Young adulthood, Adulthood, and Old age.

  Daniel Levinson's developmental periods was another framework reviewed. In Levinson's work, age ranges were assigned to periods, such that: from birth to 17 years of age was 'childhood/adolescence', from 17 years old to 40 years old was the 'early adult era', from 40 to 60 years old was the 'middle adult era', and from 60 years old until death was 'late adult era'.

  George Vaillant, another cited theoretician, described the aging process through the perspective of an ever-widening ripple from a stone dropped in water. Vaillant's visualization is organized among the aging stages of: Adolescence, Young adulthood, Middle age, and Old age.

  Gene D. Cohen reflected on the aging process, as it started from the middle of a lifetime. Valuing the potential of older generations, Cohen's model progressed through four phases: Mid-life re-evaluation, Liberation, Summing-up, and Encore.

  Altogether, the author's work paralleled the objectives of several renowned theoreticians to model the human lifetime, while demonstrating the unique characteristics of each model.

- Vemuri et al. (2018) investigated the human lifetime experience with gut microbial diversity and how it is impacted through the aging process. The lifetime was reviewed in the stages of: Infancy, Childhood, Preadolescence, Adulthood. The research focused on microbial diversity experienced by individuals in the elderly period of adulthood.

- Jacoby (2015) discussed five stages of employment for an individual employee. The stages, comprehensively labelled, "The [Human Resources] Lifetime," are: Recruitment, Education, Motivation, Evaluation, Celebration. These stages are encountered by the employee throughout their employment experience.

All these research works focused on the progression, in part or in whole, of an individual lifetime.

From the perspective of a collection of lifetimes, Kompanichenko (1994) approached the modern state of humankind existence from a compelling point of view for future civilization development. According to the research perspective, previous and current humankind activity belongs to the first stage of growth; comparable to an individual human life between birth and 18 years old. The upcoming stages for humankind, as presented by the author, are the:

- Stage of internal development. Reaching maturity.
- Maturity stage (stationary state)
- Stage of ageing

For an individual human, the research identifies the following stages of the human lifetime:

1. "Human in embryo" (Origination of a system.)
2. "Growth of human. Ends in reaching puberty and maximum body size." (*Stage of growth, increase of size.*)
3. "Growing up of human, acquiring skills of independent life, reproduction of progeny, reaching peak of existence (maturity)." (*Stage of internal development, reaching maturity.*)
4. "Stability of human's mature organism functioning, steady holding by man of a certain social niche." (*Stage of maturity, stationary state.*)

5. "Ageing, weakening of physical conditions with retention (or suppression of weakening of) intellectual conditions and cultural experience." (*Stage of ageing.*)

6. "Death." (Dying of a system.)

The author drew a parallel in describing humankind existence with the lifetime experienced by an individual human.

*2.1.17 Research Pillars Summary*

This first part of the literature review has identified and discussed relevant works at the convergence of this research work's three pillar topics (i.e., Stochastic Processes, Lifetime Experience, and Sex Trafficking). In all, the review was completed according to the sixteen components that were defined at the onset of the discussion in Figure 3 and Table 5. Multiple literature sources in this review have substantiated the suitability of Markov Chain modeling for sequences of experiences throughout and during an individual's lifetime. More specifically, important takeaways from this section were:

- Markov Chain modeling for criminal activity is established in literature.
- Lifetime experience modeling is established in literature.
- Markov Chain modeling for the lifetime experience of human trafficking and sex trafficking is an existing gap in literature and a promising approach to such social problems.
- There are pre-exploitation, exploitation, and post-exploitation experiences for sex trafficking victims.
- Literature surrounding victim trafficking experience modeling has taken various approaches.
  - Disjoint model of human trafficking (Zimmerman, Hossain, and Watts, 2011):

- Recruitment
- Travel and Transit
- Exploitation
- Detention
- Integration or Re-integration
- Re-trafficking in some cases

o Five stages of human trafficking (Greenbaum, 2014):
- Pre-departure stage
- Travel and transit stage
- Destination stage
- Detention, deportation, and criminal evidence stage
- Integration and reintegration stage

o <u>Stages when exploited by dating partner</u> (Rothman, Bazzi, and Bair-Merritt, 2015):
- Prior to dating
- Early phase dating
- Late phase dating

- No comprehensive, interconnected lifetime sex trafficking victimization model was found in the literature.

This concludes the literature review of the sixteen categories surrounding the pillar topics of this research. The following section is a more focused literature review on the specific experiences involved with sex trafficking victimization.

## 2.2 Victimization Stages

### 2.2.1 The General Lifetime Experience Model

A basic, common-sense framework for evaluating any human lifetime experience is shown in Figure 5. An initial starting state (i.e., General Population) and a single termination state (i.e., Death), are consistently states present in a human lifetime experience model. The starting state may be visited initially or after state departure, depending on the nature of the evaluated experience. Between the starting and terminal states is an "experience" sub-process, modeled for a specific experience that may or may not be experienced by the population of individuals being modeled. If a member of the starting, General Population, state will not observe the experience in their individual lifetime, there is an experience bypass between the starting and terminal states; the lifetime then being spent in the starting state.

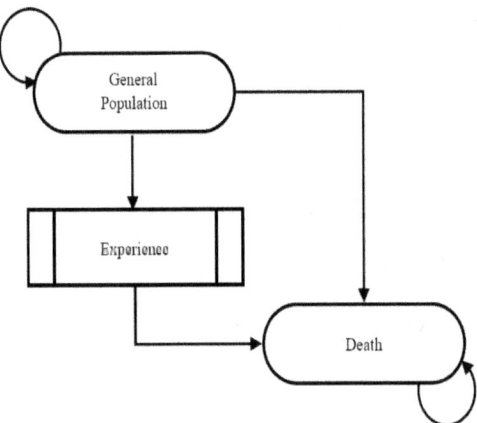

*Figure 5: General Lifetime Experience Model*

### 2.2.2 Macro Victimization Stages

In this next step, the previous model is developed towards the topic of this research To comprehensively model the lifetime experience of sex trafficking victimization, consideration is required for all Victim-experienced scenarios and stages. As a result, the macro-level development of the research model includes pre-victimization, victimization, and post-victimization stages (see Figure 6).

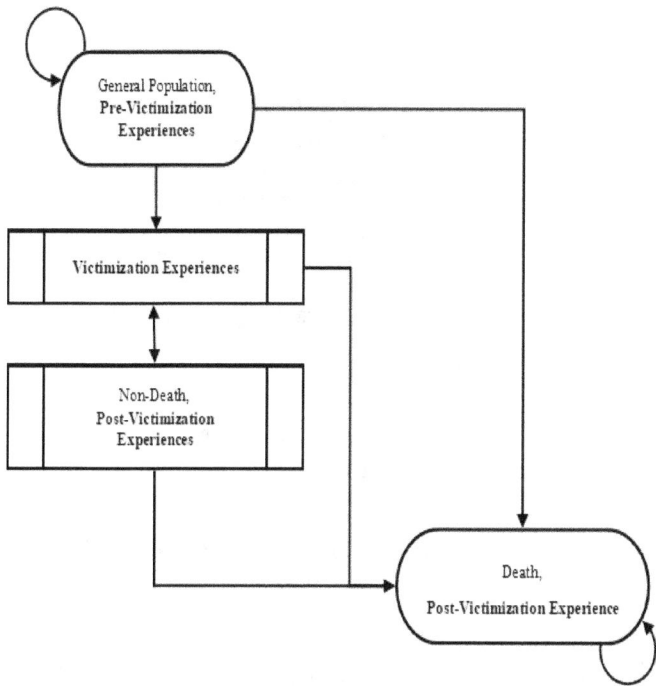

*Figure 6: Sex Trafficking Victimization Lifetime Experience Model – Macro*

Pre-Victimization

Within the sex trafficking victimization model, pre-victimization is a general source population to the victimization experience. The modeled population may be defined through any selection of individual characteristics (e.g., gender, economic class, residential security, etc.).

Pre-victimization may include risk-altering experiences. Felitti et al. (1998) spoke to the Adverse Childhood Experiences (ACE) framework, addressing the connection between negative childhood events and the resulting impact on the individual's future. Figure 7 is the visualization presented in their work. A primary conclusion of the study was that as the number of adverse experiences in childhood increases, the risk then also increases for negative future health and well-being outcomes.

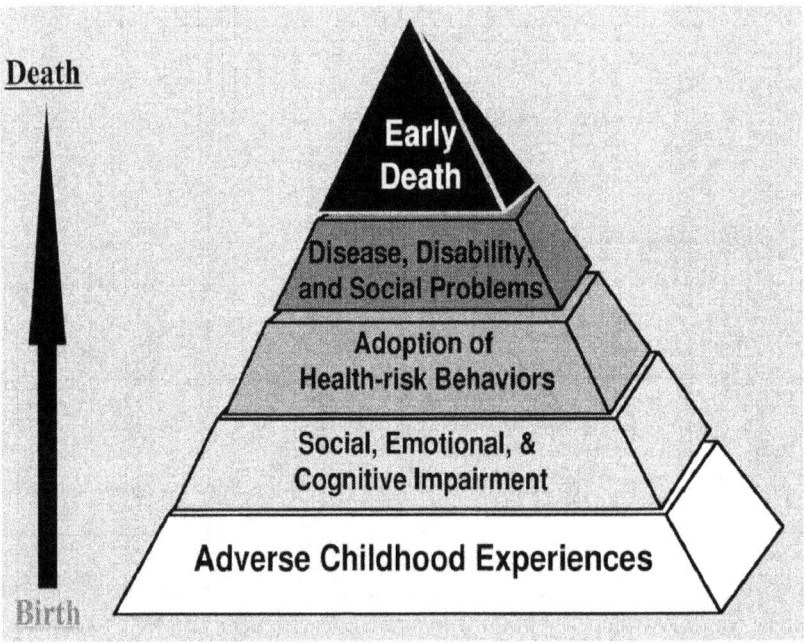

*Figure 7: "Potential influences throughout the lifespan of adverse childhood experiences" (Felitti et al., 1998)*

Several points of research have addressed influential factors on the initial risk of victimization in sex trafficking (Reid, 2012; Rothman, Bazzi, and Bair-Merritt, 2015; Sprang and Cole, 2018).

This research is developed to comprehensively model the individual's lifetime. Risk for victimization is the connecting factor of the individual to the experience of any form of sex trafficking victimization.

Victimization

Sex trafficking victimization is summarized as the sequential stages of *Recruitment*, *Trafficking*, and *Exploitation* (Kleemans and Smit, 2014; Mancuso, 2014; Baarda, 2016; Konrad et al., 2017). Each of the victimization stages summarize a variety of different types of trafficking experiences.

*Recruitment* is a summary term for entry to victimization by means of force, coercion, deception, kidnapping, pimping, recruitment, or commercial sex acts below the age of 18 (Hickle and Roe-Sepowitz, 2017). *Trafficking* may, but does not necessarily, include physical relocation (Reid, 2012). *Trafficking* and *Exploitation* are a cyclic pair of victim experiences where victimization occurs and another person benefits from the exploitation (United Nations, 2000). Hurtado, Iranzo Dosdad, and Gómez Hernández (2018) presented a detailed discussion of *Exploitation*, as viewed under different policies and laws.

Post-Victimization

The early stage of post-victimization is *Intervention*. *Intervention* may take different forms and be successful or unsuccessful.

Palmer and Foley (2017) state, "… each girl reaches a 'critical moment' in which they are conscious of making a decision, seeking help and reclaiming control despite the perpetual threats of violence and intimidation." This statement identifies those pivotal moments between victimization and post-victimization which occur in the lifetime experience, and not a gradual transition between victimization and post-victimization stages. Additionally, an important observation of their research was, "There can be no simple return to 'normal', pre-exploitation life; a new normal must be worked out but one which is safe." Therefore, post-victimization stages are different and independent of pre-victimization stages.

*Intervention* may involve only the victim or also another person(s). Successful intervention requires that the victim to be mentally ready for intervention. An established framework named, "Stages of Change" (a.k.a. "Transtheoretical Model"), involves the individual progressing through three stages to make a change (DiClemente et al., 1991). These stages are:

1. Pre-contemplation
2. Contemplation
3. Preparation

Recent work has taken focus to customize the *Stages of Change* framework to the specific application area of sex trafficking. Wilson and Nochajski (2018) identified four stages of change required for female victim departures from several international sexual exploitation settings:

1. Denial
2. Hopeful
3. Actively working
4. Perseverance

The victim mindset must be in a state of readiness for change for any intervention event to be successful. The intervention may or may not be initiated by the victim.

According to Muraya and Fry (2016), post-victimization should address the needs of the individual, which may include:

1. Rescue

2. Recovery

3. Reintegration and Repatriation.

*Rescue* could be via raids, victim escape, or hotline systems, and should include support for basic needs (e.g., "food, clothing, medical attention, if necessary, rest, and safe shelter"). *Recovery* are the elements of physical and mental health care service, as well as legal and safe and secure accommodation. *Reintegration* is defined as an exhaustive, multi-faceted support system to help the individual successfully return to society. *Repatriation*, as needed, may happen at any point during the post-victimization process, and it is prescribed when it is in the best interest of the individual. These post-victimization stages may overlap and could span from days to more than a decade by the researchers' estimate. A more detailed itemization of relevant research for aftercare services for victims is included in their research.

Survivor accounts of factors leading to their successful intervention included being believed, the availability of a trustworthy, non-judgmental individual, and a conscious moment of decided need for change (Palmer and Foley, 2017). In this same research, presented as a review of three child sexual exploitation accounts, observation of how victims sought help presented in various forms of distress (i.e., behavior changes, physical deterioration, emotional and psychological deterioration, and social isolation). Once intervened and exploitation has ended, the challenges for the victimized individual do not end, as they endure a process of repeatedly communicating their encounter to professionals, service providers, and courts, as well as facing the associated challenge of any investigation.

For interventions involving detainment, Zimmerman, Hossain, and Watts (2011) define a *detention stage* as, "a period when an individual is in the custody or detention of a state authority—or obliged to collaborate with authorities, such as under the restrictions placed on individuals who agree to cooperate with police in exchange for temporary residency."

Residential treatment programs are one type of resource for victims, post-victimization. These programs serve to treat the victim in the present, as well as aim to reduce their risk of revictimization (Thomson et al., 2011). For a sexually exploited female children residential treatment program in New England, most individuals arrive through the juvenile court system (Thomson et al., 2011).

While *Intervention* includes the short-term services and support for a victim to stabilize and depart the cycle of exploitation, *Survivor* is a long-term status of post-victimization life. Among the burdens for survivors is the need for *Integration or Reintegration*. The ECRE (2002) defines:

> "*Integration* [and *reintegration*] are 'long-term and multidimensional stages of either integrating into a host country [or reintegrating into a home country setting], which are not achieved until the individual becomes an active member of the economic, cultural, civil and political life of a country and perceives that he or she has oriented and is accepted'."

As a survivor attempts to attain a 'normal' life, a risk of re-trafficking exists (Adams, 2011; Zimmerman, Hossain, and Watts, 2011). Those trafficked are at risk for different reasons, such as financial and employment hardship, trafficking familiarity, and social stigmatization.

*Rehabilitation*, *Reintegration*, and *Repatriation* coincide in the lifetime of the victimization experience. A summative status of *Survivor* is defined to represent the ongoing, long-term post-victimization state.

Consequences endured by sex trafficking survivors in post-victimization stages included mental health (i.e., confusion, PTSD, suicidal thoughts) and social inclusion problems (Palmer and Foley, 2017). On a positive note, these same survivors proceeded to complete education studies, demonstrate thoughtfulness to their futures, and consent to sexual relationships.

*2.2.3 Identifying Micro Stages within Macro Victimization Literature*

The previous section identified distinct stages within the pre-victimization, victimization, and post-victimization macro elements of sex trafficking victimization literature. Namely, General Population, Recruitment, Trafficking, Exploitation, Intervention, and Survivor lifetime components. Figure 8 visually organizes these identified micro components within their macro victimization stages.

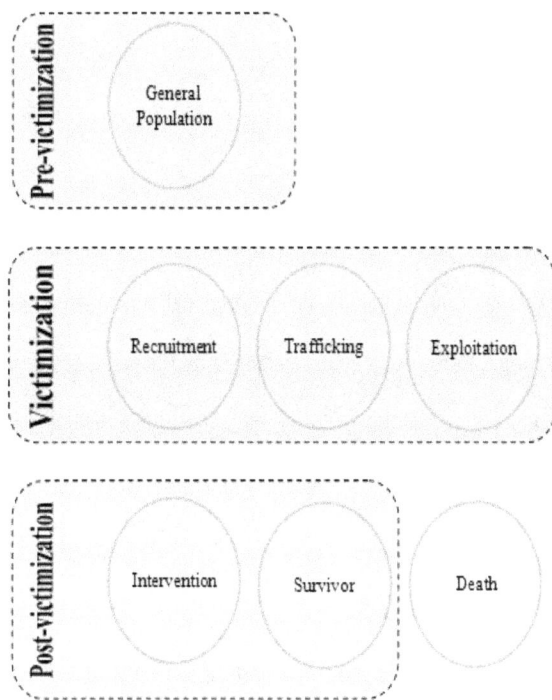

*Figure 8: Components of Macro Victimization Stages*

The first stage of pre-victimization collectively holds individuals in the General Population classification for any duration up until any form of victimization begins or death occurs. Recruitment, Trafficking, and Exploitation are the collection of events that can contribute towards an individual's victimization. Following any victimization events, Intervention and Survivor events account for any of an individual's post-victimization status. Death is a component which could follow pre-victimization, victimization, or post-victimization occurrences.

The next section addresses the micro-level stage definitions for sex trafficking victimization. The stages must be clearly defined, respect independence among stages, and accommodate the diversity of sex trafficking scenarios as well as the variety of victimization methodologies employed by traffickers.

*2.2.4 Micro Victimization Stages*

In the following, the distinct states of the victimization model are defined.

General Population

This research assumes all born individuals start in *General Population*. The starting state in any human experience model may be the entire global population or a clearly defined subset thereof. It is important to respect the considered starting population when identifying the value for the victimization risk probabilities. For example, the initial victimization risk probability will be calculated differently between a *General Population* which includes the entire World's population as opposed to a *General Population* that is defined as strictly female, homeless individuals.

The duration an individual stays in a starting, general population state will depend both on the risk of sex trafficking victimization, as well as the risk of mortality.

Recruitment

A unified global effort against sex trafficking is driven by organized strategies to define and overcome the problem. The United Nations (2000) provided a strong, comprehensive definition of human trafficking. From the definition, sex trafficking *Recruitment* entails:

"... threat or use of force or other forms of coercion, of abduction, of fraud, of deception, of the abuse of power or of a position of vulnerability or of the giving or receiving of payments or benefits to achieve the consent of a person having control over another person..." (United Nations, 2000)

To be articulate, further definitions are required. To quote Reid (2012):

"The U.S. Department of Health and Human Services [HHS] defines *force, fraud,* and *coercion* as follows:

- *Force* involves the use of rape, beatings and confinement to control victims. Forceful violence is used especially during the early stages of victimization, known as the "seasoning process," which is used to break victims' resistance to make them easier to control.

- *Fraud* often involves false offers that induce people into trafficking situations. For example, women and children will reply to advertisements promising jobs as waitresses, maids, and dancers in other countries and are then trafficked for purposes of prostitution once they arrive at their destinations.

- *Coercion* involves threats of serious harm to, or physical restraint of, any person; any scheme, plan or pattern intended to cause a person to believe that failure to perform an act would result in serious harm to or physical restraint against any person; or the abuse or threatened abuse of the legal process."

Trafficking

Dahal et al. (2015) referenced a definition of trafficking from the SAARC Convention on Preventing and Combatting Trafficking in Women and Children for Prostitution:

> "The convention defines *trafficking* as 'the transportation, selling or buying of women and children for (forced) prostitution within and outside a country for monetary or other considerations with or without the consent of the person subjected to trafficking'."

Reid's (2012) detailed review identified the common misconceptions of the *Trafficking* component of sex trafficking, stating:

> "Due to the conventional meaning of the term trafficking, a widespread misconception is that sex trafficking always involves the clandestine movement of individuals across international borders. Although the movement of sex trafficking victims is commonly practiced to hamper detection of criminal activities by local law enforcement and to disorient the victims, it is not a necessary component of sex trafficking. In reality, many victims "destined" for exploitation in sex trafficking in North America are not trafficked into the region from other countries, but rather are trafficked domestically within their home country."

*Trafficking* includes the means used to facilitate *Exploitation* events.

Exploitation

With regards to sex trafficking, the United Nations (2000) definition of human trafficking offered the following definition of *Exploitation*:

> "Exploitation shall include, at a minimum, the exploitation of the prostitution of others or other forms of sexual exploitation…"

The 'other forms of sexual exploitation' in the previous definition refers to non-prostitution forms of exploitation. Reid (2012) identified that, "Commercial sexual activity may include prostitution, the production of pornography, stripping and nude dancing, or live sex shows."

Intervention

*Intervention* is an encompassing term for any combination of resources used towards extraction of a victim from victimization. Unfortunately, intervention events are not always successful. The U.S. Department of Justice (2017) identified in a national strategy report for anti-trafficking:

> "Because commercial sex is already illegal in most locations, it is more likely that law enforcement will encounter potential victims. However, victim identification may be hampered because minors may say they are over the age of 18, and adults may conceal the use of force, fraud, and coercion."

Law enforcement is one form of intervention resource.

Several literature works have discussed the intervention potential for medical systems to victims, as well as tourism industry to sex trafficking activities (these research works were previously discussed).

An important observation is the lack of literature addressing the existing sex trafficking victimization intervention methodologies. An even more meaningful lack in research exists for evaluating the effectiveness among different intervention methods for (i) initial identification of victims and (ii) successfully intervening an individual from returning to victimization. It is beyond the scope of this research, but very important for future research, to address this gap to best aid victimization intervention efforts as well as inform policymakers of resource allocation best-practices within and among intervention entities.

Due to the variety of intervention types, the model of this research assumes a single step duration of each intervention event for the modeled individual. A successful intervention occurs when the individual transitions to the *Survivor* state. An unsuccessful intervention results in the individual returning to the cycle of *Trafficking* and *Exploitation*.

Survivor

A *Survivor* can be defined as any individual previously recruited into sex trafficking, who has subsequently been intervened <u>successfully</u> through their own or other intervention efforts. This state is reoccurring for the remainder of the individual's lifetime, assuming there is no incident of re-trafficking.

Death

*Death* is the inevitable end to the individual human lifetime. Therefore, *Death* is the final, absorptive state of the lifetime experience model. The model of this research assumes *Death* is a realized risk from most transition states in the model. Death during intervention was not an identified risk in the literature.

*2.2.5 Flow Among States*

Building the connections among the seven defined states (i.e., General Population, Recruitment, Trafficking, Exploitation, Intervention, Survivor, and Death) was an incremental process of piecing together the various aspects of literature. The following summarizes important flows that have been identified in literature:

- Various factors can elevate the risk of initial victimization (Reid, 2012; Rothman, Bazzi, and Bair-Merritt, 2015; Sprang and Cole, 2018).
- Sequential flow through Recruitment, Trafficking, Exploitation (Zimmerman, Hossain, and Watts, 2011; Kleemans and Smit, 2014; Mancuso, 2014; Baarda, 2016; Konrad et al., 2017).
- Post-victimization to include any combination of rescue, recovery, reintegration, and repatriation (Muraya and Fry, 2016). All of which may overlap.
- Re-trafficking is a risk to survivors (Adams, 2011; Thomson et al., 2011; Zimmerman, Hossain, and Watts, 2011).
- Numerous health consequences exist for victims and survivors (Thomson et al., 2011; Palmer and Foley, 2017; Jung, 2017; Lamb-Susca and Clements, 2018; Moore et al., 2019).
- Changes in risk of death is not clearly investigated throughout the different stages of victimization. Though, there is justification for future research. Consider, "I felt that committing suicide was better than selling my body." - Trafficked Female (Dahal et al., 2015).

Altogether, literature cited was the basis for defining the transition events that occur in the lifetime experience of sex trafficking victimization.

## 2.3 Anti-trafficking Approaches

A thorough review of anti-trafficking initiatives and policies is beyond the scope of this research. However, two popular anti-trafficking concepts are the '4P Paradigm' and the 'Nordic' model. While the first is a system for categorizing anti-trafficking approaches, the latter is a policy strategy that varies in acceptance domestically and internationally.

### 2.3.1 '4P Paradigm'

The 4P Paradigm outlines the four categories of anti-trafficking initiatives and activities. The '4Ps' are: Prevention, Protection, Prosecution, and Partnership. Table 10 summarizes the definitions of each "P" (Konrad et al., 2017).

*Table 10: Definitions of the "4Ps" (Konrad et al., 2017)*

| Category | Definition |
| --- | --- |
| Prevention | "involves fostering public awareness and carrying out educational campaigns aimed at conveying the nature and gravity of human trafficking, as well as providing alternative vocational opportunities for at-risk persons, particularly women and girls." |
| Protection | "includes the rescue, rehabilitation, and reintegration of victims into society." |
| Prosecution | "refers to the just creation and enforcement of anti-trafficking laws and punishment of those convicted of trafficking." |
| Partnership | "refers to the critical necessity of collaboration and information sharing, both within and across geographical and political boundaries, to successfully fight this epidemic." |

### 2.3.2 'Nordic' Model (a.k.a. Swedish Model)

Anti-trafficking members will often refer to, discuss, and sometimes contend (Kingston and Thomas, 2019; Calderaro and Giametta, 2019), whether the United States would benefit from implementing the "Nordic Model" structure of sex trafficking policies, as implemented in other nations. Though it does not address all forms of sex trafficking (e.g., familial sex trafficking), the intention of the "Nordic Model" is to impact the prostitution forms of sex trafficking by criminalizing the purchase of sexual services. Independent, entrepreneurial sex workers have a valid claim that this model will reduce demand, impacting their non-exploitative business of exchanging sexual services for compensation. However, in terms of a sex trafficking victimization experience model, the impact of presumably reducing demand while also easing the pathway of intervention is a two-folded approach of support to anti-trafficking objectives.

*2.3.3 Research Contributions towards Policy*

This research maintains a technical focus of developing and exercising a model to provide policy- and decision-makers, as well as anti-trafficking analysts, a methodical approach to understanding how results of policy or changes may affect the lifetime experience of sex trafficking victimization. The gamut of policy evaluation and measuring the impact thereof requires expertise beyond this research scope. However, with that expertise, the inputs for this work may be accurately derived. Value of this research's methodology, tools, and parameters can be observed with each instance of assessing these expert-derived inputs.

**2.4 Research Significance**

The key literature gap addressed in this research is at the intersection of Markov Chain modeling, lifetime experiences, and sex trafficking (see Table 5, Category 8). More specifically, the completed literature review is sufficient foundation to model, analyze, and understand the sex trafficking victimization lifetime experiences of trafficked females in the United States. In the upcoming sections, the model will be defined and further prepared for Markov analysis. After model preparation, select theoretical analysis results are presented. The theoretical modeling discussion is followed by an application of the research model structure to a select case study dataset. The results and methods of this research contribute towards anti-trafficking best practices through a design that allows for more thorough understanding of sex trafficking victimization experiences in individual lifetimes. The research also introduces a modeling approach and methodology that is easily adaptable to model other human lifetime experiences.

**2.5 Research Assumptions**

Certain assumptions are required for this research to be applied to a DTMC design. Among the assumptions are those specific to Markov Chain modeling, as well as assumptions for analysis and interpretation as it pertains to sex trafficking. These assumptions are:

- Memoryless: The formulated Markov Chain model observes the Markov Property of memoryless state transition probabilities. As to say, the first-order Markov model developed assumes no past information of entity statuses influence the future transitions, only the current state.

- Homogeneity: Time homogenous Markov chains have consistent transition probabilities throughout the modeling period. Beyond the scope of this research, it would be valuable to relax this assumption. Factors, such as and especially "age", would be better modeled in an inhomogeneous (i.e., time-dependent) Markov chain, once there is suitable data (e.g., Markov chain with age as a factor; Shauly et al., 2011).

- North American Victims: Sex trafficking victimization experience modeled for individuals into and within North America. This includes both domestic victims, as well as internationally sourced victims.

- Female Victims: This research is heavily based on the more substantial literature basis for female victims of sex trafficking. Males and non-binary individuals are also sex trafficked. This model has not been investigated for its suitability to male and non-binary populations.

- Implications of Adulthood Not Modeled: The age of 18 years old defines the difference between "woman" and "girl". This research is built for the entire lifetime, so 18 years old is arbitrary to the model. However, there are significant judicial and social service differences between adolescents and adults. This effect is beyond the scope of this research.

- Familial Sex Trafficking (i.e., trafficking by a family member): has certain unique characteristics related to before, during, and after exploitation (Sprang and Cole, 2018). For example, children trafficked are often younger than non-familial trafficked victims, "recruitment" could be considered the exercise of parental control or other threats, "trafficking" may be only planning with no movement of the victim, and post-exploitation, the victim may have regular interactions with the trafficker. Review of the literature suggests this research model is suitable for modeling familial trafficking. However, close attention is required to state definitions and the associated risk and transition parameters assigned.

- "Victim" Independence of "Trafficker" Classification: This research does not take any special consideration to victims who also are, or become, traffickers. The analysis is solely focused on victims and the victimization process experienced as individuals.

- Starting State is General Population: Regardless of the type of trafficking, this model assumes that a potential victim's lifetime always begins with birth into an initial, General Population state. This already is a relaxed assumption, as the formulations presented in this research are correct for any starting state (e.g., evaluating for individuals already in victimization status rather than including pre-victimization time in an analysis effort). Interpretation is the only change.

- Each Intervention is One Step Duration: Due to the variety and varying length of post-victimization experiences among victims (Muraya and Fry, 2016), the Intervention stage is assumed to be one period. If the Intervention event is successful, the remaining post-victimization activities occur in the Survivor state. If the Intervention event is unsuccessful, the victim returns to victimization processes.

- <u>Monthly Step Size</u>: Another loose assumption is for analysis to be completed in a monthly step size. A change to step size simply implies a change to inputted transition probabilities.

This research sets precedent for subsequent research to further contributions from modeling. One approach to extend this research may be to relax any of these stated assumptions.

### 2.6 Literature Review Summary

While a comprehensive model for individuals experiencing sex trafficking victimization is lacking, individual elements of the lived experiences within sex trafficking victimization are evidenced, sometimes repeatedly, by literature.

The initial review was a broad approach, reviewing an expansive sixteen categories. The categories were formed by combinations of the three pillar topics of this research: namely, Stochastic Processes, Lifetime Experiences, and Sex Trafficking. The following are key observations from this review.

- Markov Chain modeling of experiences throughout and during an individual's lifetime are diversely present in literature.
- <u>Disjoint model of human trafficking</u> (Zimmerman, Hossain, and Watts, 2011):
    - Recruitment
    - Travel and Transit
    - Exploitation
    - Detention
    - Integration or Re-integration

- o Re-trafficking in some cases
- Five stages of human trafficking (Greenbaum, 2014):
  - o Pre-departure stage
  - o Travel and transit stage
  - o Destination stage
  - o Detention, deportation, and criminal evidence stage
  - o Integration and reintegration stage
- Stages when exploited by dating partner (Rothman, Bazzi, and Bair-Merritt, 2015):
  - o Prior to dating
  - o Early phase dating
  - o Late phase dating

Thereafter, the discussion focused on the stages of sex trafficking victimization. From a macro-view, the three stages of victimization are:

1. Pre-Victimization
2. Victimization
3. Post-Victimization

The stages are sequential, yet potentially reoccurring between Victimization and Post-Victimization stages. Existing literature, organized according to these three stages, identified detailed events within both the Victimization and Post-Victimization stages. Within Victimization, there are the states:

- Recruitment
- Trafficking
- Exploitation

And within Post-Victimization, there are the states:

- Intervention
- Survivor
- Death

Definitions for Recruitment, Trafficking, Exploitation, Intervention, Survivor, and Death states are detailed, such that each state is independent and all-encompassing for the vast variety of sex trafficking scenarios and methodologies imposed by sex trafficking traffickers.

No single literature article defined the connections among the defined states. Yet, the combination of several literature articles presents a more unified understanding of the relationship of flow among the defined states. The primary connections developed in literature include:

- Various factors can elevate the risk of initial victimization.
- Sequential flow through Recruitment, Trafficking, and Exploitation.
- Post-victimization includes any combination of rescue, recovery, reintegration, and repatriation. Any of which may overlap.
- Re-trafficking is a risk to survivors.
- Numerous health consequences exist for victims and survivors.

The selected methodological approach of Markov Chains respects the discrete time, finite state space requirements of modeling sex trafficking victimization during an individual's lifetime. With this approach, there are specific assumptions adopted for this research. The following summarizes those assumptions.

- Memoryless
- Homogeneity

- North American victims
- Female victims
- Implications of adulthood not modeled
- Familial Sex Trafficking (i.e., trafficking by a family member) is accounted for
- "Victim" independence of "Trafficker" classification
- Starting state is *General Population*
- Each intervention is one step duration
- Monthly step size

These assumptions, considered valid and reasonable, support the progression of the completed literature review into the upcoming model definition.

The three objectives of this research (previously outlined in Chapter 1) address existing gaps in literature. To summarize the gaps identified in the literature that are addressed by the objectives of this research:

- Identified literature lacks a comprehensive lifetime model of the sex trafficking victimization experience of an individual (i.e., Research Objective 1).
- Without comprehensive models, understanding is limited regarding the complete impact of social and policy changes within the sex trafficking system to both individuals as well as the collective group (i.e., Research Objective 2).
- While the theory of modeling is justified, a step further is required to develop the model in a usable format for anti-trafficking and policy experts alike (i.e., Research Objective 3).

In the next chapter, the fully interconnected lifetime model resulting from the literature review is defined. The chapter will cover the design and mathematical considerations of further defining the model into a DTMC. Thereafter, a case study is introduced and applied to demonstrate modeling capabilities as well as lead the observation process through a series of sensitivity analysis exercises.

# CHAPTER 3

## METHODOLOGY

In the previous chapter, a foundational literature review was presented surrounding the pillar topics of sex trafficking, lifetime experiences, and stochastic processes. This was followed by a detailed review of pertinent literature to this research's focus on the lifetime experiences within sex trafficking victimization. The Macro elements of sex trafficking victimization were identified to be pre-Victimization, Victimization, and post-Victimization stages. The Micro elements of sex trafficking victimization were identified to be General Population, Recruitment, Trafficking, Exploitation, Intervention, and Survivor. Risk of re-trafficking and the cyclic subprocess among Trafficking and Exploitation were among the several key relationships identified among the Micro elements and represent the potential transitions between sets of experiences during a lifetime. The resulting model is shown in Figure 9.

## 3.1 Lifetime Model of the Sex Trafficking Victimization Experience

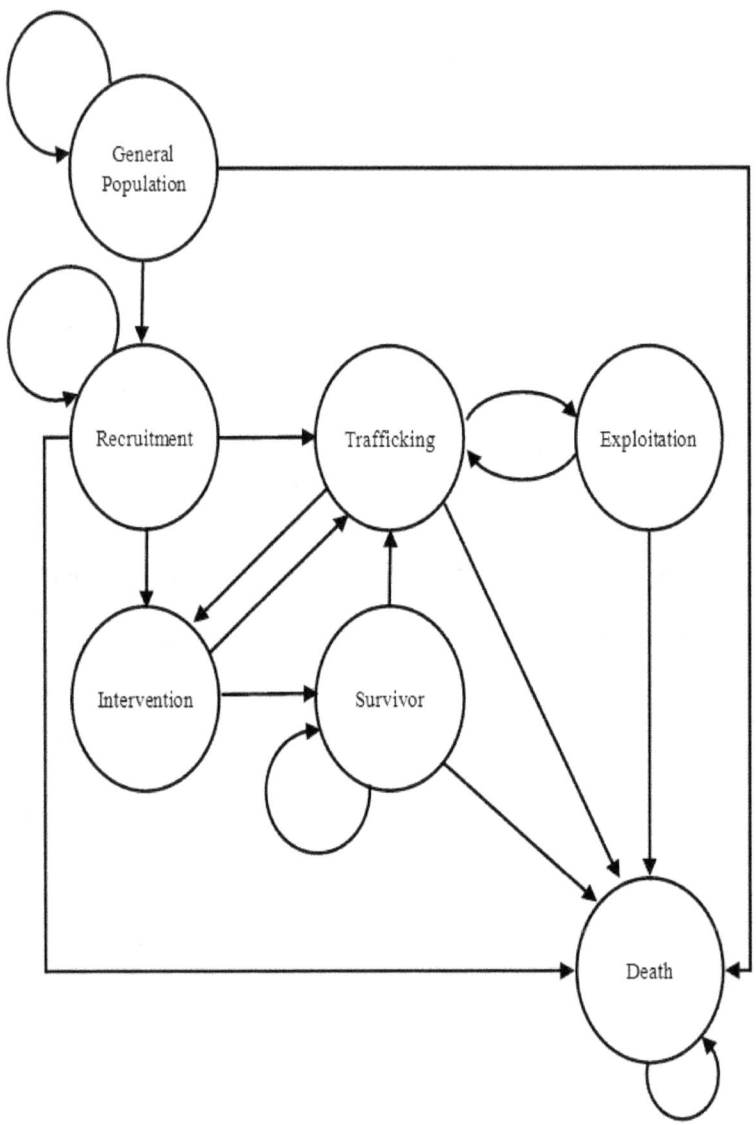

*Figure 9: Lifetime Experience Model of Sex Trafficking Victimization*

## 3.2 Modelling Entity

The model entity is an Individual, who if victimized, becomes a *Victim*. A *Victim* is any individual successfully recruited into sex trafficking victimization, for any duration of time, number of trafficking-exploitation cycles, sequence of lifetime experiences, and independent of other non-sex trafficking victimization experiences (e.g., marriage) in their lifetime. Once an individual faces victimization, they will never return to *General Population*. The Individual is also identified as a *Survivor* upon transitioning to post-victimization states.

Note, it is possible but not requisite for a *Victim* to also be a *Trafficker* (Williamson and Cluse-Tolar, 2002; Mancuso, 2014; Baarda, 2016; Crocker, 2017). The two terms of *Victim* and *Trafficker* are regarded as independent for this research.

## 3.3 Model Validation

Beyond the content of relevant literature, validation of the developed lifetime experience model of sex trafficking victimization has been completed through review of Survivor case studies and discussions with subject experts.

### *3.3.1 Survivor Case Studies*

To demonstrate the versatility and applicability of the victimization model developed through the previous literature review, this section presents mapping results of documented individual sex trafficking victimization experiences (see Table 11). Information from the case studies were partitioned to identify the sequence of state transitions. Appendix I includes the specific, extracted details leading to the flow summaries.

*Table 11: Selected Case Studies in terms of Framework, Validation of Framework*

| Researcher(s) | Year | Name | Sequence of Events During Lifetime ||||||||
|---|---|---|---|---|---|---|---|---|---|---|
| | | | 1ST | 2ND | 3RD | 4TH | 5TH | 6TH | 7TH | 8TH |
| Rothman, Bazzi, and Bair-Merritt | 2015 | Case #1 | GP | R | TE | I | S | | | |
| | | Case #2 | GP | R | TE | I | TE | I | S | |
| | | Case #3 | GP | R | TE | I | S | TE | I | S |
| | | Case #4 | GP | R | TE | I | TE | I | S | |
| UNODC | 2020 | No. USA170 | GP | R | TE | I | TE | I | | |
| | | No. USA167 | GP | R | I | | | | | |
| | | No. USA168 | GP | R | TE | I | | | | |
| | | No. USA169 | GP | R | TE | I | | | | |
| | | No. USA150 | GP | R | TE | I | | | | |
| | | No. USA171 | GP | R | TE | | | | | |
| | | No. USA165 | GP | R | TE | I | | | | |
| | | No. USA031 | GP | R | TE | I | | | | |
| | | No. USA007 | GP | R | TE | I | S | | | |
| | | No. USA046 | GP | R | TE | I | | | | |

Key: GP: General Population  TE: Trafficking and Exploitation  S: Survivor
     R: Recruitment          I: Intervention                   D: Death

Rothman, Bazzi, and Bair-Merritt (2015) presented a case study review of four individuals' sex trafficking victimization experiences, all female victims with victimization presenting through dating violence, as recorded in semi-structured interviews with the victim. UNODC (2020) human trafficking case files were filtered for relevance to sex trafficking victimization, a final/upheld "Guilty" verdict, "United States of America" for country of prosecution, and 2010-2015 verdict dates. Unlike the first four detailed accounts of victimization experiences, these court files emphasized information of the victimization experience from the prosecuted trafficker point of view and lack detail for pre- and post-victimization experiences for the victim/survivor. Nonetheless, value remains as the actions of the trafficker imply certain experiences of their victims. In all case studies, the victim/survivor is presumed alive, thus no terminality of lifetime is assumed.

Review of these cases validates the robustness and general applicability of the defined research model to accommodate a diversity of sex trafficking victimization experiences and sequences thereof. Both www.unodc.org and www.humantraffickingdata.org are recommended databases by the University of Michigan Law for prosecuted trafficking case studies. The interested analyst may observe more case studies and their fitness to the model of this research.

*3.3.2 Expert Validation*

Additional validation of the literature-developed sex trafficking victimization lifetime model has been completed. Presentation attendance and discussions with anti-trafficking experts and field personnel at the 2019 International Human Trafficking & Social Justice conference was one of the actions taken towards model validation. Several discussions have occurred through the course of this research to review the model and its components with social justice experts, law enforcement, and a sex trafficking survivor who now serves as an anti-trafficking public advocate.

**3.4 Preparing the Markov Model**

The balance of this chapter develops a methodology surrounding the model definition through standard Markov Chain techniques. Analysis presented in this chapter is motivated towards theoretical, variable-form solutions. Variable-form solutions support a tool-based design for evolving datasets as well as driving generic conclusions for the research's model structure. Upcoming chapters will further use these variable-form solutions and approaches to evaluate a case study dataset.

A Markov Chain is a stochastic process represented by a graph built of states and arc transitions, accompanied by a probability matrix for those transitions (Ross, 2010). The use of Markov Chains for Sociological problems, such as the lifetime experience of AIDS/HIV progression (Apenteng and Ismail, 2015), is chartered territory. In a similar sense, the Lifetime

Experience Model of Sex Trafficking Victimization is approached as a Markov model, observing key model characteristics:

- Discrete-time Markov chain (DTMC)
- Finite state space
- First-order, memoryless

The composition of Figure 10-Figure 12 outlines the developing model for analysis.

In Figure 10(a), the previously defined model of the relationship among the sex trafficking victimization experience states are outlined with labelled nodes and transition arcs. Figure 10(b) outlines the categorization of individual states among the macro stages of pre-victimization, victimization, and post-victimization.

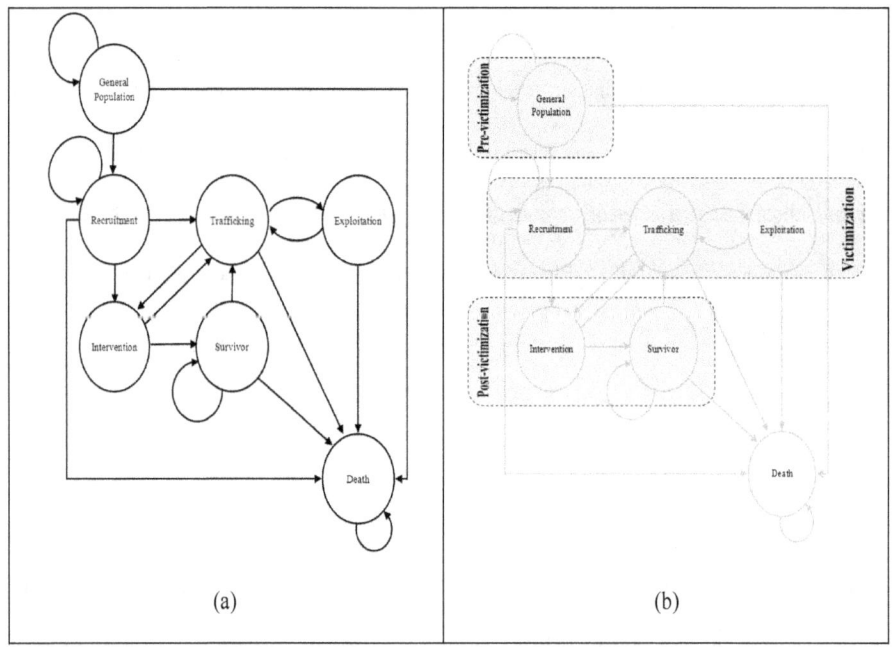

*Figure 10(a-b): Development of the Lifetime Experience of Sex Trafficking Victimization Model*

Figure 11(a) labels observed literature and industry jargon on relevant elements of the developed model. To respect the principles of Markov methodologies and the characteristics previously mentioned, Figure 11(b) highlights the subprocess of *Trafficking-Exploitation*. The subprocess is typically a more rapidly transitioning event, relative to transitions among the other model states.

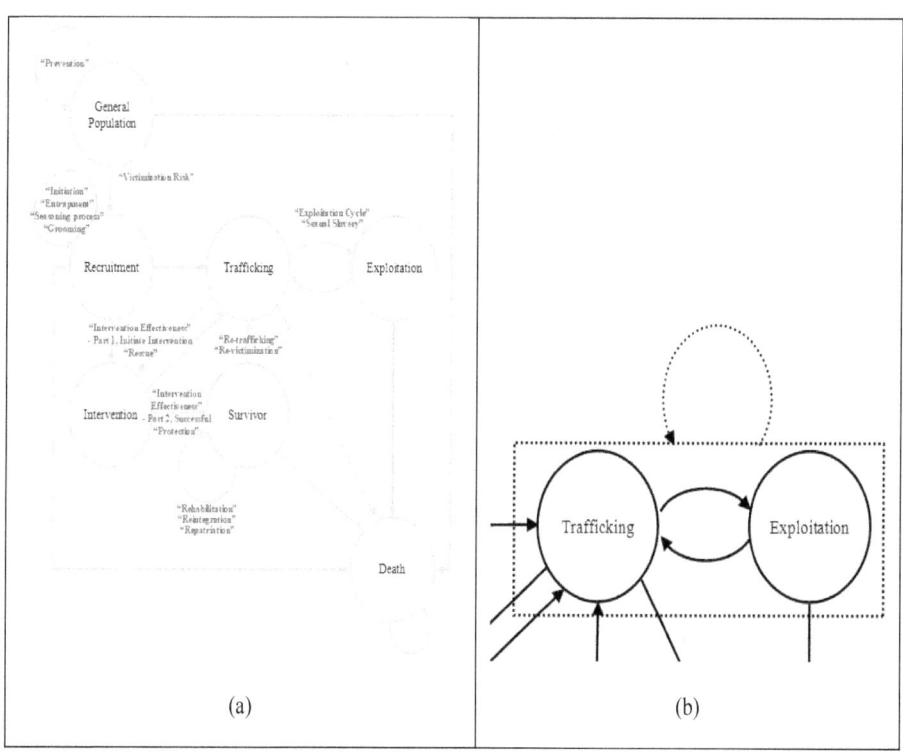

*Figure 11(a-b): Development of the Lifetime Experience of Sex Trafficking Victimization Model*

To maintain consistency throughout the modeling analysis, the subprocess of Figure 11(b) is condensed into a single state, as shown in Figure 12(a) and Figure 12(b). One final model preparation step is shown in Figure 12(b), where all states and transition arcs are labelled. With State 3 condensed, the model of this research is a six-state, DTMC.

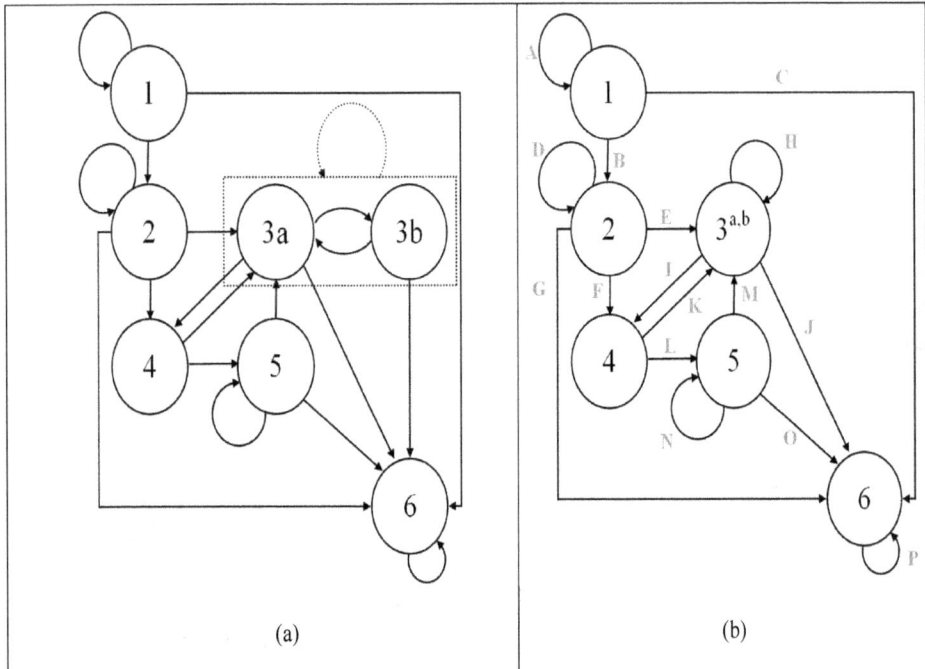

*Figure 12(a-b): Development of the Lifetime Experience of Sex Trafficking Victimization Model*

### 3.4.1 States and Transitions

The results displayed in the previous figures can be summarized in tabular format. Table 12 records the state descriptions for the six states in the DTMC model. Table 13 records the interpretation of each transition arc, labelled "A" – "P".

*Table 12: State Identification*

| State | State Description |
|---|---|
| 1 | General Population |
| 2 | Recruitment |
| 3 | Trafficking-Exploitation (sub-cycle) |
| 4 | Intervention |
| 5 | Survivor |
| 6 | Death |

*Table 13: Transition Definitions*

| Arc | States (From, To) | Transition Interpretation |
|---|---|---|
| A | (1, 1) | No victimization has occurred. |
| B | (1, 2) | Successful recruitment of individual. |
| C | (1, 6) | Mortality risk for general population individuals. |
| D | (2, 2) | Ongoing recruitment events, pre-exploitation. |
| E | (2, 3) | Transition from recruitment to trafficking-exploitation activities. |
| F | (2, 4) | Intervention event to recruited individual. |
| G | (2, 6) | Mortality risk for recruited individuals. |
| H | (3, 3) | Ongoing trafficking-exploitation events. |
| I | (3, 4) | Intervention event to exploited individual. |
| J | (3, 6) | Mortality risk for exploited individuals. |
| K | (4, 3) | Unsuccessful intervention event. (i.e., victim returns to exploitive situation) |
| L | (4, 5) | Successful intervention event. |
| M | (5, 3) | Survivor's return to exploitation. (This does not include independent sex work) |
| N | (5, 5) | Ongoing post-victimization status as a Survivor. |
| O | (5, 6) | Mortality risk for survivor individuals. |
| P | (6, 6) | Once death has occurred, the lifetime is complete and remains at death state. |

### 3.4.2 Probability Transition Matrix

Let $\{X_n, n = 0,1,2,...\}$ be the state of a *Victim* at time $n$ (Ross, 2010). Table 12 outlines all potential values, $i$, for $X_n$. The defined model is evaluated as a DTMC, assuming time homogenous, stationary state transitions. Transition probability, $P_{ij}$, is defined in Equation 1.

$$P_{ij} = P\{X_{n+1} = j \mid X_n = i, X_{n-1} = i_{n-1}, ..., X_1 = i_1, X_0 = i_0\} \quad (1)$$

Let $T$ define the set of transient states, and $Ab$ define the set of absorptive states. Then,

$$T = [1,2,3,4,5] \qquad Ab = [6] \qquad (2)$$

Using the scheme presented in Figure 12(f), transition probability matrix, **P**, is defined as follows:

$$P = \begin{bmatrix} A & B & 0 & 0 & 0 & C \\ 0 & D & E & F & 0 & G \\ 0 & 0 & H & I & 0 & J \\ 0 & 0 & K & 0 & L & 0 \\ 0 & 0 & M & 0 & N & O \\ 0 & 0 & 0 & 0 & 0 & P \end{bmatrix} \qquad (3)$$

where,

$$\sum_j P_{ij} = 1 \qquad \forall i = 1, 2, \ldots, 6 \qquad (4)$$

Partitioning transition probability matrix, $P$, among transient and absorptive structures, let

$$P = \begin{bmatrix} Q & R \\ 0 & I_r \end{bmatrix} \qquad (5)$$

Where $Q$, also known as transient probability matrix $P_T$, represents the 5x5 matrix of flow probabilities among transient states. $R$ represents the 5x1 matrix of flow from $T$ elements into the $Ab$ element. 0 represents a 1x5 zero matrix, and $I_r$ is a 1x1 Identity matrix to represent the recurrence of transition within the $Ab$ element. As a result of these definitions, $Q$ may be defined as,

$$Q = P_T = \begin{bmatrix} A & B & 0 & 0 & 0 \\ 0 & D & E & F & 0 \\ 0 & 0 & H & I & 0 \\ 0 & 0 & K & 0 & L \\ 0 & 0 & M & 0 & N \end{bmatrix} \qquad (6)$$

For this research, all transition probabilities are assumed to remain constant throughout the individual's lifetime and in variable form as coded in Table 13 (i.e. "A" – "P"). Beyond the scope of this research due to an existing lack of reliable data, a point of priority for future research should be to address the stationary assumption of this methodology. To exemplify the point, consider the sex trafficking victimization risk of a 35-year-old, employed female versus a 15-year-old, runaway homeless female. Undoubtedly, elements of the transition matrix will differ over time, both because of attributes such as age and risk factors of the victim-group modeled.

A potential approach would be to develop the model into a Markov Decision Process (MDP). Traditionally an MDP has probabilities dependent on "actions" taken as a probabilistic result of a policy. Due to the characteristics of sex trafficking victimization, probabilities may be evaluated with the victim attributes as the "action" of MDP considerations. Due to the lack of dependable victimization data for analysis at this time, the stationary assumption is upheld. As a result, analysis is done with variable representations of a single summative state transition probability for each transition arc, regardless of all other factors. To make development of an MDP worthwhile, future work should first aim to better quantify dependable values for each transition probability listed in Table 13, ideally recorded for the risk factor attributes as well as the victim attribute of age.

*3.4.3 The User*

The anticipated user of this model are academic researchers, anti-trafficking analysts, and policy-making analysts. The user of the research model and methodology should have existing comprehension in quantitative methods and use thereof for sociological applications. Having this knowledge foundation will enable the user to accurately derive model inputs and gain the most insights from model outputs.

### 3.5 Markov Model Calculations

The Markov model is approached in this chapter strictly through variable representations. Identification and analysis of variable-form solutions offers valuable, general insights of the lifetime experience model. These insights include the amount of time (i.e., in terms of steps) expected in each state before absorption (i.e. death), n-step probability of transition among states, and sensitivity analysis with rates of change and incremental variable changes. A vast variety of calculations can be set up and evaluated having a defined Markov model. In the following, a select subset of all potential calculations are defined and discussed.

*3.5.1 Expected Time in Each State Before Absorption*

Let $q_{ij}$ be the expected time a process is in state $j$, given it starts in state $i$. Then, the following calculation establishes the Fundamental Matrix, $\mathbb{Q}$, in Equation 7 (Li, 2015).

$$\mathbb{Q} = (I_T - P_T)^{-1} \qquad (7)$$

Where, $I_T$ is a 5×5 Identity matrix. Then,

$$\mathbb{Q} = (I_T - P_T)^{-1} = \left( \begin{bmatrix} 1 & 0 & 0 & 0 & 0 \\ 0 & 1 & 0 & 0 & 0 \\ 0 & 0 & 1 & 0 & 0 \\ 0 & 0 & 0 & 1 & 0 \\ 0 & 0 & 0 & 0 & 1 \end{bmatrix} - \begin{bmatrix} A & B & 0 & 0 & 0 \\ 0 & D & E & F & 0 \\ 0 & 0 & H & I & 0 \\ 0 & 0 & K & 0 & L \\ 0 & 0 & M & 0 & N \end{bmatrix} \right)^{-1} = \begin{bmatrix} I & II & III & IV & V \\ VI & VII & VIII & IX & X \\ XI & XII & XIII & XIV & XV \\ XVI & XVII & XVIII & XIX & XX \\ XXI & XXII & XXIII & XXIV & XXV \end{bmatrix} \qquad (8)$$

where, for formatting purposes, roman numerals *I* through *XXV* are used as placeholders within each of the $\mathbb{Q}$ matrix elements for the resulting variable-form equations. The complete results of the $\mathbb{Q}$ matrix is included in Appendix E.

The $\mathbb{Q}$ matrix gives the expected number of visits to a state, $j$, when starting in transient state $i$. The victimization model assumes every individual begins in *General Population* (i.e., *State 1*). Thus, only $\mathbb{Q}_{1j}$ $\forall j$ needs evaluation; namely, the set $\mathbb{Q}_{1j} = \begin{bmatrix} I & II & III & IV & V \end{bmatrix}$. Further, this model processes in equal step-sizes back to the same state or into another state. The step size selected for this research is monthly. Therefore, the expected number of visits equates directly to the expected number of months in a state before absorption (i.e., Death).

*3.5.2 Probability of Transition in n-Steps Calculations*

The transition probability, $P_{ij}$, has been defined for single-step state transitions. The Chapman-Kolmogorov methodology (Ross, 2010) is applied for defining n-step state transitions, $P_{ij}^n$, as shown in Equation 9.

$$P_{ij}^n = P\{X_{n+m} = j \mid X_m = i\} \quad \text{for } n \geq 0 \text{ and } i, j \geq 0. \quad (9)$$

Note, $P_{ij}^1 = P_{ij}$. In matrix form of the n-step state transition probabilities, $P_{ij}^n$, the matrix $P^{(n)}$ is defined. Where, $P^{(n)}$ is simply the repetitive matrix multiplication of probability transition matrix, $P$, by itself, $n$ times. As to say,

$$P^{(n)} = P^n \quad (10)$$

As mentioned, this research model assumes all modeled entities (i.e., *Victims*) originate in *State 1* of the model. Therefore, $P_{1j}^{(n)}$ $\forall j$ is of primary research interest in this work. Additional consideration could be made towards the other elements of the matrix. For example, if a research question were instead focused on the experience of re-trafficking (e.g., starting in State 5).

### 3.5.3 Expected Number of Steps Before Absorption

The expected number of steps before absorption is equivalent to the Life Expectancy of an Individual. To calculate, matrix $t_i$ is used to calculate the expected number of steps before absorption when starting in state $i$. Let,

$$t_i = \mathbb{Q}_{ij} \bullet J_{51} \qquad (11)$$

where $J_{51}$ is a 5x1 matrix of ones. Then, and assuming the starting location is State 1,

$$t_1 = \mathbb{Q}_{1j} \bullet J_{51} = \begin{bmatrix} I & II & III & IV & V \end{bmatrix} \begin{bmatrix} 1 \\ 1 \\ 1 \\ 1 \\ 1 \end{bmatrix} = I + II + III + IV + V \qquad (12)$$

### 3.5.4 Calculation Variations with Probability of Transition in n-Steps

There are several probabilities that may be of value to the anti-trafficking analyst. Recall that the probability an individual will be in any one of the six states in n-steps is 1.0. Basic measures to assess would include:

1. Probability that Individual is Alive in n-Steps.

$$P(Alive_n) = 1 - P(\text{State } 6_n) \qquad (13)$$

2. Probability that Individual is Alive and not in Victimization State in n-Steps.

$$P(Alive_n \cap \overline{Victimization_n}) = P(\text{State } 1_n) + P(\text{State } 4_n) + P(\text{State } 5_n) \qquad (14)$$

3. Probability that Individual is Victim in n-Steps.

$$P(Victimization_n) = P(\text{State } 2_n) + P(\text{State } 3_n) \qquad (15)$$

4. Probability that Individual is Alive and in Post-Victimization State in n-Steps.

$$P(Alive_n \cap Post\text{-}Victimization_n) = P(\text{State } 4_n) + P(\text{State } 5_n) \qquad (16)$$

### 3.5.5 Probability Victimization Begins Between Ages $a_i$ and $a_{ii}$

In the context of sex trafficking victimization, a calculation that may be of interest is quantifying the probability victimization will first occur between a range of ages. A fundamental characteristic of DTMCs is the assumption of independence among sequential event probabilities. Therefore, the basic probability tool, "Product Rule", applies. Transition probability B is the probability of "success", meaning $A + C = 1 - B$ is the probability of "failure". Assuming modeling step-size of monthly and ages $a_i$ and $a_{ii}$ stated as months, then the total probability victimization begins between the two ages ($\upsilon$) is:

$$\upsilon = \sum_{x=1}^{a_{ii}-a_i} B(1-B)^{x-1} \qquad (17)$$

### 3.5.6 Probability of Visiting State j before State k

The probability of visiting one state before another can be approached with conditioned systems of equations. For example, the researcher may be interested in the probability of being in State 5 before State 3. This translates into research context as the outcome of a recruited individual who departed victimization before entering into the trafficking-exploitation cycle (i.e. State 3). To demonstrate the setup and simplification for this specific probability of outcome, let $u(x)$ be the probability that State 5 is visited before State 3 when starting in State $x$. Recall,

$$P = \begin{bmatrix} A & B & 0 & 0 & 0 & C \\ 0 & D & E & F & 0 & G \\ 0 & 0 & H & I & 0 & J \\ 0 & 0 & K & 0 & L & 0 \\ 0 & 0 & M & 0 & N & O \\ 0 & 0 & 0 & 0 & 0 & P \end{bmatrix}$$

Then,

$$u(1) = Au(1) + Bu(2) + Cu(6) \quad = Au(1) + Bu(2)$$
$$u(2) = Du(2) + Eu(3) + Fu(4) + Gu(6) \quad = Du(2) + Fu(4)$$
$$u(3) = 0$$
$$u(4) = Ku(3) + Lu(5) \quad = L$$
$$u(5) = 1$$
$$u(6) = 0$$

Solving the set of equations for starting in State $x = 1$,

$$u(3) = u(6) = 0$$
$$u(5) = 1$$
$$u(4) = L$$
$$u(2) = Du(2) + FL \text{ becomes } u(2) = \frac{FL}{(1-D)}$$
$$u(1) = Au(1) + \frac{BFL}{(1-D)} \text{ becomes } u(1) = \frac{BFL}{(1-A)(1-D)}$$

Thus, the probability of visiting State 5 before State 3, when starting in State 1, is $u(1) = \frac{BFL}{(1-A)(1-D)}$. The value of variable-form solutions such as this one is universal in applying to any input dataset. However, there is an involved process to solving for the conditioned formulations based on the research question of interest.

There are virtually no limits to continue defining formulations surrounding this DTMC to support the computational needs of anti-trafficking and policy-making analysts. A collaboration to do so is slated for future research. In the following, the research focus progresses to sensitivity analysis.

*3.5.7 Sensitivity Analysis*

In this and future sections, previously defined calculations (i.e., expected time to absorption and n-step transition probabilities) are theoretically evaluated and then applied to a real-life case study dataset. Theoretical solutions offer the value of worked, variable-form solutions. While the case study application serves to demonstrate procedure of analysis and provides results for concluding on the specific dataset evaluated. Before formulation development, a review of anti-trafficking commonsense is required.

Anti-Trafficking Commonsense

The following two questions, varying in level of detail, are stated as the basis of the sensitivity analysis discussion.

*BIG PICTURE*

*How do changes in risks and rates (expressed as probabilities) impact the lifetime experiences of sex trafficking victimization?*

*FOCUSED VIEW*

*What happens in the system when select transition probabilities change? (Table 14, with reference to Figure 13)*

With these questions in mind, the set of Select Transition Probabilities are defined in Table 14 to organize sensitivity analysis points-of-interest throughout the progression of the lifetime model. These Select Transition Probabilities were mindfully selected to observe points of impact of the anti-trafficking 4P Paradigm, as reviewed by Konrad et al. (2017). A commonsense approach is applied to define the perspective sought by the anti-trafficking community.

*Table 14: Select Transition Probabilities for Sensitivity Analysis, Anti-Trafficking Perspective*

| Term | Transition Probability | Anti-Trafficking Perspective | |
|---|---|---|---|
| | | Probability Increases | Probability Decreases |
| Initial Victimization Risk | $P_{1,2} = B$ | Bad | Good |
| Intervention Rate | $P_{2,4} = F$ | Good | Bad |
| | $P_{3,4} = I$ | Good | Bad |
| Intervention Success Rate | $P_{4,5} = L$ | Good | Bad |
| Revictimization Risk | $P_{5,3} = M$ | Bad | Good |

Different objectives exist relative to wanting to increase or reduce specific transition probabilities (refer to Table 14 and corresponding Figure 13). While increasing the initial victimization risk (i.e., transition probability B) and increasing the revictimization risk (i.e., transition probability M) are undesirable outcomes for anti-trafficking perspectives, increasing intervention rates (i.e., transition probabilities F and I) and increasing the success rate of interventions (i.e., transition probability L) are desirable outcomes through the anti-trafficking perspective.

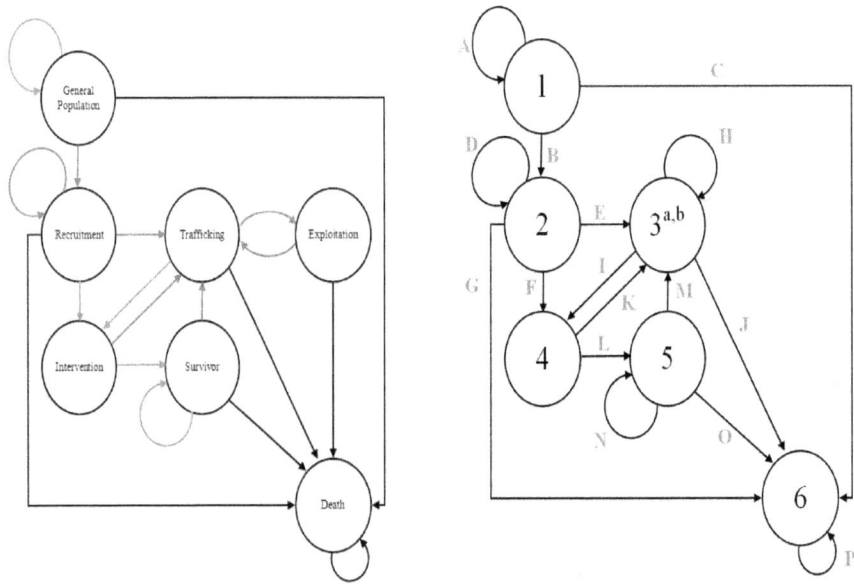

*Figure 13: Sex Trafficking Victimization Experience Model (model previously defined)*

Now to reach past commonsense for the theoretical exercises of formulating the rate of change for the Select Transition Probabilities, as well as the net difference of changes in the Select Transition Probabilities.

Rate of Change for Select Transition Probabilities

The first derivative of a function with respect to an independent variable results in the instantaneous rate of change (i.e., tangent slope) of the function with respect to that independent variable. When working with more than one independent variable, as is done in this research, a partial derivative with respect to a specific independent variable is applied to understand how a function responds to changes in that specific independent variable, all other independent variables remaining constant.

With an anti-trafficking initiative to impact individual's time spent in victimization states, select transition probabilities (Table 14) are investigated as independent variables for rate of change analysis. Due to the structure of the functions I – V for the time spent in transient states prior to absorption (i.e. assuming starting in *State 1*), an established and relevant derivation tool for this work is the "Quotient Rule". Consider a function, $f(x)$, as stated in Equation 18.

$$f(x) = \frac{G(x)}{H(x)} \qquad (18)$$

Then, the partial derivative of $f(x)$, with respect to independent variable $x$, is expressed in Equation 19.

$$\frac{df(x)}{dx} = \frac{\frac{dG(x)}{dx}H(x) - G(x)\frac{dH(x)}{dx}}{H(x)^2} \qquad (19)$$

Equation 19 is the only tool required to derive the Rate of Change calculations for the I – V formulations. The resulting rate of change formulations for the selected transition probabilities are computationally heavy to simplify/reduce. These results are recorded in Appendix G. Note that non-linear components of the results are frequent.

Net Difference of Select Transition Probability Changes

Another potentially insightful assessment of the model from a policy-perspective is the impact (expressed as a difference) of a factored increase/decrease in the state transition probabilities identified in Table 14. Variable change assessments being completed individually.

Consider a factor of change variable, $\lambda$, where $\lambda > 1$ results in a factored increase, and $0 < \lambda < 1$ results in a factored decrease. Table 15 organizes the variable-expressions resulting from this investigation on factored variable changes. Let the notation of $x$ represent each of the independent variables tested (i.e., Select Transition Probabilities – B, F, I, L, and M).

*Table 15: Impact of Factored Select Transition Probability Changes*

| What happens to… | …when select transition probability $x$ is adjusted by a multiple of $\lambda$.* (All other variables remain constant.) |
|---|---|
| I | $f_I(\lambda x) - f_I(x)$ |
| II | $f_{II}(\lambda x) - f_{II}(x)$ |
| III | $f_{III}(\lambda x) - f_{III}(x)$ |
| IV | $f_{IV}(\lambda x) - f_{IV}(x)$ |
| V | $f_V(\lambda x) - f_V(x)$ |

* Note: the select transition probability is increased when $\lambda > 1$ and decreased when $0 < \lambda < 1$.

**3.6 Case Study**

Application of the theoretical formulations to a case study dataset is presented in detail within the upcoming Results chapter. While the case study dataset used in this work may be considered arbitrary to the greater scope evaluating sex trafficking victimization for the entire or subset population effected, the essence of value is in the procedure of analysis to apply these and additional Markovian techniques in a regimented, repeatable approach to any dataset. More work towards dataset definition and additional evaluation techniques are strongly called for in future research.

**3.7 Microsoft Excel® Tool**

A MS Excel workbook has been created with built-in calculations to easily work with inputs and display outputs in a user-friendly manner. Initially, there was an intention to structure an Excel VBA Simulation as the primary foundation for analysis. However, a computational approach is much more robust. The next chapter results and analysis were obtained exclusively using the Excel Tool. The benefit of this tool being in Excel-format is the virtually limitless accessibility by users, as well as an established interface for ease of use by various disciplines of experts.

Figure 14 – Figure 16 are sequential worksheet screenshots of the Excel Tool. Figure 14 is the landing page for introduction, instruction, and inputs. The user should update/enter the transition probabilities in the white cells on this page. Without prompt then, the next two worksheets update automatically with calculations for Expected Time in Each State and Probability of Transition. Variations on the display of output are included to aid interpretation of results on each of the output worksheets. Additionally, the entire modeled probability of transition in n-steps output for 600 months (50 years) are included in tabular form on the latter worksheet.

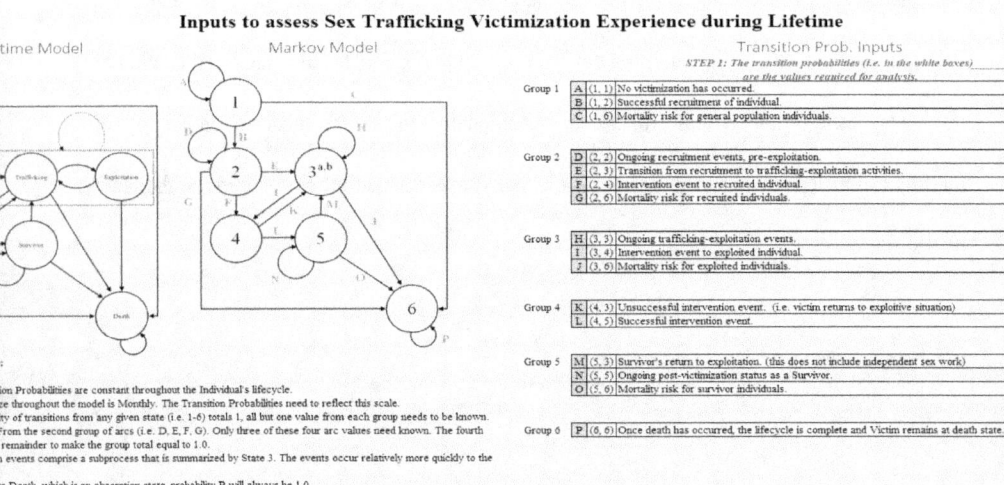

*Figure 14: Microsoft Excel® Tool – Inputs*

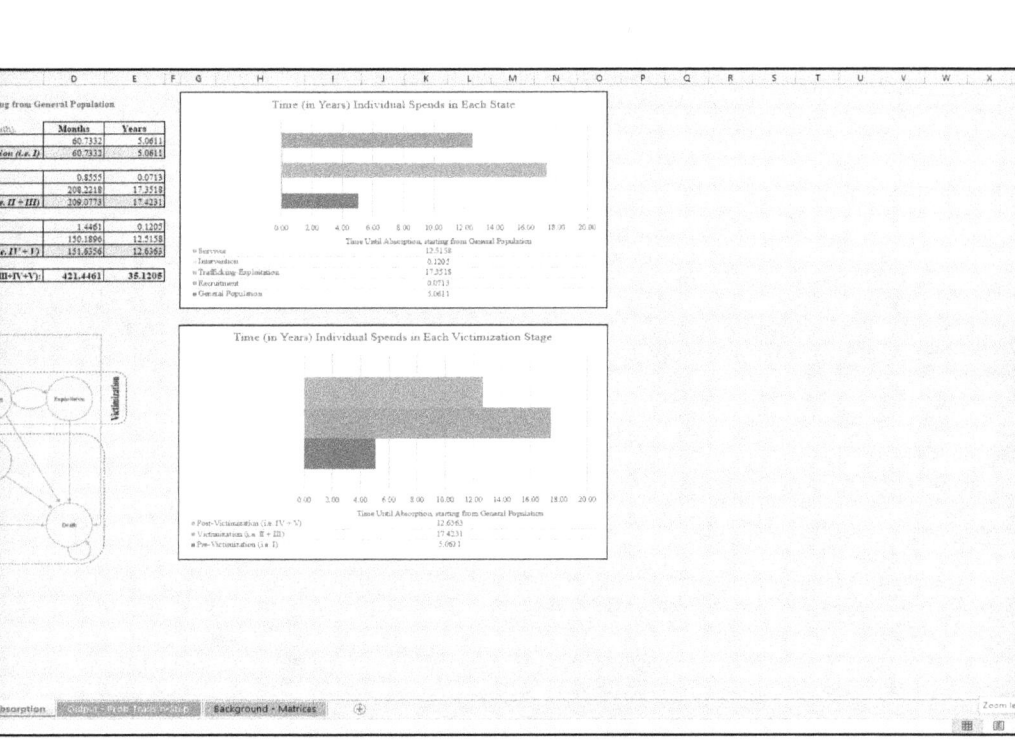

*Figure 15: Microsoft Excel® Tool – Outputs (Expected Time)*

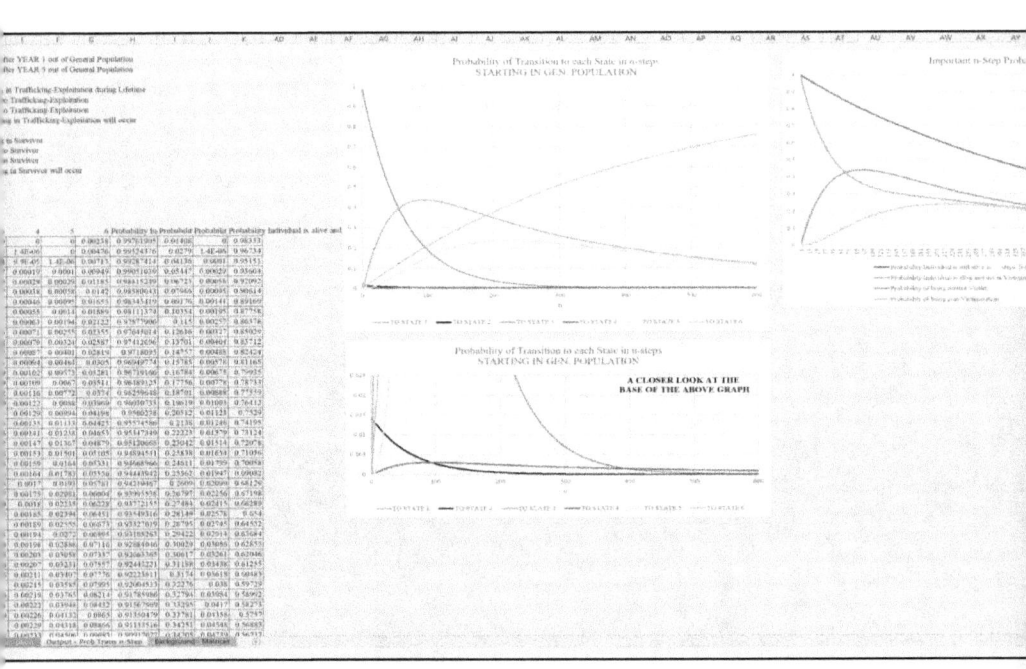

Figure 16: Microsoft Excel® Tool – Outputs (Probability of Transition)

With this Excel Tool, a variety of evaluations can be made per the needs of the analyst. This Excel Tool was the foundational point of reference for the later-discussed decision support system (DSS), implemented design as an open-source webpage design.

### 3.8 Policies for Impact

Trafficking systems are complex. Kővári and Pruyt (2014) presented a simulation model of the trafficking industry, representing all involved members of human trafficking activity. Four anti-trafficking policies were evaluated. The four policies modeled, verbatim from the literature, were:

1. "To strengthen anti-human-trafficking laws and enforcement by the existing police force."
2. "To raise the protection of trafficking victims, build rehabilitation centers, help the social reintegration of those who want to escape from prostitution, make the choice for this profession really 'free'."
3. "To ban prostitution, prosecute prostitutes, brothels and other organized forms."
4. "To ban the purchase of sex services (the Swedish model) or substantially reduce demand for sex services. In this policy in isolation, prostitutes would be protected and helped to escape their profession, not punished."

The same research emphasized the presence of uncertainty in understanding the full effects of anti-trafficking policies and measures taken against trafficking systems.

Likewise, this research evaluates sex trafficking victimization through variable representation and fluctuation, rather than limited in the scope of specific policies. Policy experts may apply this research by observing model output changes resulting from controlled variable variation (e.g., Sensitivity Analysis).

Applying logic and reason, observation of the defined lifetime model for the experiences around sex trafficking victimization (see Figure 17 for convenient reference), leads to certain resolutions towards policies.

- Transition probabilities C, G, J, O, and P are independently neutral arcs to policy changes. As to say, policy does not foreseeably impact mortality rates associated within the different stages of the lifetime model.
- B, D, E, H, K, and M are transition probabilities that anti-trafficking initiatives would aim to <u>decrease</u>.
- A, F, I, L, and N are transition probabilities that anti-trafficking initiatives would aim to <u>increase</u>.

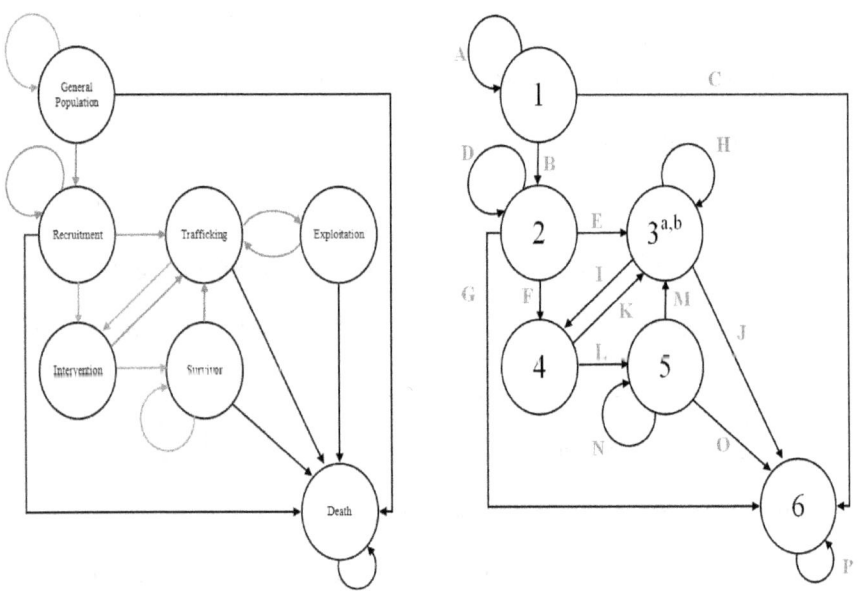

*Figure 17: Sex Trafficking Victimization Experience Model (previously defined)*

## 3.8 Methodology Summary

The defined and validated mathematical model of this research provides the ability to empirically approach a complex social dilemma; namely, the lifetime experience of sex trafficking victimization. The theoretical basis for discussion in this context space is critical as the lack of dependable data opens room for subjectivity in application-driven analysis. The key formulations that have been defined are expected duration of lifetime spent in each state, the probability of transition in n-steps, and life expectancy. Additional formulations that may be of value to anti-trafficking and policy-making experts is the definition of rate of change and net difference calculations, both forms of sensitivity analysis. The MS Excel Tool of this research can execute the calculations outlined in this chapter and is the mechanism for which the results were populated in next chapter.

CHAPTER 4

RESULTS, ANALYSIS, AND DISCUSSION

In this chapter, a combination of results, analysis, and corresponding discussion are presented with respect to a case study dataset. In this case study, validated transition probabilities are applied from the lived experiences of a sex trafficking victim. The case study is basis for discussion purposes, but the dataset itself could be used to represent an individual or the collective sum of inputs for a defined group of individuals. Further, the effort of this research is to demonstrate a process-based approach to analysis rather than conclude on this dataset alone. Any dataset could be evaluated through the following approaches.

This chapter begins with the definition of the case study dataset, along with necessary assumptions and first-round analysis via the methodology-outlined calculations of expected time in each state and probabilities of transition in n-steps. After the case study is prepared for analysis, this chapter delves into four sensitivity analysis approaches, targeting the potential points of interests of different academic and anti-trafficking community members. The chapter comes to an end with observations from the results in terms of the anti-trafficking community and the implemented decision support system to support future analyst endeavors within this research space.

**4.1 Case Study Background**

Ms. Liz Williamson is an anti-trafficking advocate who speaks publicly as a Survivor of FCST. Eubanks (2015) of The Clarion-Ledger, published on an interview regarding Ms. Williamson's lived experiences. The article gave all necessary input to outline Ms. Williamson's lived experiences in terms of the inputs for this research's model. Towards the end of 2021, contact was made with Ms. Williamson who generously gave her time to validate the details identified in Table 16. In the table, the progression of life events are defined with the associated elements of validation.

*Table 16: A Validated Account of Ms. Liz Williamson's Lived Sex Trafficking Experiences*

| Order of Events | States | Duration | Duration (months) | Validated Modeling Structure |
|---|---|---|---|---|
| 1 | General Population | 5 years and 11 months | 71 months | -- |
| 2 | Recruitment | 1 month | 1 month | Recruitment (force, fraud, coercion) started 1 month before 6-year-old victimization timeline. |
| 3 | Exploitation | 12 years | 144 months | Exploitation started as of 6th birthday. Turned 18 years old at departure for college. |
| 4 | Intervention | 1 month | 1 month | 1 month intervention (model limitation) which includes a duration for elements of preparation taken to stop exploitation. |
| 5 | Survivor | 4 months | 4 months | Assume college started in the fall and there were 4 months as a survivor before winter break. |
| 6 | Exploitation | 4 years | 48 months | College lasted exactly 4 years. |
| 7 | Intervention | 1 month | 1 month | Left situation to a homeless shelter. 1-month intervention (model limitation) with balance recognized as a survivor. |
| 8 | Survivor | Ongoing | | 5 months in a shelter before joining the adoptive family. This event continues. |

Ms. Williamson's experiences are evaluated as a case study in the following analysis. Certain, supplementary assumptions were required for modeling, defined as follows.

**4.2 Assumptions**

*4.2.1 Step Size*

The step size for the case study analysis is assumed to be monthly.

*4.2.2 Life Expectancy*

Assume life expectancy of sex trafficking victim is 35 years (Potterat et al., 2004).

### 4.2.3 Monthly Risk of Death

Following the assumption of victim life expectancy is the need to define the assumption of monthly risk of death for victims. The Social Security Administration (SSA.gov, 2019) reported the annual risk of death for females in the United States. This data is plotted in Figure 18. If modeling were not assumed to be time-homogenous, this risk of death dataset could be applied.

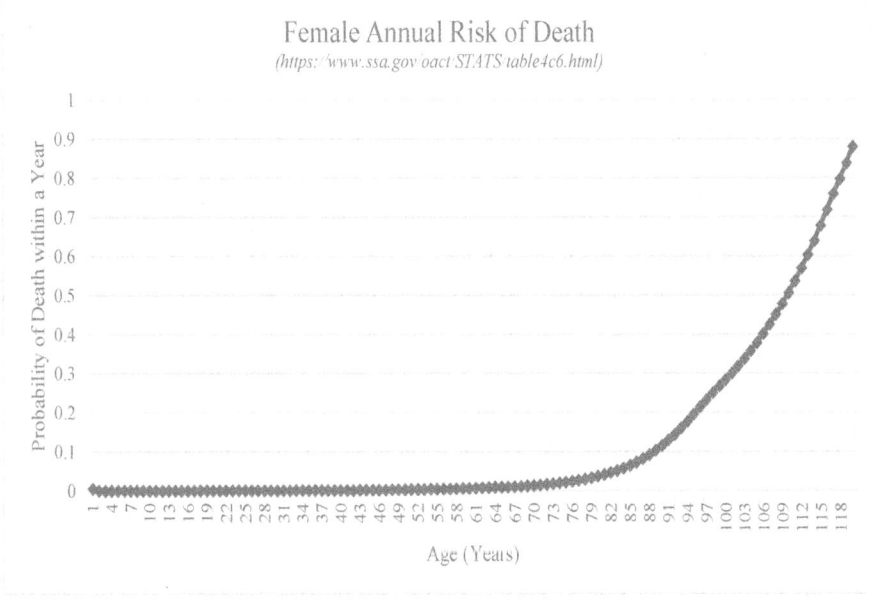

*Figure 18: U.S.A. Female Annual Risk of Death (SSA.gov, 2019)*

Instead, to respect the homogenous and 35-year life expectancy assumptions for this case study, the monthly risk of death is calculated as a constant and assumed to be:

$$\text{Monthly Risk of Death} = \frac{1}{35*12} = 0.002380952 \qquad (20)$$

Further, literature is lacking around the differences between C, O, G, and J probabilities of death. This would be a valuable scope of contribution in future research. For now, due to an absence of literature as well as no observation of death in Ms. Williamson's lifespan, the assumption is made that $P(C) = P(O) = P(G) = P(J) = 0.002380952$.

### 4.2.4 Transition Probabilities D, F, and K

D, F, K transition flows have not occurred throughout Ms. Williamson's lifetime experiences. Assume that $P(D) = P(F) = P(K) = 0.0001$ to mean that although possible, these transition probabilities are improbable.

### 4.3 DTMC Transition Probabilities

Combining the validated lifetime events of Ms. Liz Williamson (Table 16) with the outlined assumptions, it is possible to organize and define all transition probabilities, A-P, for this case study's base dataset.

State 1: General Population

- $A = 1 - B - C$ ("Complement Rule")

- $B = \dfrac{1}{71} = 0.014084507$ (direct experience)

- $C = 0.002380952$ (time-homogenous assumption)

State 2: Recruitment

- $D = 0.0001$ (assumption)

- $E = 1 - D - F - G$ ("Complement Rule")

- $F = 0.0001$ (assumption)

- $G = 0.002380952$ (time-homogenous assumption and equivalent death risk assumption)

State's 3, 4, and 5 are transient states that may observe more than one visit back to state after departure. The Markov Chain relationship of each state's departing probabilities summing to one and the stated assumption of death risk reduces the number of probabilities needing identified.

State 3: Trafficking & Exploitation

- $H = 1 - I - J$ ("Complement Rule")

- $I_i = \left\{ \dfrac{1}{144}, \dfrac{1}{48} \right\} = \{0.00694444, 0.02083333\}$ (direct experiences)

Ms. Williamson was both exploited and re-exploited. Ms. Williamson also achieved the Survivor state twice in her lifetime. In the current homogeneous form of a DTMC, modeling is unable to represent varying values of risk over time in a single, modeled lifetime. To address the different experiences within the same lifetime, the model is evaluated at both observed levels of risk to define a range for the collective risk probability for the entire lifetime. The comparative approach offers insight into the bounds of the population represented by Ms. Liz Williamson's experiences.

- $J = 0.002380952$ (time-homogenous assumption and equivalent death risk assumption)

State 4: Intervention

- $K = 0.0001$ (assumption)

- $L = 1 - K$ ("Complement Rule")

State 5: Survivor

- $M_i = \left\{ \dfrac{1}{138}, \dfrac{1}{4} \right\} = \{0.00724638, 0.25\}$ (direct experiences)

Ms. Williamson experienced being a Survivor twice. The first time, she remained a Survivor for four months before being re-exploited by a romantic partner in college. After escaping exploitation, for the second time, Ms. Williamson remains a Survivor into present day. Therefore, the balance of 138 months in the assumed life expectancy of 35 years is allocated to the second Survivor duration for analysis.

- $N = 1 - M - O$ ("Complement Rule")
- $O = 0.002380952$ (time-homogenous assumption and equivalent death risk assumption)

State 6: Death

- $P = 1.0$ (MC probability relationship)

### 4.4 Initial Testing Framework

The first element of analysis with the case study dataset includes four initial test scenarios, as outlined in Table 17. These values are a direct result of the preceding definition of the A-P case study transition probability values. The testing centers around transition probabilities I and M, each defined at two treatment levels that occurred in Ms. Liz Williamson's lifetime. One of the four scenarios is identified as the Base Case going into later points of case study analysis.

*Table 17: Initial Testing Framework and Naming Convention, Base Case*

| | | Scenario | | | |
|---|---|---|---|---|---|
| | | 1 | 2 | 3 | 4 |
| Transition Probability | I | 0.00694444 | 0.00694444 | 0.02083333 | 0.02083333 |
| | M | 0.00724638 | 0.25000000 | 0.00724638 | 0.25000000 |
| | | \multicolumn{4}{|c|}{Applying naming convention $S_{Liz}$(Transition Probability I, Transition Probability M)} |
| Scenario Names | | $S_{Liz}$(Low,Low) BASE CASE | $S_{Liz}$(Low,High) | $S_{Liz}$(High,Low) | $S_{Liz}$(High,High) |

### 4.4.1 Initial Results – Expected Duration in Each State, Life Expectancy

Expected total duration in each state (in months) is identified in Table 18 for each of the four scenarios. Variation is not seen in Expected Time in States 1 and 2. Notable variation is seen in Expected Time in States 3, 4, and 5. Life Expectancy (i.e., absorption from the transient states) varies less than half a year among the scenarios. Further, an element of validation is revealed in the Life Expectancy which is in every scenario near the 35-year assumption.

*Table 18: Initial Results for Expected Duration in Each State, Life Expectancy (months)*

|  | Scenario | | | |
|---|---|---|---|---|
|  | 1 | 2 | 3 | 4 |
| State 1 | 60.7332 | 60.7332 | 60.7332 | 60.7332 |
| State 2 | .8555 | .8555 | .8555 | .8555 |
| State 3 | 208.2218 | 348.8141 | 113.2837 | 331.0838 |
| State 4 | 1.4461 | 2.4224 | 2.3602 | 6.8977 |
| State 5 | 150.1896 | 9.5972 | 245.1277 | 27.3276 |
| Life Expectancy | 421.4461 | 422.4225 | 422.3602 | 426.8977 |

### 4.4.2 Initial Results – Probability of Transition in n-Steps

Now to investigate the probability of transition in n-steps for the four scenarios, the results for maximum probabilities in States 3 and 5 are shown in Table 19. The tested scenarios reveal differences in the maximum probabilities of being in States 3 and 5 throughout a lifetime as well as when those maximums occur.

*Table 19: Maximum Probabilities of Transition in n-Steps for State 3, State 5*

|  | Scenario | | | |
|---|---|---|---|---|
|  | 1 | 2 | 3 | 4 |
| Max Prob of being in State 3 | 0.4367 | 0.5974 | 0.2858 | 0.5615 |
| When max prob of being in State 3 (month) | 94 | 138 | 62 | 138 |
| Max Prob of being in State 5 | 0.2364 | 0.0164 | 0.4084 | 0.0463 |
| When max prob of being in State 5 (month) | 222 | 143 | 182 | 143 |

The next aspect of Probability of Transition in n-Steps is displayed in Table 20. From the table output, the following observations are made.

- With exception of Scenario 3 - $S_{Liz}$(High, Low), States 1, 3, and 6 encompass all maximum likelihoods throughout the lifetime of an individual.

- An interesting occurrence is seen in Scenario 3 - $S_{Liz}$ (High, Low), and to a lesser degree in Scenario 1 - $S_{Liz}$ (Low, Low). The low level of transition probability M results in a notable increase in likelihood of being in State 5 in n-steps. This is highly desirable for anti-trafficking concerns when realizing that there is a drop in the likelihood of being in State 3 under the same circumstances.

*Table 20: Probability of Transition to each State in n-Steps starting in General Population, Month-by-Month*

Key: ──── TO STATE 1 ──── TO STATE 2 ──── TO STATE 3 ──── TO STATE 4 ──── TO STATE 5 ──── TO

State 1: General Population, State 2: Recruitment, State 3: Trafficking-Exploitation, State 4: Intervention, State 5: Surv

| Scenario 1: $S_{Liz}$(Low,Low) | Scenario 2: $S_{Liz}$(Low,High) |

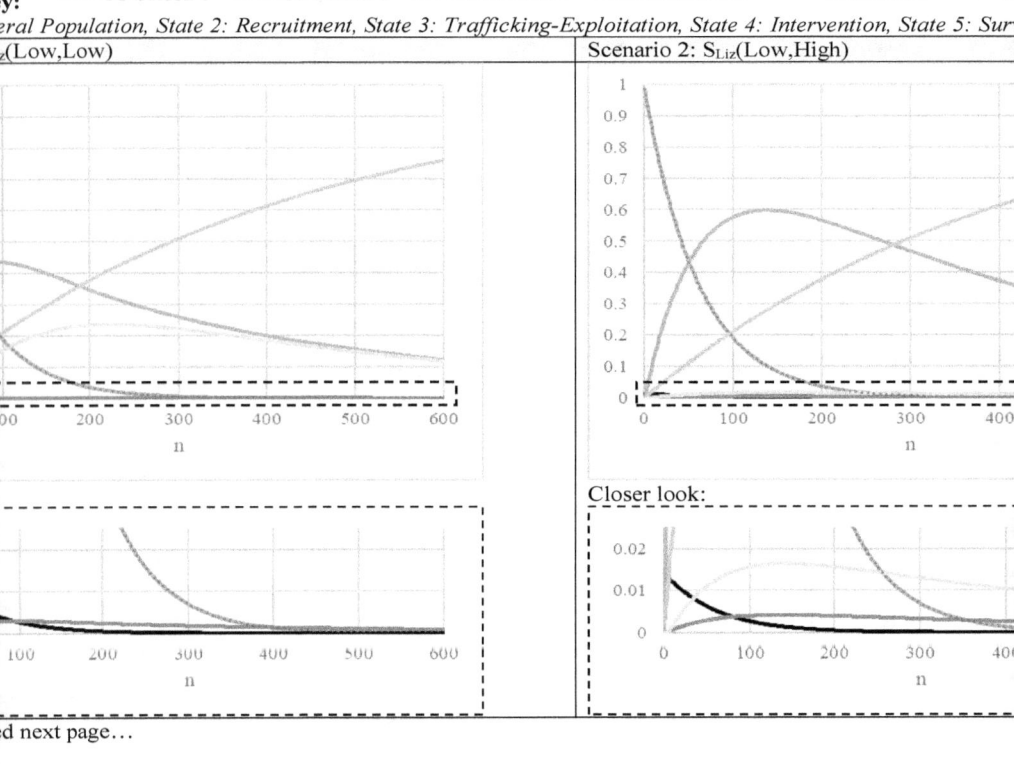

Closer look:

...continued next page...

**0 (continued): Probability of Transition to each State in n-Steps starting in General Population, Month-by-Month**

TE 1 ——TO STATE 2 ———— TO STATE 3 ———— TO STATE 4 ———— TO STATE 5 ———— TO STATE 6

*ulation, State 2: Recruitment, State 3: Trafficking-Exploitation, State 4: Intervention, State 5: Survivor, St*

,Low) | Scenario 4: $S_{Liz}$(High,High)

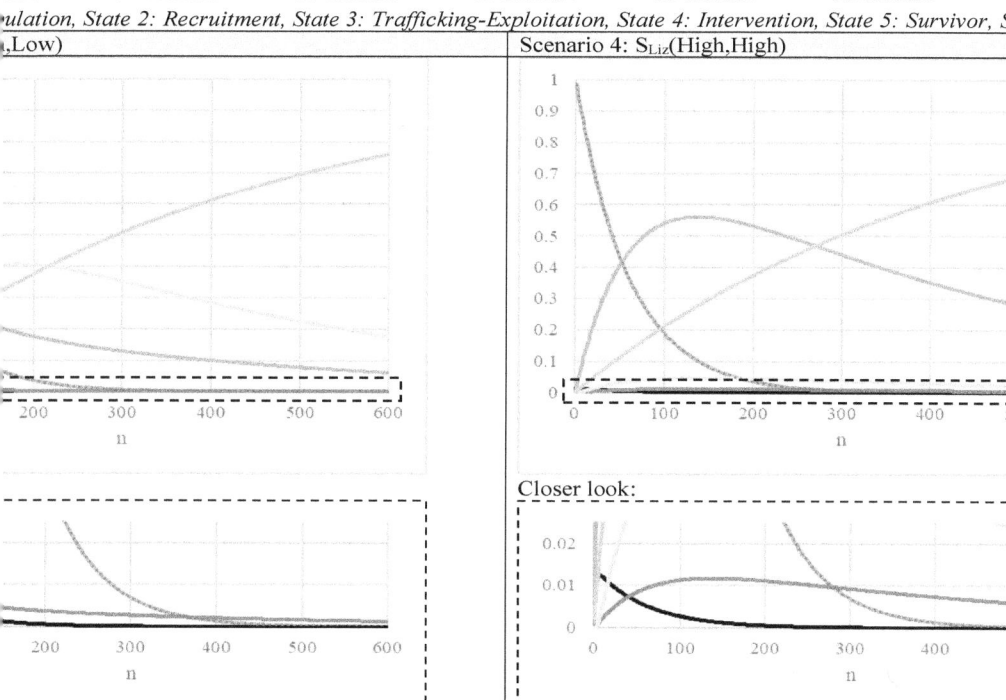

Closer look:

Now to observe rate of changes within Probability of Transition in n-Steps. States 1, 3, 5 and 6 have notable changes over the span of time evaluated. Working with discrete rate of change results led the following review over the individual's lifetime into States 1, 3, 5, and 6. These results are displayed in Table 21. Observations from these results include:

- The magnitude of expected rate of change converges towards zero in all four scenarios from start to end of an individual's lifetime.
- The expected rate of change into State 5 has notable shifts among all four scenarios.
- The expected rate of change into States 1, 3, and 6 initiates at the same levels among all four scenarios.
- The expected rate of change into States 1, 3, and 6 shifts gradually throughout lifetime, as seen in the intersection points between each state's plotted data.

Table 21: Rate of Change in n-Step Probability of Transition from General Population, Month-by-Month

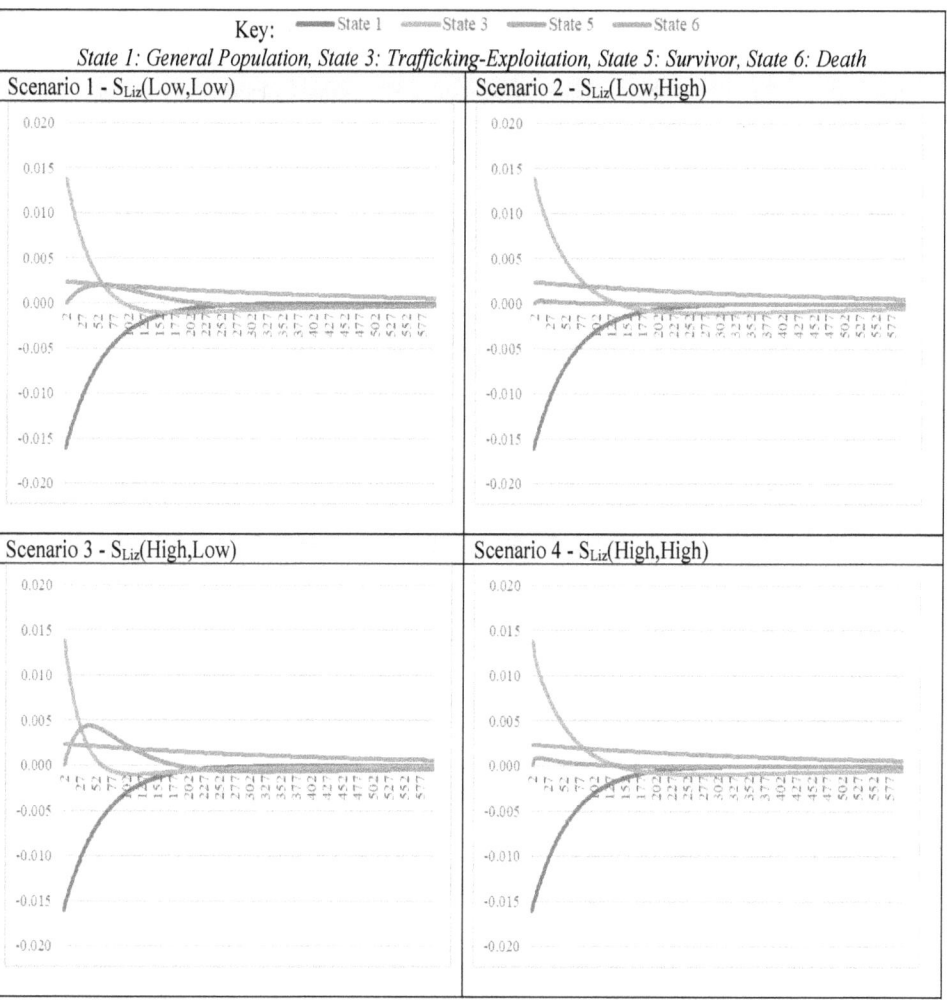

Recall several of the significant n-step probability calculations from the Methodology chapter. Specifically,

1. Probability that Individual is Alive in n-Steps

2. Probability that Individual is Alive and not in Victimization State in n-Steps

3. Probability that Individual is Victim in n-Steps

4. Probability that Individual is Alive and in Post-Victimization State in n-Steps.

These calculation results for the four scenarios are displayed in Table 22. The first calculation is essentially a constant, as the likelihood of death is constant through all tested scenarios. The three other calculations all have changes in the results. The second probability of being alive and not in a victimization state is ever decreasing throughout the lifetime. The third and fourth probabilities both have an increasing-to-decreasing trend over the course of the modeled lifetime. These are only foundational observations of the visual results. Distribution estimation and numerical analysis would be a worthwhile future research endeavor for these and other analysis figures.

Table 22: Significant n-Step Probability Calculations Starting in General Population, Month-by-Month

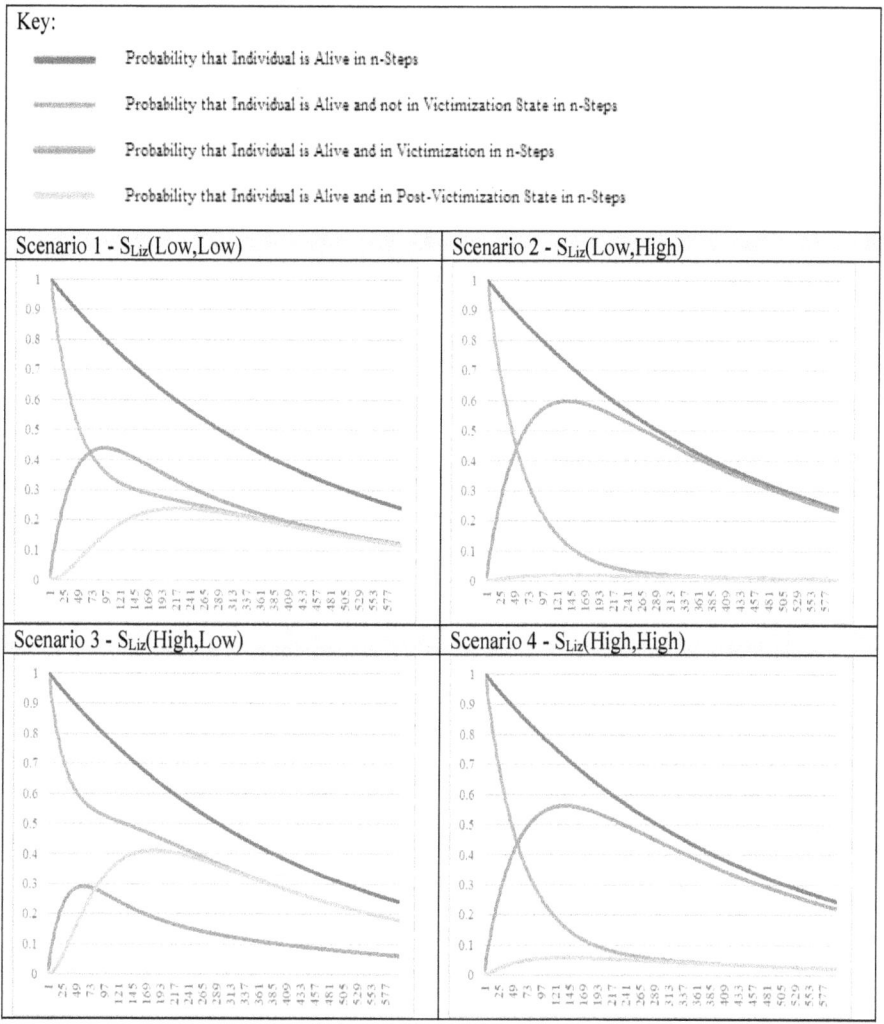

### 4.6 Sensitivity Analysis for Base Case: Scenario 1 - $S_{Liz}$(Low,Low)

The analysis discussion thus far has centered on the specific case study of Ms. Williamson's lived experiences, with four scenarios applied for evaluation of expected time in each state and the probability of transition in n-steps. Having the case study initial assessment complete, the remainder of analysis takes direct focus on sensitivity analysis of the base case towards the final research objective of this work; sensitivity analysis to assess the individual P's of the 4P Paradigm (i.e. Prevention, Protection, Prosecution, and Partnership) (Konrad et al., 2017).

Important Notes:

- "Select Transition Probabilities" in this analysis are transition probabilities B, F, I, L, and M.
- The Markov Chain modeling requirement for all transition arcs leaving any node to sum to 1.0 was respected with the relationships displayed in Table 23 (e.g., a change to probability B would result in an equal and opposite adjustment to probability A).

*Table 23: Summary of Maintaining Sum of Departing Transition Probability Requirement*

| |
|---|
| $\Delta B = -\Delta A$ |
| $\Delta F = -\Delta E$ |
| $\Delta I = -\Delta H$ |
| $\Delta L = -\Delta K$ |
| $\Delta M = -\Delta N$ |

- Sensitivity analysis centers on Scenario 1 - $S_{Liz}$(Low,Low) which was arbitrarily selected as the "Base Case" among the four scenarios.

#### 4.6.1 Sensitivity Analysis Organization

The collective hierarchy chart in Table 24 displays an outline for the sensitivity analysis completed. The first tier refers to the separation of Sensitivity Analysis Approaches 1 and 2.

Each of these approaches then are broken down into the levels displayed in the second tier. For ease of formatting, a third tier is defined for the BFILM comparative analysis within each of the approaches.

There are two questions to approach this sensitivity analysis section. There is an overlap of the concept of the questions, but both are valuable considerations to determine what the expected gain or loss would be from changes in the select transition probabilities BFILM. The purpose of question differentiation is to cater the analysis to the larger audience who may be motivated by different perspectives.

1. What is the net impact on key parameters when select transition probabilities BFILM are changed in 20% increments? (Sensitivity Analysis Approach 1)

2. What is the net impact on key parameters when select inputs (BFILM) are changed in 0.0002 increments? (Sensitivity Analysis Approach 2)

*Table 24: Structure for Sensitivity Analysis, 3-Tier Organization*

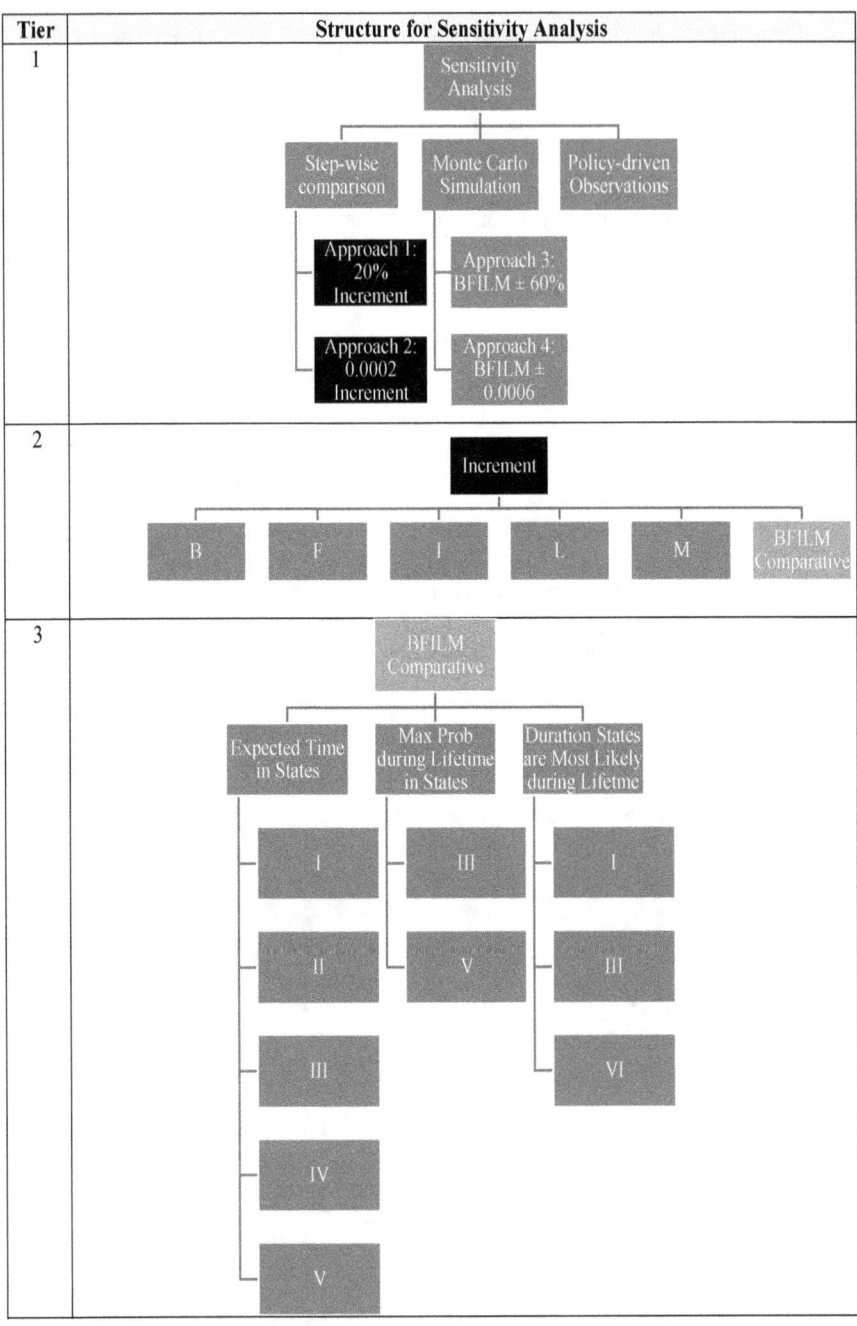

### 4.6.2 Sensitivity Analysis – Approach 1 (Increments of 20%)

Transition Probability B

Table 25 displays the sensitivity analysis output for transition probability B, when varied in 20% increments. The value of transition probability B at these variations is indicated in the header of each column. From review of the values, the following observations are made for the levels of transition probability B tested.

- Expected Time in State 1 decreases as B increases, varying more than 84 months (7 years).
- Expected Time in State 2 does fluctuate but remains as less than one month in duration.
- Expected Time in State 3 increases with B, varying just over 49 months (4 years).
- Expected Time in State 4 does fluctuate but remains a one-to-two-month duration.
- Expected Time in State 5 increases with B, varying by 35 months (nearly 3 years).
- Life Expectancy follows expectation to vary very little due to the risk of death (i.e., absorption) being held constant.
- The maximum probability of being in State 3 during the victim's lifetime nearly doubles between the smallest and largest B levels tested. A difference of 25.37%.
- The maximum probability of being in State 5 during the victim's lifetime varies 9.33%.
- Over the 600 months (50 years) modeled for the individual's lifespan, notable shifts occur among States 1, 3, and 6 in state location with highest likelihood in n-steps.
  - The duration of State 1 being most likely in n-steps has a decrease of 116 months (9.67 years) between the lowest and highest levels of B.
  - At the lowest level of B, State 3 no longer has a range of highest likelihood.

*Table 25: Sensitivity Analysis Output – B at 20%*

| | | .4B =0.0056 | .6B =0.0085 | .8B =0.0113 | B =0.0141 | 1.2B =0.0169 | 1.4B =0.0197 | 1.6B =0.0225 |
|---|---|---|---|---|---|---|---|---|
| Expected Time in State (mths) | 1 | 124.7699 | 92.3220 | 73.2678 | 60.7332 | 51.8609 | 45.2504 | 40.1346 |
| | 2 | 0.7030 | 0.7803 | 0.8256 | 0.8555 | 0.8766 | 0.8924 | 0.9045 |
| | 3 | 171.1078 | 189.9138 | 200.9571 | 208.2218 | 213.3640 | 217.1953 | 220.1602 |
| | 4 | 1.1883 | 1.3189 | 1.3956 | 1.4461 | 1.4818 | 1.5084 | 1.5290 |
| | 5 | 123.4194 | 136.9840 | 144.9495 | 150.1896 | 153.8986 | 156.6621 | 158.8007 |
| Life Expectancy (mths) | | 421.1884 | 421.3190 | 421.3957 | 421.4461 | 421.4818 | 421.5085 | 421.5290 |
| Max Prob of being in State | 3 | 0.2734 | 0.3421 | 0.3946 | 0.4367 | 0.4717 | 0.5014 | 0.5271 |
| | 5 | 0.1683 | 0.2005 | 0.2216 | 0.2364 | 0.2472 | 0.2553 | 0.2616 |
| When State is most likely among all states. (Highest curve on graph) | 1 | 0 - 149 | 0 - 100 | 0 - 71 | 0 - 55 | 0 - 45 | 0 - 38 | 0 - 33 |
| | 2 | - | - | - | - | - | - | - |
| | 3 | - | 101 - 168 | 72 - 182 | 56 - 188 | 46 - 190 | 39 - 190 | 34 - 190 |
| | 4 | - | - | - | - | - | - | - |
| | 5 | - | - | - | - | - | - | - |
| | 6 | 150 - 600 | 169 - 600 | 183 - 600 | 189 - 600 | 191 - 600 | 191 - 600 | 191 - 600 |

Note Figure 19. In the base case, 50.4% of the individual's lifetime is expected to be in non-victimization states (i.e., States 1, 4, and 5), with the balance of 49.6% expected lifetime duration to be in victimization states (i.e., States 2 and 3). A non-linear relationship is observed among the results. Gains of up to 8.8% of an entire lifetime from victimization into non-victimization duration by reducing B by 60%, while the cost of B increasing 60% is expected to have a loss of 2.8% of non-victimization into victimization duration.

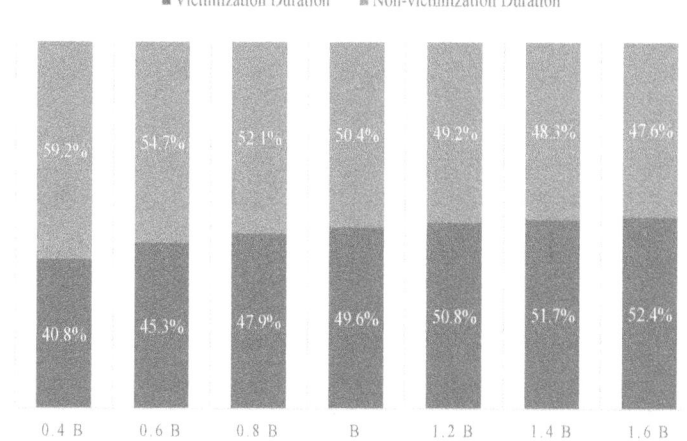

*Figure 19: Division of Victimization versus Non-victimization Duration During Individual's Lifetime, Transition Probability B Sensitivity Analysis (20%)*

Transition Probability F

Table 26 displays the sensitivity analysis output for transition probability F, when varied in 20% increments. The value of F at these variations is indicated in the header of each column. From review of the values, the following observations are made for the levels of F tested.

- Expected Time in State 1 is unchanged by changes in F.

- Expected Time in State 2 is unchanged by changes in F.

- Expected Time in State 3 varies slightly with changes in F, only differing by 0.0062 months between the lowest and highest tested levels.

- Expected Time in State 4 varies slightly with changes in F, only differing by 0.0001 months between the lowest and highest tested levels.

- Expected Time in State 5 varies slightly with changes in F, only differing by 0.0062 months between the highest and lowest tested levels. There is an inverse, direct relationship between the effects of changing F on Expected Time in State 3 and State 5.

- The maximum probability of being in State 3 during the victim's lifetime is unchanged by changes in F.

- The maximum probability of being in State 5 during the victim's lifetime is unchanged by changes in F.

- Over the 600 months (50 years) modeled for the individual's lifespan, no shifts occur for the state location with highest likelihood in n-steps by changing F.

*Table 26: Sensitivity Analysis Output – F at 20%*

| | | .4F =0.00004 | .6F =0.00006 | .8F =0.00008 | F =0.0001 | 1.2F =0.00012 | 1.4F =0.00014 | 1.6F =0.00016 |
|---|---|---|---|---|---|---|---|---|
| Expected Time in State (mths) | 1 | 60.7332 | 60.7332 | 60.7332 | 60.7332 | 60.7332 | 60.7332 | 60.7332 |
| | 2 | 0.8555 | 0.8555 | 0.8555 | 0.8555 | 0.8555 | 0.8555 | 0.8555 |
| | 3 | 208.2249 | 208.2239 | 208.2228 | 208.2218 | 208.2208 | 208.2198 | 208.2187 |
| | 4 | 1.4460 | 1.4460 | 1.4461 | 1.4461 | 1.4461 | 1.4461 | 1.4461 |
| | 5 | 150.1865 | 150.1875 | 150.1885 | 150.1896 | 150.1906 | 150.1916 | 150.1927 |
| Life Expectancy (mths) | | 421.4461 | 421.4461 | 421.4461 | 421.4461 | 421.4461 | 421.4462 | 421.4462 |
| Max Prob of being in State | 3 | 0.4367 | 0.4367 | 0.4367 | 0.4367 | 0.4367 | 0.4367 | 0.4367 |
| | 5 | 0.2364 | 0.2364 | 0.2364 | 0.2364 | 0.2364 | 0.2364 | 0.2364 |
| When State is most likely among all states. (highest curve on graph) | 1 | 0 - 55 | 0 - 55 | 0 - 55 | 0 - 55 | 0 - 55 | 0 - 55 | 0 - 55 |
| | 2 | - | - | - | - | - | - | - |
| | 3 | 56 - 188 | 56 - 188 | 56 - 188 | 56 - 188 | 56 - 188 | 56 - 188 | 56 - 188 |
| | 4 | - | - | - | - | - | - | - |
| | 5 | - | - | - | - | - | - | - |
| | 6 | 189 - 600 | 189 - 600 | 189 - 600 | 189 - 600 | 189 - 600 | 189 - 600 | 189 - 600 |

In Figure 20, it is apparent that varying transition probability F in 20% increments makes no notable difference on the breakdown of victimization to non-victimization proportions of lifetime for the individual.

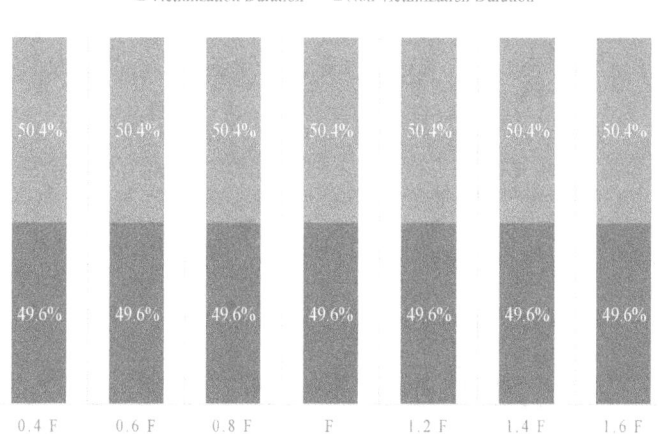

*Figure 20: Division of Victimization versus Non-victimization Duration During Individual's Lifetime, Transition Probability F Sensitivity Analysis (20%)*

Transition Probability I

Table 27 displays the sensitivity analysis output for transition probability I, when varied in 20% increments. The value of I at these variations is indicated in the header of each column. From review of the values, the following observations are made for the levels of I tested.

- Expected Time in State 1 is unchanged by changes in transition probability I.

- Expected Time in State 2 is unchanged by changes in transition probability I.

- Expected Time in State 3 decreases as transition probability I is increased, varying over 111 months (9.3 years). This demonstrates the importance of intervention (i.e., represented by transition probability I), as compared to the previous biggest impact on State 3 expected duration of roughly 49 months (4 years) that was observed previously from varying transition probability B. This will be further discussed in later line plots.

- Expected Time in State 4 varies increases by 1.0761 months as transition probability I is increased from lowest to highest level.
- Expected Time in State 5 has a substantial impact by varying transition probability I. More than 111 months (9.3 years) difference is observed in this expected time, where expected time in State 5 increases as transition probability I increases.
- Life Expectancy follows expectation to vary very little due to the risk of death (i.e., absorption) being held constant.
- The maximum probability of being in State 3 during the individual's lifetime decreases by 15.2% between the lowest and highest levels of transition probability I.
- The maximum probability of being in State 5 during the individual's lifetime varies 18.97%.
- Over the 600 months (50 years) modeled for the individual's lifespan, notable shifts occur among States 1, 3, and 6 in state location with highest likelihood in n-steps.
    - The duration of State 1 being most likely in n-steps has an increase of 9 months between the lowest and highest levels of transition probability I.
    - The duration of State 3 being most likely in n-steps is nearly halved between the lowest and highest levels of transition probability I, dropping from a duration of 183 months to 97 months.
    - As the duration decreases for State 3 being most likely in n-steps, a notable increase occurs in the duration of State 6 being most likely in n-steps.

*Table 27: Sensitivity Analysis Output – I at 20%*

|  |  | .4I =0.0028 | .6I =0.0042 | .8I =0.0056 | I =0.0069 | 1.2I =0.0083 | 1.4I =0.0097 | 1.6I =0.0111 |
|---|---|---|---|---|---|---|---|---|
| Expected Time in State (mths) | 1 | 60.7332 | 60.7332 | 60.7332 | 60.7332 | 60.7332 | 60.7332 | 60.7332 |
|  | 2 | 0.8555 | 0.8555 | 0.8555 | 0.8555 | 0.8555 | 0.8555 | 0.8555 |
|  | 3 | 278.1545 | 250.1497 | 227.2682 | 208.2218 | 192.1210 | 178.3315 | 166.3889 |
|  | 4 | 0.7727 | 1.0424 | 1.2627 | 1.4461 | 1.6011 | 1.7339 | 1.8488 |
|  | 5 | 80.2568 | 108.2617 | 131.1432 | 150.1896 | 166.2904 | 180.0799 | 192.0225 |
| Life Expectancy (mths) |  | 420.7728 | 421.0424 | 421.2628 | 421.4461 | 421.6012 | 421.7339 | 421.8489 |
| Max Prob of being in State | 3 | 0.5270 | 0.4924 | 0.4626 | 0.4367 | 0.4138 | 0.3935 | 0.3753 |
|  | 5 | 0.1207 | 0.1658 | 0.2039 | 0.2364 | 0.2645 | 0.2889 | 0.3104 |
| When State is most likely among all states. (highest curve on graph) | 1 | 0 - 51 | 0 - 53 | 0 - 54 | 0 - 55 | 0 - 57 | 0 - 59 | 0 - 60 |
|  | 2 | - | - | - | - | - | - | - |
|  | 3 | 52 - 235 | 54 - 216 | 55 - 201 | 56 - 188 | 58 - 176 | 60 - 166 | 61 - 158 |
|  | 4 | - | - | - | - | - | - | - |
|  | 5 | - | - | - | - | - | - | - |
|  | 6 | 236 - 600 | 218 - 600 | 202 - 600 | 189 - 600 | 178 - 600 | 167 - 600 | 159 - 600 |

Note Figure 21. As previously mentioned, in the base case, 50.4% of the individual's lifetime is expected to be in non-victimization states (i.e., States 1, 4, and 5), with the balance of 49.6% expected lifetime duration to be in victimization states (i.e., States 2 and 3). A non-linear relationship is observed among the results. Gains of 10.0% of an entire lifetime from victimization into non-victimization duration by increasing transition probability I by 60%, while the cost of transition probability I decreasing by 60% is expected to have a loss of 16.7% of non-victimization into victimization duration.

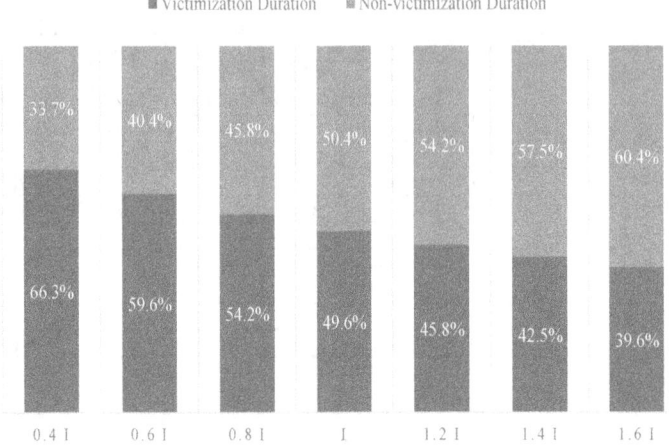

*Figure 21: Division of Victimization versus Non-victimization Duration During Individual's Lifetime, Transition Probability I Sensitivity Analysis (20%)*

Transition Probability L

Table 28 displays the sensitivity analysis output for transition probability L, when varied in 20% increments. The value of transition probability L at these variations is indicated in the header of each column. From review of the values, the following observations are made for the levels of transition probability L tested.

- Expected Time in State 1 is unchanged by changes in transition probability L.
- Expected Time in State 2 is unchanged by changes in transition probability L.
- Expected Time in State 3 decreases as transition probability L is increased, varying nearly 70 months (5.8 years) for just the partial spectrum tested (60% variation compared to the previous 120% variation for B, F, and I transition probabilities).

- Expected Time in State 4 decreases by 0.4856 months as transition probability L is increased from lowest to base levels. Due to the structure of the model assuming a one-month duration in the intervention state, each month increment can be considered as a measurement of frequency as well. At the lowest level of transition probability L, an individual is expected have nearly two instances of intervention in their lifetime.

- Expected Time in State 5 nearly doubles when varying transition probability L between the lowest and base levels. Nearly 70 months (5.8 years) difference is observed, where expected time in State 5 increases as transition probability L increases.

- Life Expectancy follows expectation to vary very little due to the risk of death (i.e., absorption) being held constant.

- The maximum probability of being in State 3 during the individual's lifetime decreases by 8.88% between the lowest and base levels of transition probability L.

- The maximum probability of being in State 5 during the individual's lifetime nearly doubles from lowest to base levels of transition probability L. The difference is 11.6%, increasing from lowest to base levels.

- Over the 600 months (50 years) modeled for the individual's lifespan, notable shifts occur among States 1, 3, and 6 in state location with highest likelihood in n-steps.
  - The duration of State 1 and State 6 maximum likelihood in n-steps increases as transition probability L increases.
  - The duration of State 3 maximum likelihood decreases from both bounds.

*Table 28: Sensitivity Analysis Output – L at 20%*

|  |  | .4L<br>=0.4000 | .6L<br>=0.5999 | .8L<br>=0.7999 | L<br>=0.9999 | 1.2L<br>> 1.0 | 1.4L<br>> 1.0 | 1.6L<br>> 1.0 |
|---|---|---|---|---|---|---|---|---|
| Expected Time in State (mths) | 1 | 60.7332 | 60.7332 | 60.7332 | 60.7332 | | | |
|  | 2 | 0.8555 | 0.8555 | 0.8555 | 0.8555 | | | |
|  | 3 | 278.1587 | 250.1522 | 227.2693 | 208.2218 | | | |
|  | 4 | 1.9317 | 1.7373 | 1.5783 | 1.4461 | | | |
|  | 5 | 80.2527 | 108.2592 | 131.1421 | 150.1896 | | | |
| Life Expectancy (mths) |  | 421.9318 | 421.7373 | 421.5784 | 421.4461 | | | |
| Max Prob of being in State | 3 | 0.5255 | 0.4915 | 0.4622 | 0.4367 | N/A | N/A | N/A |
|  | 5 | 0.1204 | 0.1656 | 0.2037 | 0.2364 | | | |
| When State is most likely among all states. (highest curve on graph) | 1 | 0 - 51 | 0 - 53 | 0 - 54 | 0 - 55 | | | |
|  | 2 | - | - | - | - | | | |
|  | 3 | 52 - 235 | 54 - 216 | 55 - 201 | 56 - 188 | | | |
|  | 4 | - | - | - | - | | | |
|  | 5 | - | - | - | - | | | |
|  | 6 | 236 - 600 | 217 - 600 | 202 - 600 | 189 - 600 | | | |

Note Figure 22. As previously mentioned, in the base case, 50.4% of the individual's lifetime is expected to be in non-victimization states (i.e., States 1, 4, and 5), with the balance of 49.6% expected lifetime duration to be in victimization states (i.e., States 2 and 3). A non-linear relationship is observed among the results. Cost of transition probability L decreasing 60% is a loss of 16.5% of non-victimization into victimization duration.

# BREAKDOWN OF LIFETIME, L @ 20%

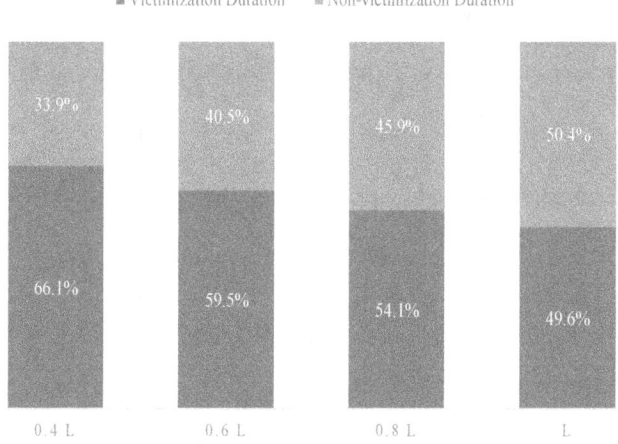

*Figure 22: Division of Victimization versus Non-victimization Duration During Individual's Lifetime, Transition Probability L Sensitivity Analysis (20%)*

Transition Probability M

Table 29 displays the sensitivity analysis output for transition probability M, when varied in 20% increments. The value of transition probability M at these variations is indicated in the header of each column. From review of the values, the following observations are made for the levels of transition probability M tested.

- Expected Time in State 1 is unchanged by changes in transition probability M.
- Expected Time in State 2 is unchanged by changes in transition probability M.
- Expected Time in State 3 increases as transition probability M is increased. The total increase from lowest to highest levels of M is more than 84 months (7 years).
- Expected Time in State 4 increases by 0.5877 months as transition probability M is increased from lowest to highest levels.

- Expected Time in State 5 decreases as transition probability M is increased. The total decrease is comparable to the magnitude of change in Expected Time in State 3, more than 84 months (7 years).
- Life Expectancy follows expectation to vary very little due to the risk of death (i.e. absorption) being held constant.
- The maximum probability of being in State 3 during the individual's lifetime increases by 3.42% between the lowest and base levels of transition probability M.
- The maximum probability of being in State 5 during the individual's lifetime decreases 11.28% from lowest to highest levels of transition probability M.
- Over the 600 months (50 years) modeled for the individual's lifespan, notable shifts occur among States 1, 3, and 6 in state location with highest likelihood in n-steps.
    - The duration of State 1 maximum likelihood in n-steps varies slightly over the levels tested.
    - The duration of State 3 and State 6 maximum likelihood has notable changes over the levels tested.

Table 29: Sensitivity Analysis Output – M at 20%

|  |  | .4M =0.0029 | .6M =0.0043 | .8M =0.0058 | M =0.0072 | 1.2M =0.0087 | 1.4M =0.0101 | 1.6M =0.0116 |
|---|---|---|---|---|---|---|---|---|
| Expected Time in State (mths) | 1 | 60.7332 | 60.7332 | 60.7332 | 60.7332 | 60.7332 | 60.7332 | 60.7332 |
|  | 2 | 0.8555 | 0.8555 | 0.8555 | 0.8555 | 0.8555 | 0.8555 | 0.8555 |
|  | 3 | 154.7992 | 176.3819 | 193.8276 | 208.2218 | 220.3007 | 230.5814 | 239.4375 |
|  | 4 | 1.0751 | 1.2250 | 1.3461 | 1.4461 | 1.5300 | 1.6013 | 1.6628 |
|  | 5 | 203.6122 | 182.0295 | 164.5838 | 150.1896 | 138.1107 | 127.8300 | 118.9739 |
| Life Expectancy (mths) |  | 421.0751 | 421.2250 | 421.3462 | 421.4461 | 421.5300 | 421.6014 | 421.6629 |
| Max Prob of being in State | 3 | 0.4196 | 0.4252 | 0.4310 | 0.4367 | 0.4424 | 0.4482 | 0.4538 |
|  | 5 | 0.3053 | 0.2784 | 0.2557 | 0.2364 | 0.2198 | 0.2052 | 0.1925 |
| When State is most likely among all states. (highest curve on graph) | 1 | 0 - 56 | 0 - 56 | 0 - 56 | 0 - 55 | 0 - 55 | 0 - 55 | 0 - 55 |
|  | 2 | - | - | - | - | - | - | - |
|  | 3 | 57 - 168 | 57 - 175 | 57 - 181 | 56 - 188 | 56 - 194 | 56 - 199 | 56 - 205 |
|  | 4 | - | - | - | - | - | - | - |
|  | 5 | - | - | - | - | - | - | - |
|  | 6 | 169 - 600 | 176 - 600 | 182 - 600 | 189 - 600 | 195 - 600 | 200 - 600 | 206 - 600 |

Note Figure 23. In the base case, 50.4% of the individual's lifetime is expected to be in non-victimization states (i.e., States 1, 4, and 5), with the balance of 49.6% expected lifetime duration to be in victimization states (i.e. States 2 and 3). A non-linear relationship is observed among the results. Gains of 12.6% of an entire lifetime from victimization into non-victimization duration by decreasing transition probability M by 60%, while the cost of transition probability M increasing 60% is expected to have a loss of 7.4% of non-victimization into victimization duration.

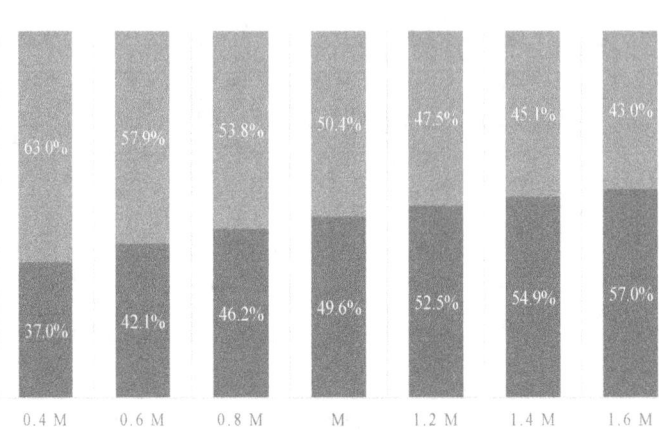

*Figure 23: Division of Victimization versus Non-victimization Duration During Individual's Lifetime, Transition Probability M Sensitivity Analysis (20%)*

Select Transition Probabilities, Expected Time in each State

The following brings together the previous tabular results on each metric. Both a two-dimensional and isometric view are included as it is difficult to differentiate stacked results in two dimensions alone.

In Figure 24, observe that Expected Time in State 1 is only impacted by changes in transition probability B. If the risk of victimization is reduced, the expected time before victimization greatly increases. The relationship is non-linear to the benefit of units of decrease making a greater magnitude of effect than comparable units of increase.

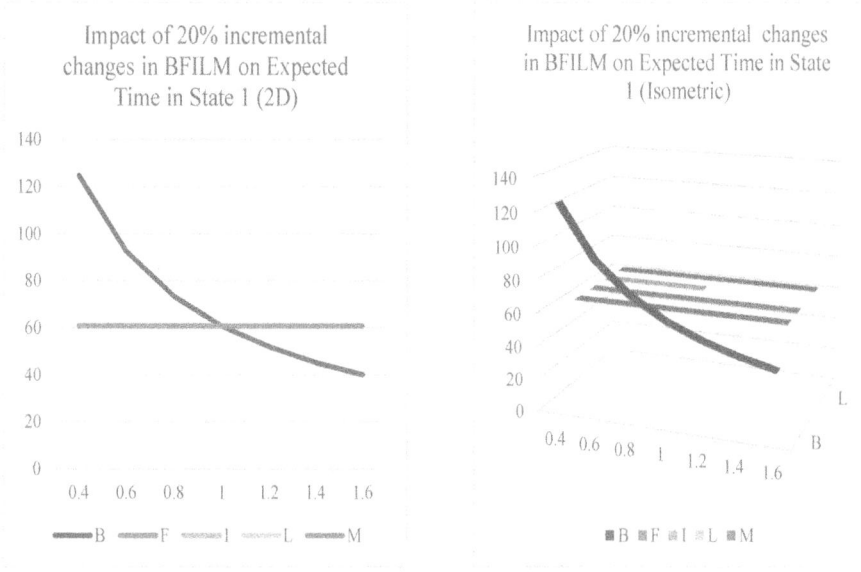

*Figure 24: Impact of BFILM changes on Expected Time in State 1, 20% Increments*

As with Expected Time in State 1, the risk of victimization is the only transition probability tested that impacts the Expected Time in State 2 (Figure 25). As the risk of initial victimization reduces, less time is expected for the individual in the recruitment state.

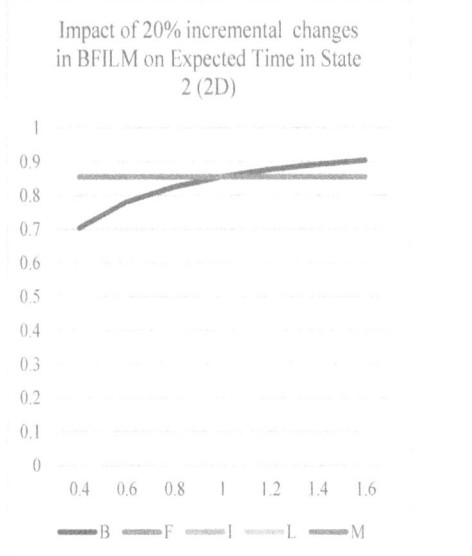 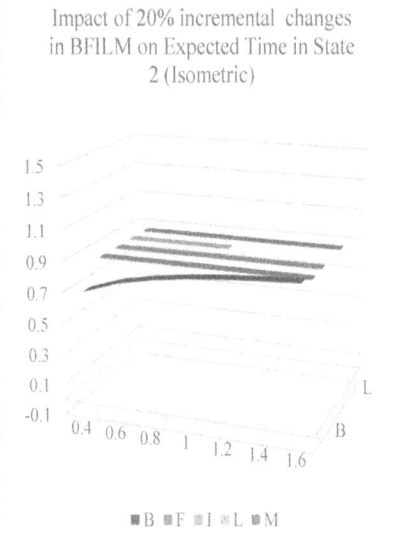

*Figure 25: Impact of BFILM changes on Expected Time in State 2, 20% Increments*

The interesting relationships of transition probabilities within the model become more complex and interactive when approaching the discussion of Expected Time in State 3. Refer to Figure 26.

- With the objective to reduce the expected time in State 3:
    o B and M are best when minimized
    o F is irrelevant
    o L and I are best when maximized.
- The effect of changes in L and I are comparable from the lowest to base levels tested.
- Changes in transition probability I have the greatest magnitude of impact than B, F, L and M.

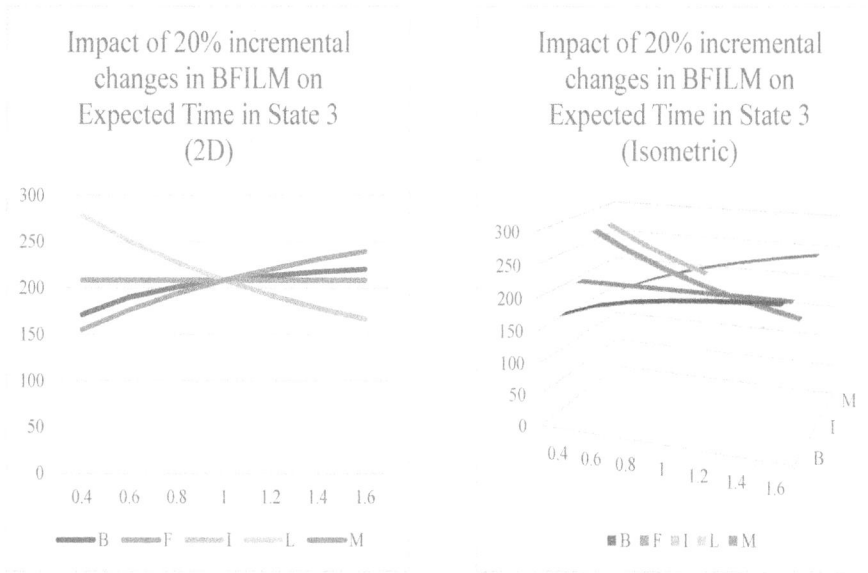

*Figure 26: Impact of BFILM changes on Expected Time in State 3, 20% Increments*

Expected Time in State 4 is the next aspect for observation (Figure 27). Each visit to State 4 (i.e. Intervention) is assumed to be a 1 month duration. Therefore, we would objectively aim to reduce the expected duration in, and therefore expected number of visits to, State 4. Of the tested increments, reducing transition probability I best achieves this objective. Transition probabilities B and M reach the same conclusion, to a lesser extent. Changes to transition probability F has no effect. The higher levels of transition probability L supports the desired outcome to lower Expected Time in State 4.

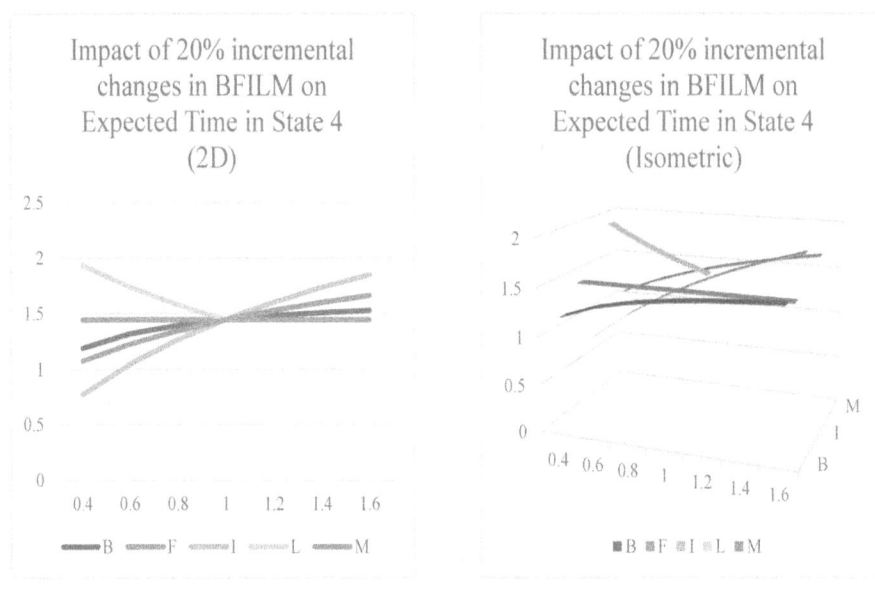

*Figure 27: Impact of BFILM changes on Expected Time in State 4, 20% Increments*

The objective related to duration in State 5 is less straightforward. While it is more desirable for an individual to spend time in State 5 than in State 3, it is less desirable to spend time in State 5 than in State 1. Thus, the observations for Figure 28 are made without a set objective. Transition probabilities B, I and L have a positive relationship with Expected Time in State 5. Transition probability M has a negative relationship with Expected Time in State 5. Transition probability F has no effect on Expected Time in State 5.

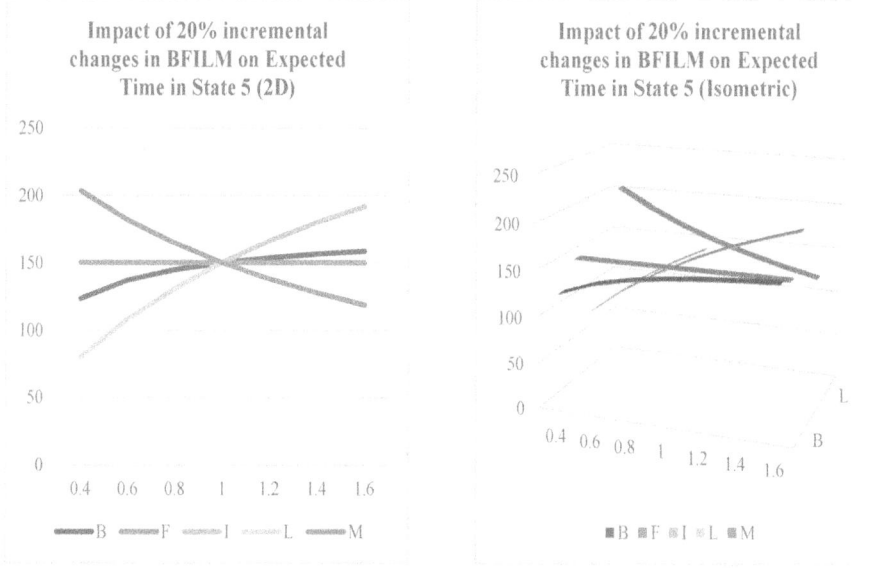

*Figure 28: Impact of BFILM changes on Expected Time in State 5, 20% Increments*

Select Transition Probabilities, Maximum Probability of Transition in n-Steps

In this section, senstivity analysis of maximum probabilities of transition in n-steps are reviewed. Recall the results matrix that was introduced in Table 20. The two elements of these graphs of particular interest in terms of maximums is the probabilities of being in States 3 and 5 in n-steps. As mentioned previously, it is desireable for an objective to minimize the maximum probability of being in State 3 in n-steps throughout an individual's lifetime. However, there is more of a complex relationship for the objective around the maximum probability of being in State 5 in n-steps throughout an individual's lifetime. On one hand, we want to maximize the likelihood of post-victimization as opposed to victimization likelihood. But simultaneously minimize the maximum likelihood of post-victimization relative to the likelihood of pre-victimization. These are key factors to consider during the current evaluation.

In Figure 29, the maximum probability for being in State 3 throughout an individual's lifetime is assessed through sensitivity analysis on the BFILM transition probabilities. The following are observed.

- Transition probability B has the greatest net effect on this maximum, followed by transition probabilities I and L.
- Transition probability M has little effect on maximum probability in this case.
- Transition probability F has no effect on maximum probability in this case.
- Decreasing transition probabilities B and M aid the objective to minimize the maximum.
- Increasing transition probabilities I and F aid the objective to minimize the maximum.

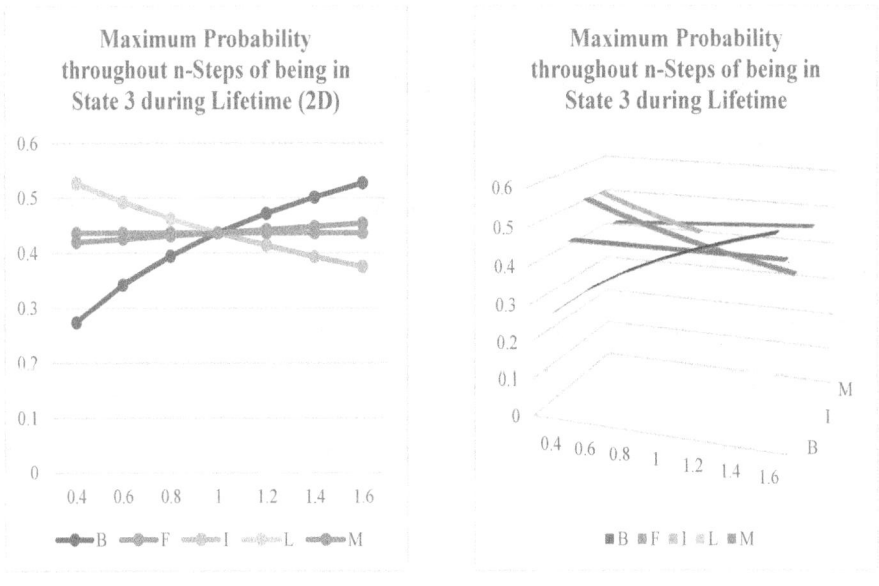

*Figure 29: Impact of BFILM changes on Maximum Probability of Being in State 3, 20% Increments*

In Figure 30, the maximum probability for being in State 5 throughout an individual's lifetime is assessed through sensitivity analysis on the BFILM transition probabilities. The following are observed.

- In order of the greatest net effect on this maximum, transition probability I, M and then B.
- Transition probability L follows similar effect as transition probability I.
- Transition probability F has no effect on maximum probability in this case.

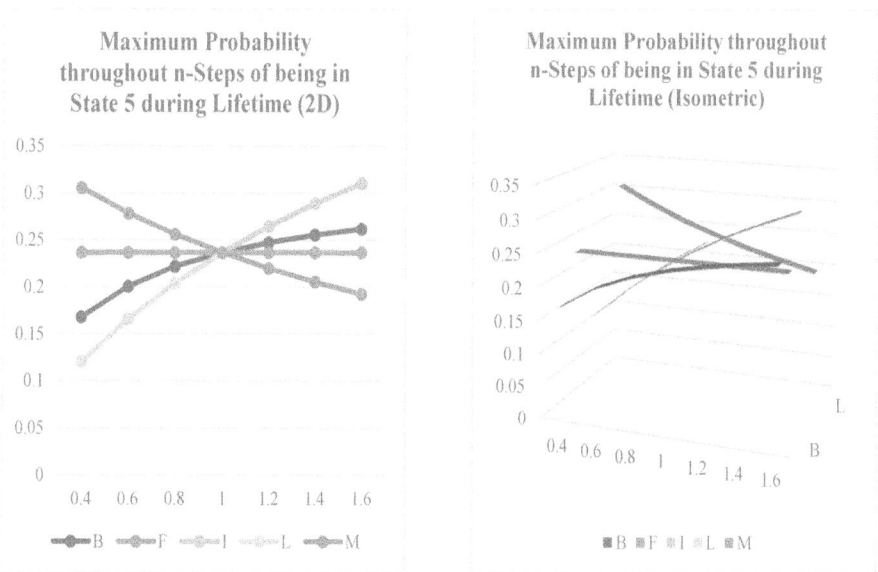

*Figure 30: Impact of BFILM changes on Maximum Probability of Being in State 5, 20% Increments*

Select Transition Probabilities, Life Expectancy

Summarized by Figure 31, life expectancy shows minimal variation at the tested increments. The maximum variation of all expectancies is less than 2.5 months. Life expectancy is only expected to have notable changes when the risk of death (i.e., probability of transition to the absorption state) fluctuates.

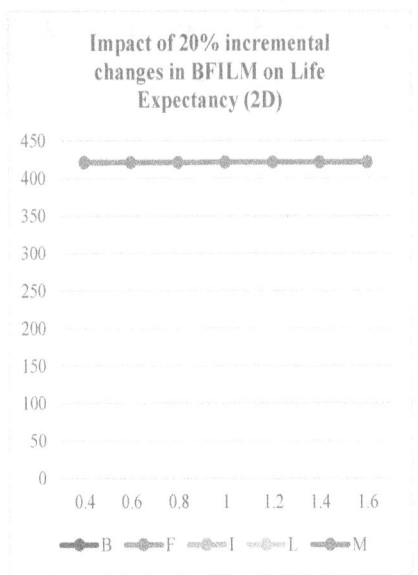 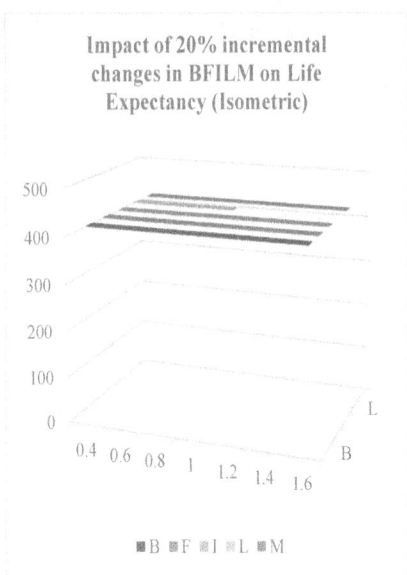

*Figure 31: Impact of BFILM changes on Expected Lifespan, 20% Increments*

Select Transition Probabilities, State with Maximum Likelihood in n-Steps

The final discussion of this 20% increment section is focused on the duration States remain most likely for the individual to be in after n-steps. Figure 32 summarizes these results that were numerically displayed in Tables 25 – 29 previously. To navigate the figure, note that the x-axis marks the duration of each State indicated as the maximum likelihood during an individual's lifetime. The rows of the figure are broken into each of the transition probability collections (i.e. transition probability ±60%). A special note is that there are three vertical lines to portray the Base Case durations in months to provide point-of-reference for observations.

- The duration of State 2, 4, and 5 being most likely among all other states is consistently zero months.

- The duration of State 1 being most likely among all other states as a base case is 55 months.

- o Varying transition probability B has the greatest effect on this duration.
- o Varying transition probability I and L have some effect on this duration.
- o Varying transition probabilities F and M have no effect on this duration.
- o With the objective to increase duration where State 1 is most likely in n-steps, reducing transition probability B is the most significant action. Increasing transition probabilities, I and L have a positive effect.
- The duration of State 3 being most likely among all other states as a base case is 133 months.
  - o Varying transition probability B has the greatest effect on this duration, followed by transition probability I.
  - o Varying transition probabilities L and M also influence this duration.
  - o Varying transition probability F has no effect on this duration.
  - o With the objective to reduce duration where State 3 is most likely in n-steps, reducing transition probabilities B and M while increasing transition probabilities I and L are desired.
- The duration of State 6 being most likely among all other states has a strong, direct relationship to the duration of State 3 being most likely.

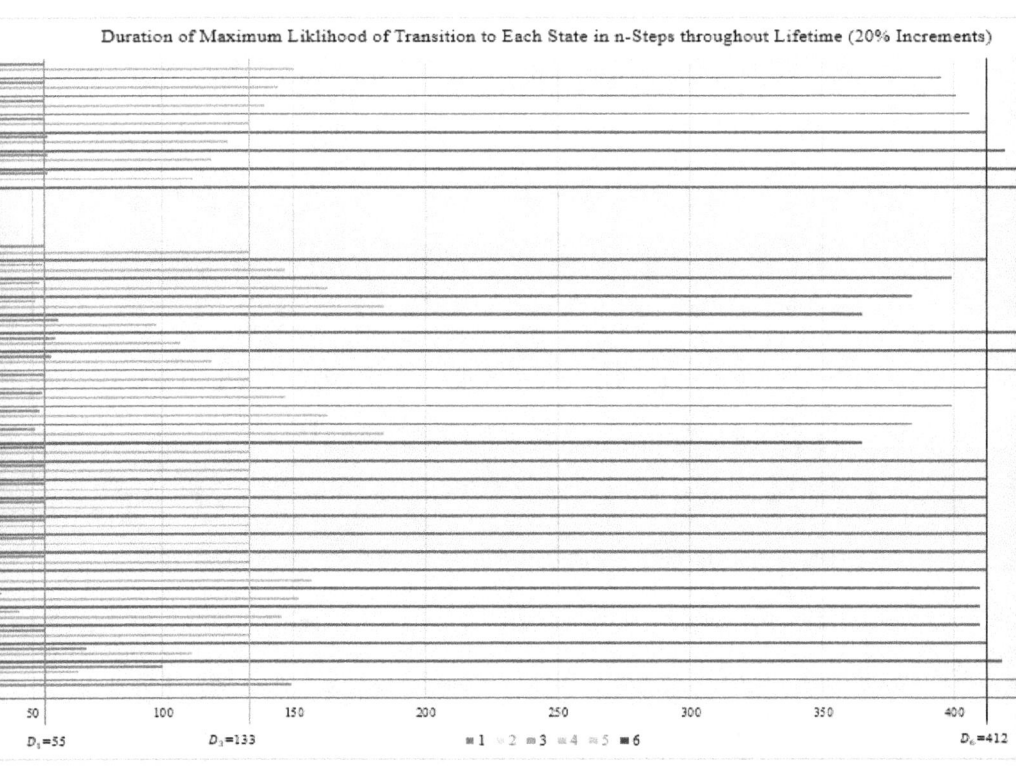

*Figure 32: Impact of BFILM changes on Maximum Likelihood of Transition, 20% Increments*

Select Transition Probabilities, Summary of Results

Table 30 summarizes the findings of the sensitivity analysis performed to identify the impact of varying the select transition probabilities in relative 20% increments. Transition probability B has the most impactful effect on the parameters evaluated, followed by transition probability I. Transition probability F has no notable impacts, while transition probabilities L and M are impactful on certain parameters.

*Table 30: Summary of Comparative BFILM Sensitivity Analysis, 20% Increment*

| | Expected Time in State | | | | | Max Prob of Being in State during Lifetime | | Duration State is Most Likely during Lifetime | | | | | |
|---|---|---|---|---|---|---|---|---|---|---|---|---|---|
| | 1 | 2 | 3 | 4 | 5 | 3 | 5 | 1 | 2 | 3 | 4 | 5 | 6 |
| B | ▣ | ▣ | • | • | • | ▣ | • | ▣ | o | ▣ | o | o | • |
| F | o | o | o | o | o | o | o | o | o | o | o | o | o |
| I | o | o | ▣ | ▣ | ▣ | • | ▣ | • | o | • | o | o | ▣ |
| L | o | o | • | • | • | • | • | • | o | • | o | o | • |
| M | o | o | • | • | • | • | • | o | o | • | o | o | • |

| KEY | | Total Frequencies | | | | |
|---|---|---|---|---|---|---|
| | | B | F | I | L | M |
| Most impactful | ▣ | 5 | 0 | 5 | 0 | 0 |
| Notable impact | • | 5 | 0 | 3 | 8 | 7 |
| No notable impact | o | 3 | 13 | 5 | 5 | 6 |

Keep in mind that the 20% increments of the preceding analysis are relative to each individual transition probability starting values in the Base Case scenario. In the next section, this relative aspect is removed, fluctuating each select transition probability by consistent increments of 0.0002.

*4.6.3 Sensitivity Analysis – Approach 2 (Increments of 0.0002)*

In this second sensitivity analysis section, a complementary analysis is performed to the previous section. Unlike the previous section, here the select transition probabilities are changed in equivalent increments (i.e. 0.0002) to allow for a different perspective of comparison. Again, analysis is performed on the Base Case. Findings will overlap with the previous, but more comparable to one another since the step sizes between levels are consistent, with a maximum total span of 0.0012 in transition probabilities tested. Discussion of results in this section that replicate the findings of the previous section are excluded due to redundancy.

Transition Probability B

The range of transition probability B interpreted in the previous analysis spanned from the lowest level of 0.0056 to the highest level of 0.0225; a difference of 0.0169, compared to the span of 0.0012 displayed in Table 31. This span is narrower, leaving the highest value of interpretation of these results in the comparison of all five select transition probabilities.

*Table 31: Sensitivity Analysis Output – B at 0.0002*

| | | B-.0006 =0.0135 | B-.0004 =0.0137 | B-.0002 =0.0139 | B =0.0141 | B+.0002 =0.0143 | B+.0004 =0.0145 | B+.0006 =0.0147 |
|---|---|---|---|---|---|---|---|---|
| Expected Time in State (mths) | 1 | 63.0300 | 62.2453 | 61.4800 | 60.7332 | 60.0043 | 59.2928 | 58.5979 |
| | 2 | 0.8500 | 0.8519 | 0.8537 | 0.8555 | 0.8572 | 0.8589 | 0.8606 |
| | 3 | 206.8906 | 207.3454 | 207.7890 | 208.2218 | 208.6442 | 209.0566 | 209.4594 |
| | 4 | 1.4368 | 1.4400 | 1.4431 | 1.4461 | 1.4490 | 1.4519 | 1.4547 |
| | 5 | 149.2294 | 149.5574 | 149.8774 | 150.1896 | 150.4943 | 150.7917 | 151.0822 |
| Life Expectancy (mths) | | 421.4369 | 421.4401 | 421.4431 | 421.4461 | 421.4461 | 421.4519 | 421.4547 |
| Max Prob of being in State | 3 | 0.4284 | 0.4312 | 0.4340 | 0.4367 | 0.4394 | 0.4420 | 0.4447 |
| | 5 | 0.2336 | 0.2346 | 0.2355 | 0.2364 | 0.2373 | 0.2381 | 0.2390 |
| When State is most likely among all states. (highest curve on graph) | 1 | 0 - 58 | 0 - 57 | 0 - 56 | 0 - 55 | 0 - 55 | 0 - 54 | 0 - 53 |
| | 2 | - | - | - | - | - | - | - |
| | 3 | 59 - 187 | 58 - 187 | 57 - 187 | 56 - 188 | 56 - 188 | 55 - 188 | 54 - 188 |
| | 4 | - | - | - | - | - | - | - |
| | 5 | - | - | - | - | - | - | - |
| | 6 | 188 - 600 | 188 - 600 | 188 - 600 | 189 - 600 | 189 - 600 | 189 - 600 | 189 - 600 |

In Figure 33, the trend of change in percent is shown for breakdown of an individual's lifetime expected between victimization and non-victimization states. This interval, again, is narrower than previously analyzed.

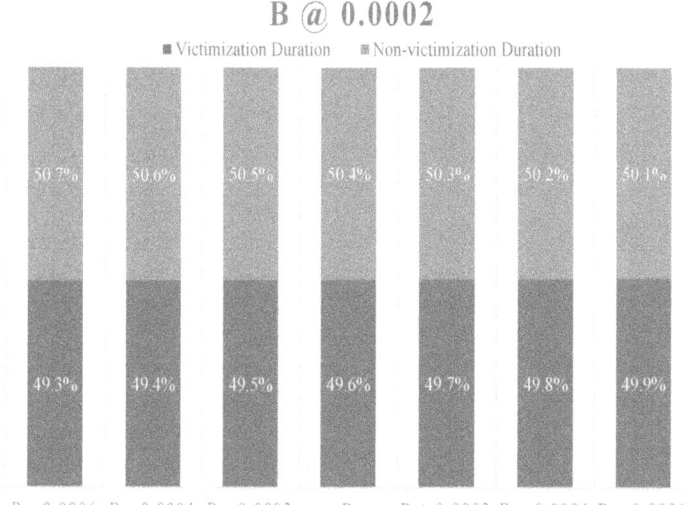

*Figure 33: Division of Victimization versus Non-victimization Duration During Individual's Lifetime, Transition Probability B Sensitivity Analysis (0.0002)*

Transition Probability F

The range of transition probability F interpreted in the previous analysis spanned from the lowest level of 0.00004 to the highest level of 0.00016; a difference of 0.00012, compared to the one-sided span of 0.0006 displayed in Table 32. This span is much wider, resulting in both value of this interpretation as well as in the comparison of this among all five transition probabilities analyzed. Additional observations to the previous section are noted from this table.

- Expected Time in State 3 varies just over 0.03 months because of changes in transition probability F.
- Expected Time in State 4 varies by 0.0001 months with each increment.
- Expected Time in State 5 varies by less than 0.03 months among the levels tested.

- The maximum probability of being in State 3 during the victim's lifetime varies by 0.0002 among the levels tested.

*Table 32: Sensitivity Analysis Output – F at 0.0002*

|  |  | F-.0006 = <0.0 | F-.0004 = <0.0 | F-.0002 = <0.0 | F =0.0001 | F+.0002 =0.0003 | F+.0004 =0.0005 | F+.0006 =0.0007 |
|---|---|---|---|---|---|---|---|---|
| Expected Time in State (mths) | 1 |  |  |  | 60.7332 | 60.7332 | 60.7332 | 60.7332 |
|  | 2 |  |  |  | 0.8555 | 0.8555 | 0.8555 | 0.8555 |
|  | 3 |  |  |  | 208.2218 | 208.2115 | 208.2012 | 208.1908 |
|  | 4 |  |  |  | 1.4461 | 1.4462 | 1.4463 | 1.4464 |
|  | 5 |  |  |  | 150.1896 | 150.1999 | 150.2102 | 150.2205 |
| Life Expectancy (mths) |  |  |  |  | 421.4461 | 421.4462 | 421.4463 | 421.4464 |
| Max Prob of being in State | 3 | N/A | N/A | N/A | 0.4367 | 0.4366 | 0.4366 | 0.4365 |
|  | 5 |  |  |  | 0.2364 | 0.2364 | 0.2364 | 0.2364 |
| When State is most likely among all states. (highest curve on graph) | 1 |  |  |  | 0 - 55 | 0 - 55 | 0 - 55 | 0 - 55 |
|  | 2 |  |  |  | - | - | - | - |
|  | 3 |  |  |  | 56 - 188 | 56 - 188 | 56 - 188 | 56 - 188 |
|  | 4 |  |  |  | - | - | - | - |
|  | 5 |  |  |  | - | - | - | - |
|  | 6 |  |  |  | 189 - 600 | 189 - 600 | 189 - 600 | 189 - 600 |

Refer to Figure 34. At a resolution level of tenths of percent, there is no observable impact of victimization versus non-victimization time during the individual's lifetime by changes in transition probability F.

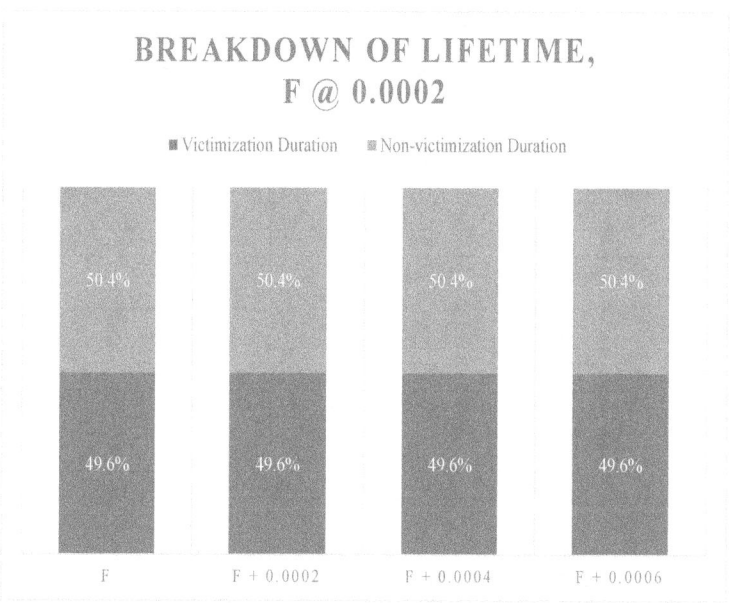

*Figure 34: Division of Victimization versus Non-victimization Duration During Individual's Lifetime, Transition Probability F Sensitivity Analysis (0.0002)*

Transition Probability I

The range of transition probability I interpreted in the previous analysis spanned from the lowest level of 0.0028 to the highest level of 0.0111; a difference of 0.0083, compared to the span of 0.0012 displayed in Table 33. The span is much narrower, leaving the highest value of interpretation in the comparison of all five transition probabilities analyzed.

*Table 33: Sensitivity Analysis Output – I at 0.0002*

| | | I-.0006 =0.0063 | I-.0004 =0.0065 | I-.0002 =0.0067 | I =0.0069 | I+.0002 =0.0071 | I+.0004 =0.0073 | I+.0006 =0.0075 |
|---|---|---|---|---|---|---|---|---|
| Expected Time in State (mths) | 1 | 60.7332 | 60.7332 | 60.7332 | 60.7332 | 60.7332 | 60.7332 | 60.7332 |
| | 2 | 0.8555 | 0.8555 | 0.8555 | 0.8555 | 0.8555 | 0.8555 | 0.8555 |
| | 3 | 216.0435 | 213.3718 | 210.7653 | 208.2218 | 205.7390 | 203.3146 | 200.9467 |
| | 4 | 1.3708 | 1.3965 | 1.4216 | 1.4461 | 1.4700 | 1.4933 | 1.5161 |
| | 5 | 142.3679 | 145.0396 | 147.6461 | 150.1896 | 152.6724 | 155.0968 | 157.4647 |
| Life Expectancy (mths) | | 421.3708 | 421.3966 | 421.4216 | 421.4461 | 421.4700 | 421.4934 | 421.5162 |
| Max Prob of being in State | 3 | 0.4475 | 0.4438 | 0.4402 | 0.4367 | 0.4332 | 0.4298 | 0.4265 |
| | 5 | 0.2230 | 0.2275 | 0.2320 | 0.2364 | 0.2407 | 0.2449 | 0.2490 |
| When State is most likely among all states. (highest curve on graph) | 1 | 0 - 55 | 0 - 55 | 0 - 55 | 0 - 55 | 0 - 56 | 0 - 56 | 0 - 56 |
| | 2 | - | - | - | - | - | - | - |
| | 3 | 56 - 193 | 56 - 191 | 56 - 189 | 56 - 188 | 57 - 186 | 57 - 183 | 57 – 182 |
| | 4 | - | - | - | - | - | - | - |
| | 5 | - | - | - | - | - | - | - |
| | 6 | 194 - 600 | 192 - 600 | 190 - 600 | 189 - 600 | 187 - 600 | 184 - 600 | 183 - 600 |

In Figure 35, the trend of change in percent is shown for breakdown of an individual's lifetime expected between victimization and non-victimization states. This interval, again, is narrower than previously analyzed.

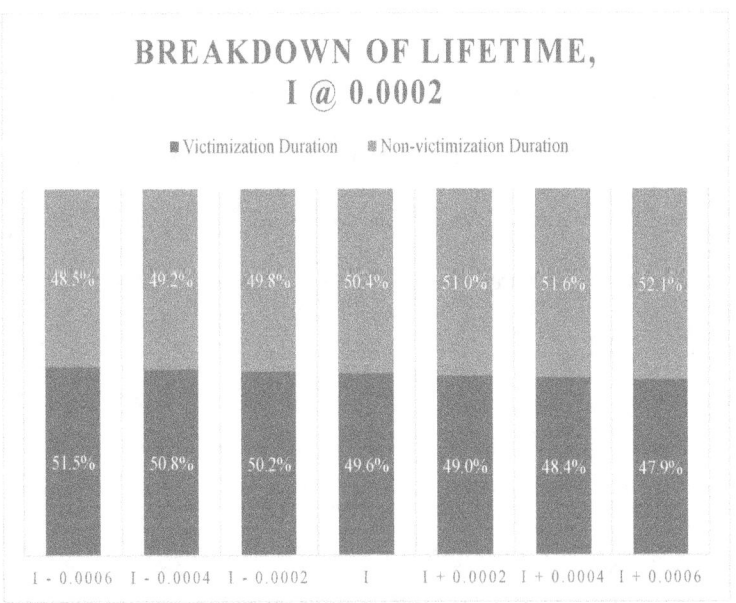

*Figure 35: Division of Victimization versus Non-victimization Duration During Individual's Lifetime, Transition Probability I Sensitivity Analysis (0.0002)*

Transition Probability L

The range of transition probability L interpreted in the previous analysis spanned from the lowest level of 0.4000 to the highest level of 0.9999; a difference of 0.5999, compared to the span of 0.0006 displayed in Table 34. This span is narrower, leaving the highest value of interpretation in the comparison of all five transition probabilities analyzed.

*Table 34: Sensitivity Analysis Output – L at 0.0002*

| | | L-.0006 =0.9993 | L-.0004 =0.9995 | L-.0002 =0.9997 | L =0.9999 | L+.0002 > 1.0 | L+.0004 > 1.0 | L+.0006 > 1.0 |
|---|---|---|---|---|---|---|---|---|
| Expected Time in State (mths) | 1 | 60.7332 | 60.7332 | 60.7332 | 60.7332 | | | |
| | 2 | 0.8555 | 0.8555 | 0.8555 | 0.8555 | | | |
| | 3 | 208.2742 | 208.2567 | 208.2393 | 208.2218 | | | |
| | 4 | 1.4464 | 1.4463 | 1.4462 | 1.4461 | | | |
| | 5 | 150.1372 | 150.1547 | 150.1721 | 150.1896 | | | |
| Life Expectancy (mths) | | 421.4465 | 421.4463 | 421.4462 | 421.4461 | | | |
| Max Prob of being in State | 3 | 0.4368 | 0.4367 | 0.4367 | 0.4367 | N/A | N/A | N/A |
| | 5 | 0.2363 | 0.2363 | 0.2364 | 0.2364 | | | |
| When State is most likely among all states. (highest curve on graph) | 1 | 0 - 55 | 0 - 55 | 0 - 55 | 0 - 55 | | | |
| | 2 | - | - | - | - | | | |
| | 3 | 56 - 188 | 56 - 188 | 56 - 188 | 56 - 188 | | | |
| | 4 | - | - | - | - | | | |
| | 5 | - | - | - | - | | | |
| | 6 | 189 - 600 | 189 - 600 | 189 - 600 | 189 - 600 | | | |

At the level of resolution displayed in Figure 36, there are no insights as to the impact of changes in transition probability L on the percent breakdown of an individual's lifetime in terms of victimization time and non-victimization time.

# BREAKDOWN OF LIFETIME, L @ 0.0002

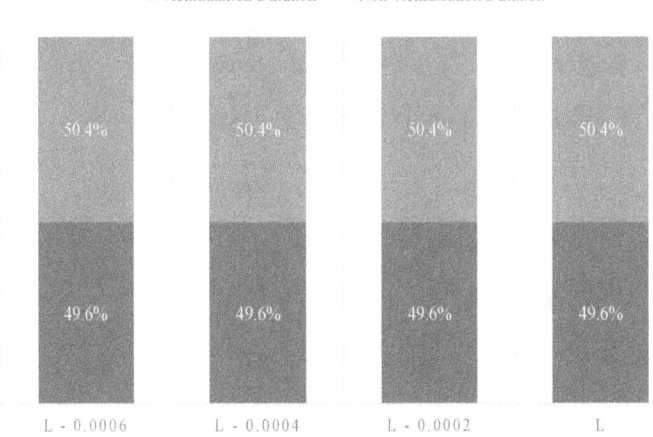

*Figure 36: Division of Victimization versus Non-victimization Duration During Individual's Lifetime, Transition Probability L Sensitivity Analysis (0.0002)*

Transition Probability M

The range of transition probability M interpreted in the previous analysis spanned from the lowest level of 0.0029 to the highest level of 0.0116; a difference of 0.0087, compared to the span of 0.0012 displayed in Table 35. This span is much narrower, leaving the highest value of interpretation in the comparison of all five transition probabilities analyzed.

*Table 35: Sensitivity Analysis Output – M at 0.0002*

|  |  | M-.0006 =0.0066 | M-.0004 =0.0068 | M-.0002 =0.0070 | M =0.0072 | M+.0002 =0.0074 | M+.0004 =0.0076 | M+.0006 =0.0078 |
|---|---|---|---|---|---|---|---|---|
| Expected Time in State (mths) | 1 | 60.7332 | 60.7332 | 60.7332 | 60.7332 | 60.7332 | 60.7332 | 60.7332 |
|  | 2 | 0.8555 | 0.8555 | 0.8555 | 0.8555 | 0.8555 | 0.8555 | 0.8555 |
|  | 3 | 202.5795 | 204.5068 | 206.3870 | 208.2218 | 210.0129 | 211.7617 | 213.4698 |
|  | 4 | 1.4069 | 1.4203 | 1.4333 | 1.4461 | 1.4585 | 1.4707 | 1.4825 |
|  | 5 | 155.8319 | 153.9046 | 152.0244 | 150.1896 | 148.3985 | 146.6497 | 144.9416 |
| Life Expectancy (mths) |  | 421.4070 | 421.4203 | 421.4334 | 421.4461 | 421.4586 | 421.4707 | 421.4826 |
| Max Prob of being in State | 3 | 0.4343 | 0.4351 | 0.4359 | 0.4367 | 0.4375 | 0.4383 | 0.4391 |
|  | 5 | 0.2440 | 0.2414 | 0.2389 | 0.2364 | 0.2340 | 0.2316 | 0.2292 |
| When State is most likely | 1 | 0 - 55 | 0 - 55 | 0 - 55 | 0 - 55 | 0 - 55 | 0 - 55 | 0 - 55 |
|  | 2 | - | - | - | - | - | - | - |

| | | | | | | | | |
|---|---|---|---|---|---|---|---|---|
| among all states. (highest curve on graph) | 3 | 56 - 185 | 56 - 186 | 56 - 187 | 56 - 188 | 56 - 188 | 56 - 189 | 56 – 190 |
| | 4 | - | - | - | - | - | - | - |
| | 5 | - | - | - | - | - | - | - |
| | 6 | 186 - 600 | 187 - 600 | 188 - 600 | 189 - 600 | 189 - 600 | 190 - 600 | 191 - 600 |

In Figure 37, the trend of change in percent is shown for breakdown of an individual's lifetime expected between victimization and non-victimization states. This interval, again, is narrower than previously analyzed.

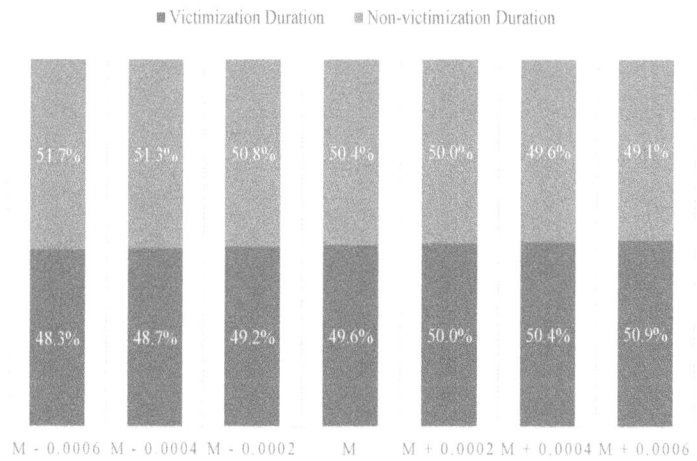

*Figure 37: Division of Victimization versus Non-victimization Duration During Individual's Lifetime, Transition Probability M Sensitivity Analysis (0.0002)*

Select Transition Probabilities, Expected Time in Each State

Doing this second sensitivity analysis sets up the following discussion for a true 'apples-to-apples' comparison in magnitude of change in transition probabilities. Keep in mind one of the questions of application that can be assessed is:

*If it is possible to change any one of these five select transition probabilities, which transition probability would be best changed per the objectives of the anti-trafficking community?*

In Figure 38 and Figure 39, the Expected Times in States 1 and 2 are only impacted by changes in transition probability B. For an anti-trafficking objective, decreasing transition probability B increases Expected Time in State 1 while decreasing Expected Time in State 2.

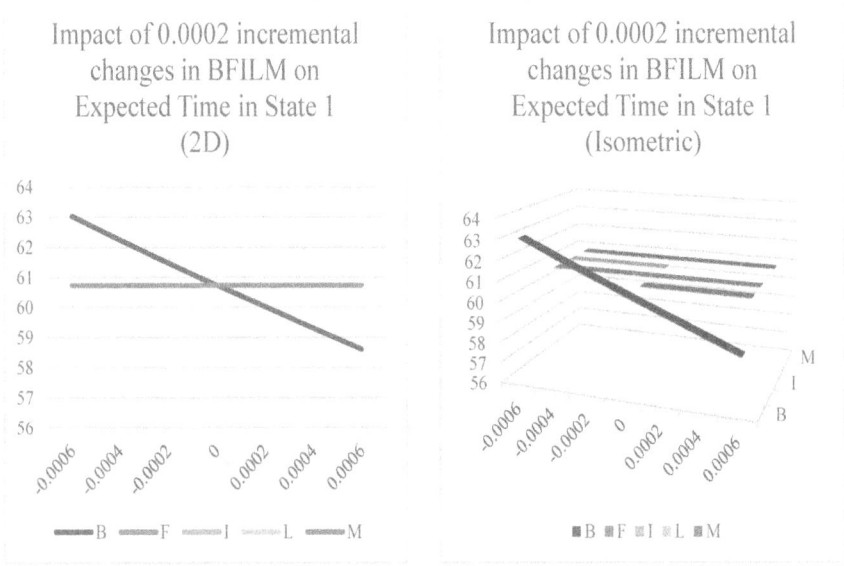

*Figure 38: Impact of BFILM changes on Expected Time in State 1, 0.0002 Increments*

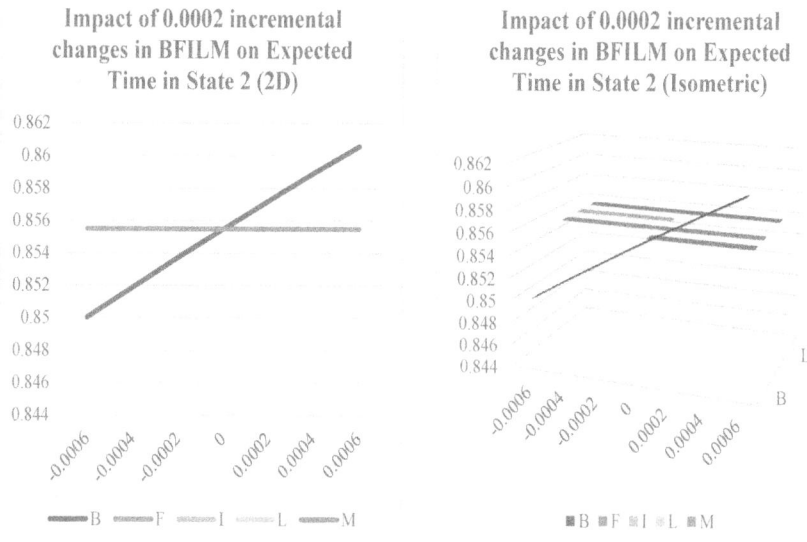

*Figure 39: Impact of BFILM changes on Expected Time in State 2, 0.0002 Increments*

In Figure 40 – Figure 42, Expected Time in States 3, 4, and 5 are all most impacted by transition probability I. For an anti-trafficking objective, increasing transition probability I decreases Expected Time in State 3, while increasing Expected Time in States 4 and 5.

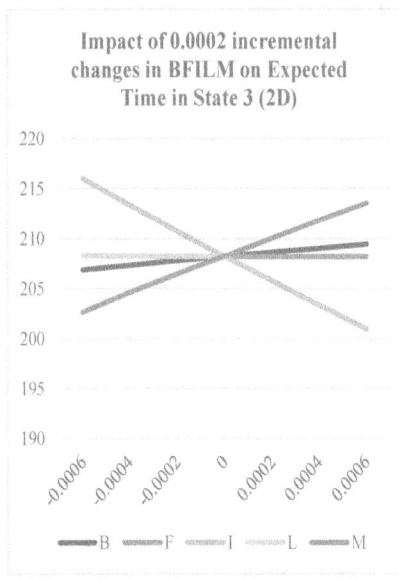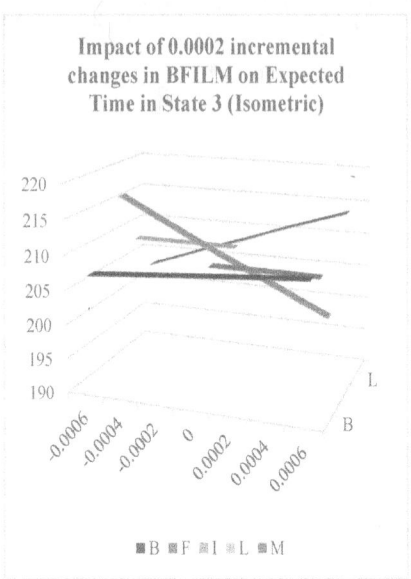

*Figure 40: Impact of BFILM changes on Expected Time in State 3, 0.0002 Increments*

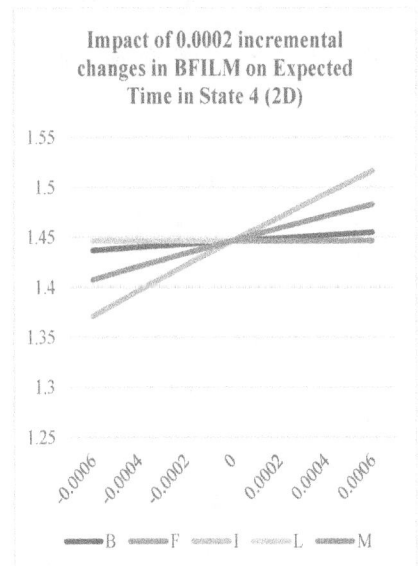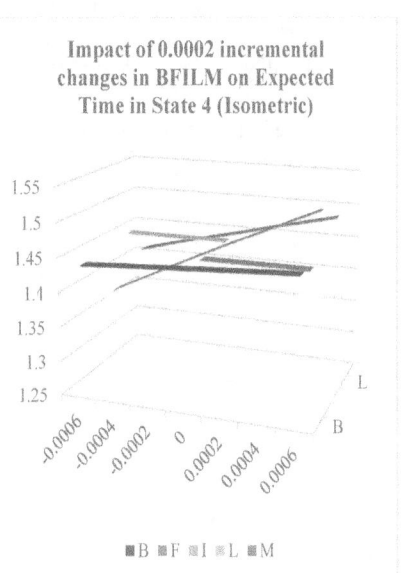

*Figure 41: Impact of BFILM changes on Expected Time in State 4, 0.0002 Increments*

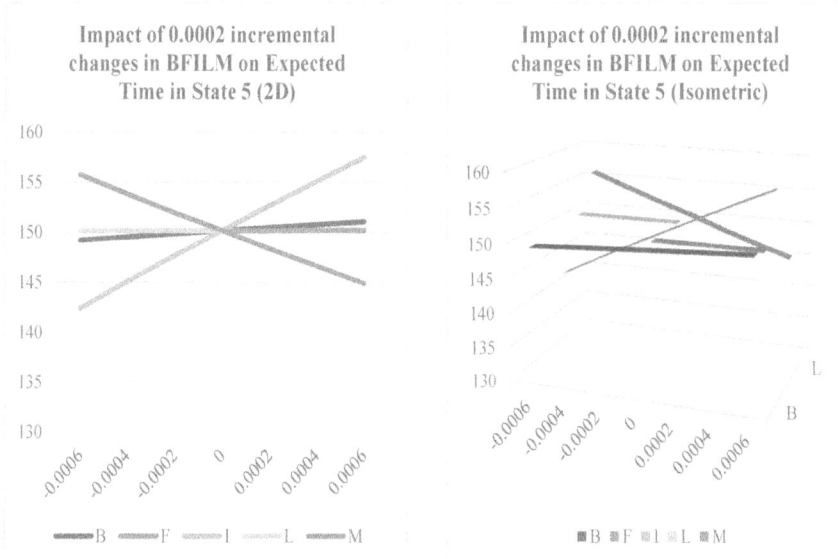

*Figure 42: Impact of BFILM changes on Expected Time in State 5, 0.0002 Increments*

A takeaway is that while transition probability B impacts Expected Time in States 1 and 2, the other transition probabilities have no impact on this Expected Time in States 1 and 2. Due to the life expectancy being controlled with little variation, the changes in Expected Time in States 3, 4, and 5 have an observable direct relationship with one another. As to say, as one changes, the others have essentially equal and opposite changes.

Select Transition Probabilities, Maximum Probability of Transition in n-Steps

In Figure 43 and Figure 44, Maximum Probability of being in State 3 and 5 during lifetime respectively, are most significantly impacted by changes in transition probability I. The second most impactful transition probability for Maximum Probability of being in State 3 is transition probability B. The second most impactful probability for Maximum Probability of being in State 5 is transition probability M.

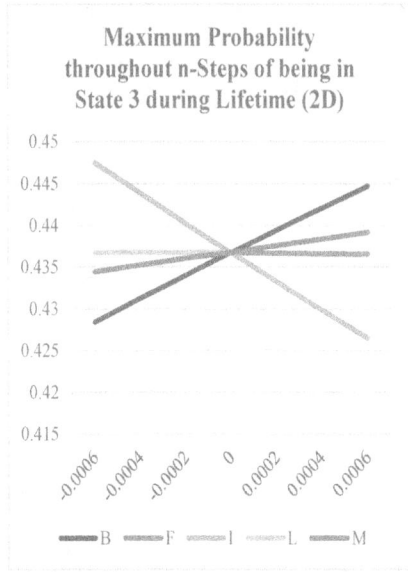 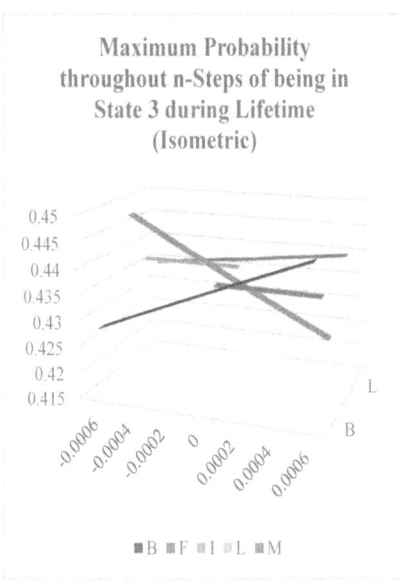

*Figure 43: Impact of BFILM changes on Maximum Probability of Being in State 3, 0.0002 Increments*

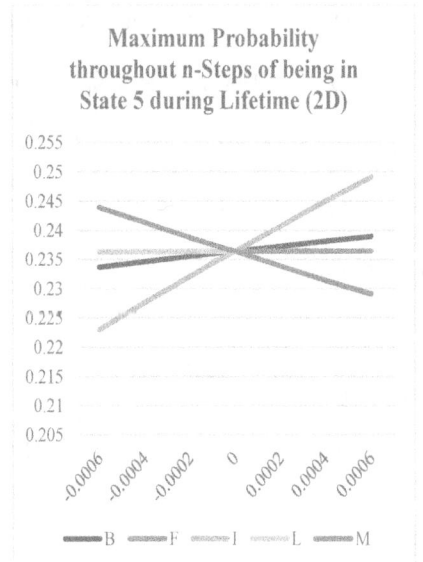 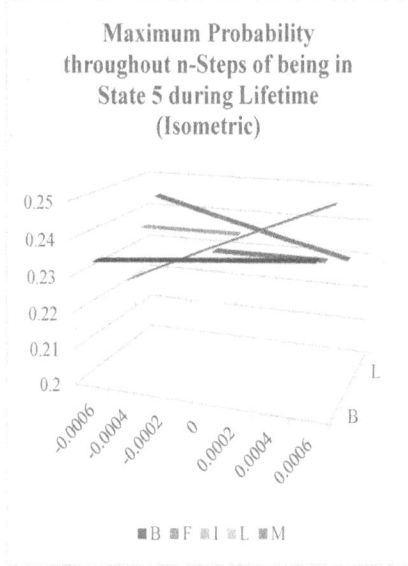

*Figure 44: Impact of BFILM changes on Maximum Probability of Being in State 5, 0.0002 Increments*

Select Transition Probabilities, Life Expectancy

As summarized in the previous section for 20% incremental impacts on life expectancy, Figure 45 re-emphasizes that life expectancy is equivalently a control variable in this sensitivity analysis.

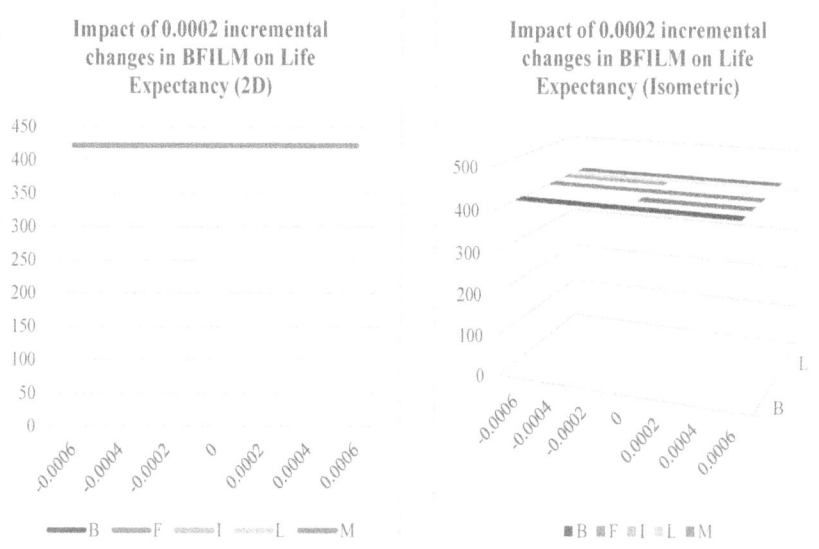

*Figure 45: Impact of BFILM changes on Expected Lifespan, 0.0002 Increments*

Select Transition Probabilities, State with Maximum Likelihood in n-Steps

The final discussion of this 0.0002 increment section and overall sensitivity analysis review is focused on the duration States remain most likely for the individual to be in after n-steps. Figure 46 summarizes these results that were numerically displayed in Tables 31 – 35. To navigate the figure, note that the x-axis marks the duration of each State indicated as the maximum likelihood during an individual's lifetime. The rows of the figure are broken into each of the transition probability collections (i.e., transition probability ±0.0006). A special note is that there are three vertical lines to portray the base case durations in months to provide point-of-reference for observations.

- The duration of State 2, 4, and 5 being most likely among all other states is consistently zero months.

- The duration of State 1 being most likely among all other states as a base case is 55 months. Varying transition probability B has the greatest effect on this duration.

- The duration of State 3 being most likely among all other states as a base case is 133 months. Varying transition probability I has the greatest effect on this duration.

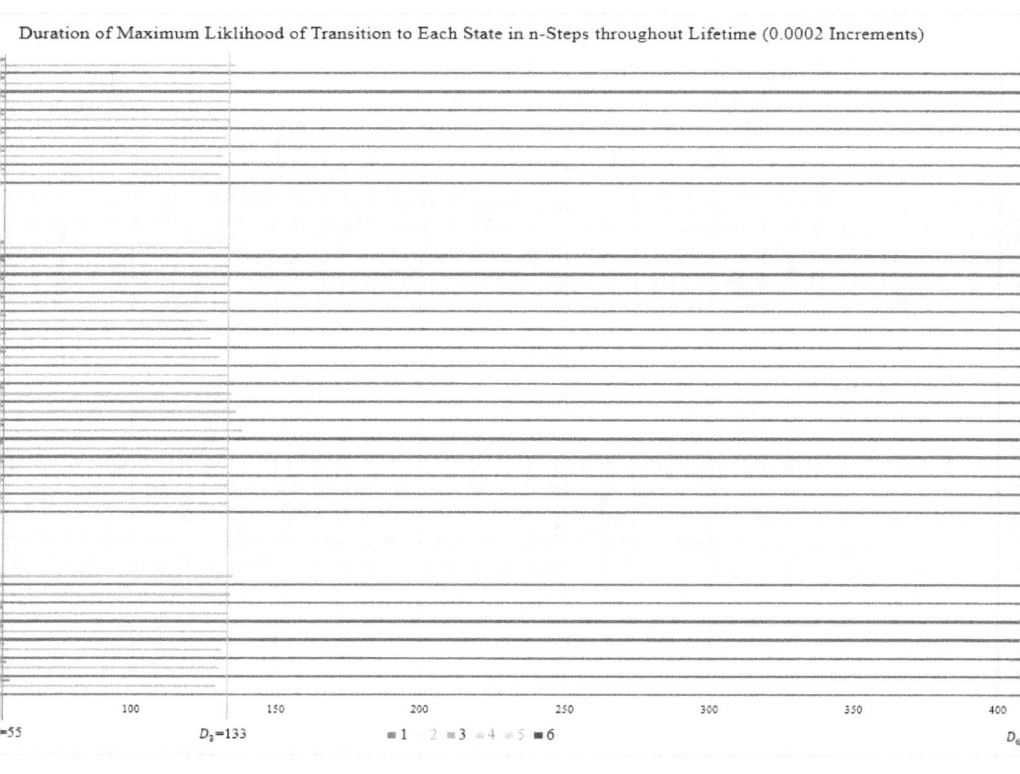

*Figure 46: Impact of BFILM changes on Maximum Likelihood of Transition, 0.0002 Increments*

Select Transition Probabilities, Summary of Results

The importance of this supplementary sensitivity analysis is captured in Table 36. In this testing scenario, transition probability I is considered the most impactful, while transition probability impacts the most parameters. Transition probabilities F and L identified with no notable impacts on any of the parameters. On the other hand, transition probability M is in between with seven notable impacts out of the parameters tested.

*Table 36: Summary of Comparative BFILM Sensitivity Analysis, 0.0002 Increment*

|   | Expected Time in State |   |   |   |   | Max Prob of Being in State during Lifetime |   | Duration State is Most Likely during Lifetime |   |   |   |   |   |
|---|---|---|---|---|---|---|---|---|---|---|---|---|---|
|   | 1 | 2 | 3 | 4 | 5 | 3 | 5 | 1 | 2 | 3 | 4 | 5 | 6 |
| B | ◙ | ◙ | ● | ● | ● | ● | ● | ◙ | ○ | ● | ○ | ○ | ● |
| F | ○ | ○ | ○ | ○ | ○ | ○ | ○ | ○ | ○ | ○ | ○ | ○ | ○ |
| I | ○ | ○ | ◙ | ◙ | ◙ | ◙ | ◙ | ● | ○ | ◙ | ○ | ○ | ◙ |
| L | ○ | ○ | ○ | ○ | ○ | ○ | ○ | ○ | ○ | ○ | ○ | ○ | ○ |
| M | ○ | ○ | ● | ● | ● | ● | ● | ○ | ○ | ● | ○ | ○ | ● |

| KEY |   |   | Total Frequencies |   |   |   |   |
|---|---|---|---|---|---|---|---|
|   |   |   | B | F | I | L | M |
| Most impactful | ◙ |   | 3 | 0 | 7 | 0 | 0 |
| Has notable impact | ● |   | 7 | 0 | 1 | 0 | 7 |
| No notable impact | ○ |   | 3 | 13 | 5 | 13 | 6 |

*4.6.4 Monte Carlo Simulation Background*

In the Excel Tool developed for this research model, the add-in software package of Crystal Ball® was used to execute Monte Carlo simulations with the element of variability introduced on the select transition probabilities, simultaneously. Each simulation was run for 5,000 iterations and the confidence level applied in analysis is 95%. In Approach 3, ±60% variability was applied to the select transition probabilities. The same procedure was followed for Approach 4, where ±0.0006 variability was applied to the select transition probabilities.

To begin to better understand the impact of uncertainty of inputs, the select transition probabilities were defined according to a Triangular distribution. The most likely, middle value is the Base Case value. Paralleling the previous incremental analysis in Approaches 1 and 2, this analysis similarly identifies the lower and upper bounds for the Triangular distribution as an equivalent increment away from the Base Case values. In the third approach, the lower bound and upper bound are 60% increments away from the base case. In the fourth approach, the lower bound and upper bound are 0.0006 increments away from the base case. Figure 47 summarizes these bounds on each of the select transition probabilities in the far-right columns. Note that for unreal bounds in these increments, the minimum of 0.00 and maximum of 1.00 were enforced in required instances.

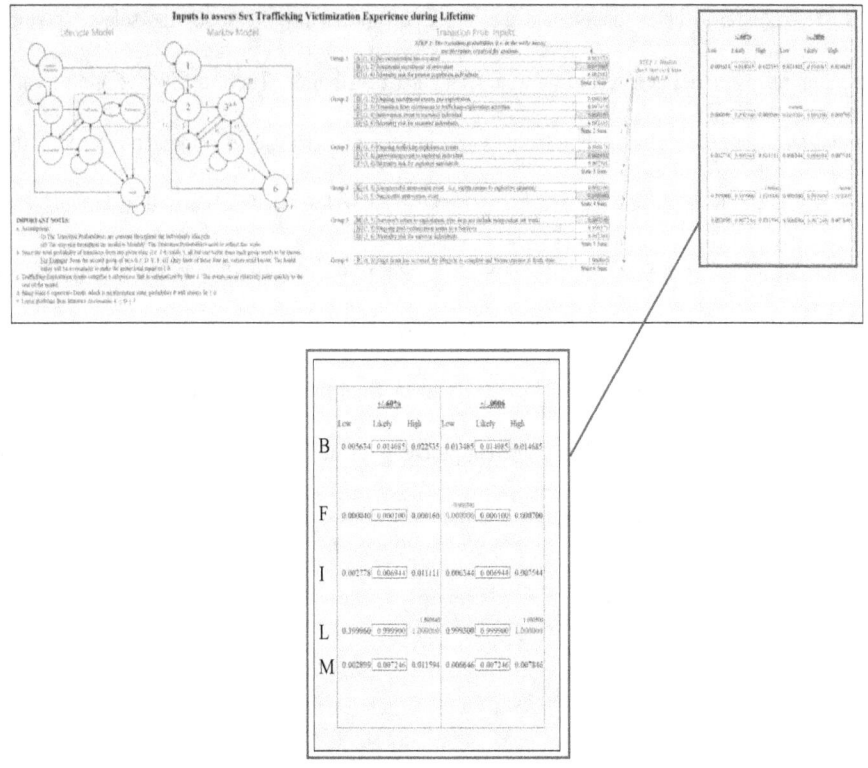

*Figure 47: Preparation for Monte Carlo Simulation and Sensitivity Analysis*

In what follows, Approach 3 and 4 will evaluate the impacts on previously discussed parameters of the select transition probabilities varying concurrently. The measured parameters are the expected time in each state, the maximum probability of being in States 3 and 5, and the sensitivity analysis associated with all of these. The defining difference between Approaches 3 and 4 parallels the differences in sensitivity analysis Approaches 1 and 2. While in Approach 3 the select transition probabilities vary as a percentage of their individual totals, in Approach 4 the select transition probabilities vary equivalently. Observations are identified.

150

*4.6.5 Sensitivity Analysis – Approach 3 (±60% Variability)*

Expected Time in Each State

Figure 48 through Figure 52 summarize the results of the simulation with the select transition probabilities assigned with Triangular distributions that ranged ±60% from the Base Case values. A notable visual observation for the graphical and numerical results lies in the skewness. State 1 expected time results have right skewness while State 2 expected time results have left skewness. The remainder of the state expected times results have less notable skewness, demonstrating a more symmetrical, bell-shape.

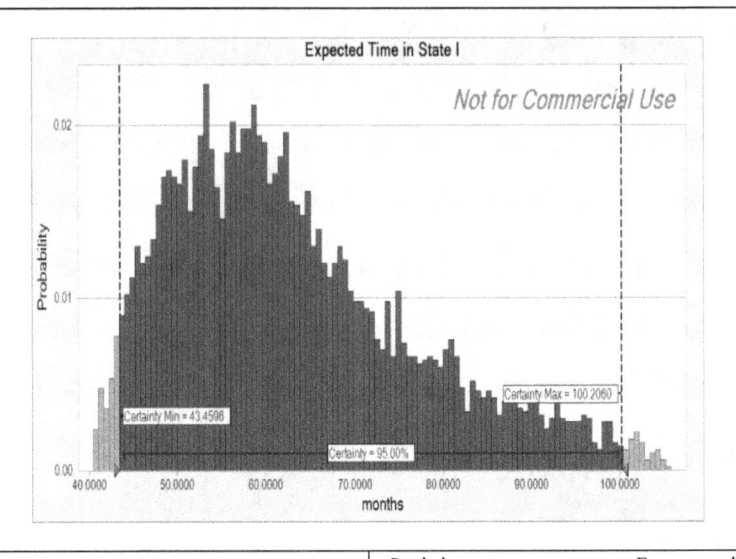

| | Statistics: | Forecast values |
|---|---|---|
| Certainty level is 95.00% | Trials | 5,000 |
| Certainty range is from 43.4596 to 100.2060 | Base Case | 60.7332 |
| | Mean | 63.8327 |
| Entire range is from 40.4000 to 122.6798 | Median | 60.6219 |
| Base case is 60.7332 | Mode | --- |
| After 5,000 trials, the std. error of the mean is 0.2119 | Standard Deviation | 14.9839 |
| | Variance | 224.5184 |
| | Skewness | 0.9766 |
| | Kurtosis | 3.67 |
| | Coeff. of Variation | 0.2347 |
| | Minimum | 40.4000 |
| | Maximum | 122.6798 |
| | Range Width | 82.2798 |
| | Mean Std. Error | 0.2119 |

*Figure 48: Collection of Crystal Ball output for Expected Time in State 1 (BFILM ± 60%)*

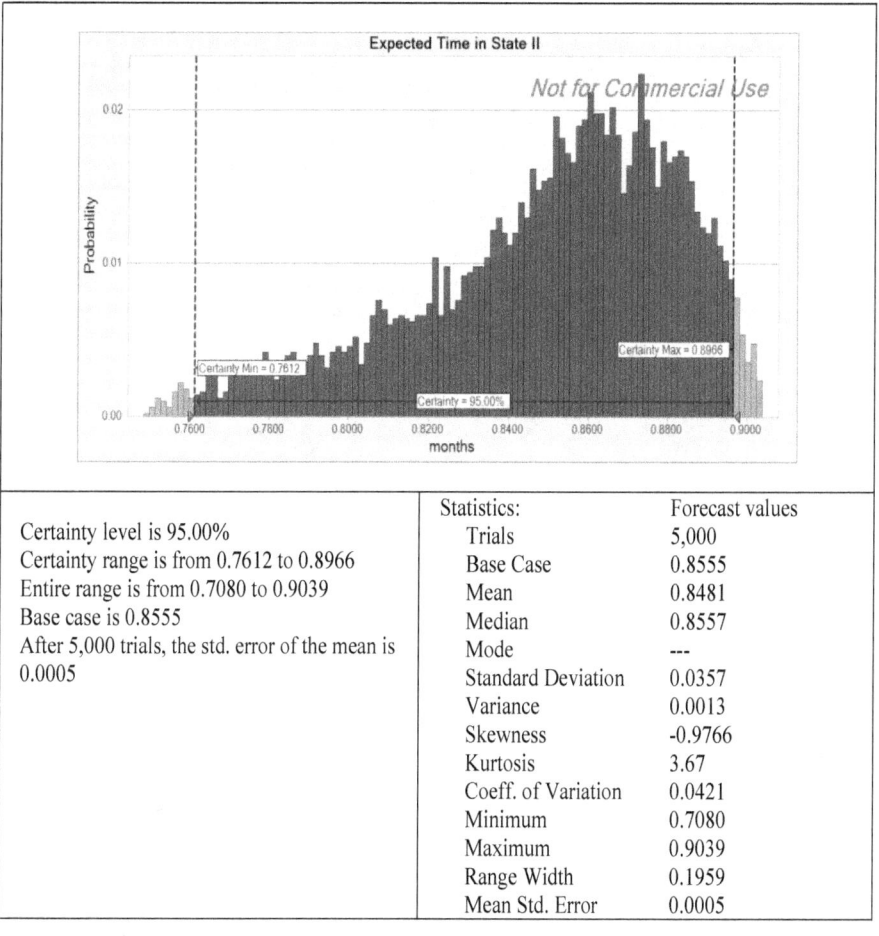

| | Statistics: | Forecast values |
|---|---|---|
| Certainty level is 95.00% | Trials | 5,000 |
| Certainty range is from 0.7612 to 0.8966 | Base Case | 0.8555 |
| Entire range is from 0.7080 to 0.9039 | Mean | 0.8481 |
| Base case is 0.8555 | Median | 0.8557 |
| After 5,000 trials, the std. error of the mean is 0.0005 | Mode | --- |
| | Standard Deviation | 0.0357 |
| | Variance | 0.0013 |
| | Skewness | -0.9766 |
| | Kurtosis | 3.67 |
| | Coeff. of Variation | 0.0421 |
| | Minimum | 0.7080 |
| | Maximum | 0.9039 |
| | Range Width | 0.1959 |
| | Mean Std. Error | 0.0005 |

*Figure 49: Collection of Crystal Ball output for Expected Time in State 2 (BFILM ± 60%)*

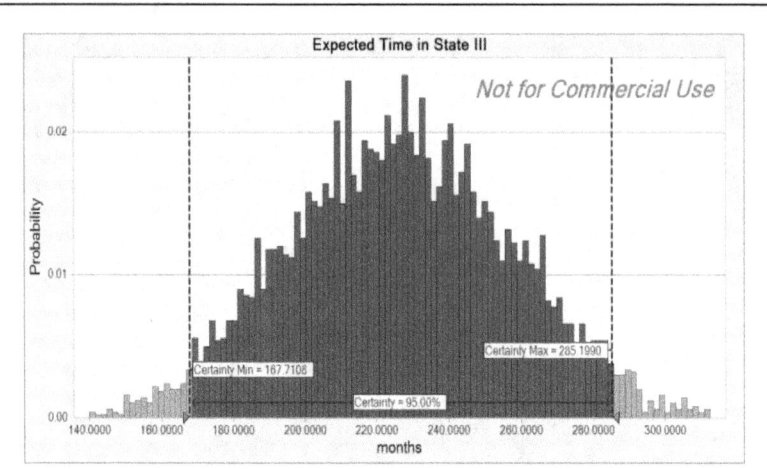

| | | Forecast |
|---|---|---|
| Certainty level is 95.00% | Statistics: | values |
| Certainty range is from 167.7108 to 285.1990 | Trials | 5,000 |
| Entire range is from 129.8165 to 335.4812 | Base Case | 208.2218 |
| Base case is 208.2218 | Mean | 226.2527 |
| After 5,000 trials, the std. error of the mean is 0.4357 | Median | 226.2296 |
| | Mode | --- |
| | Standard Deviation | 30.8076 |
| | Variance | 949.1098 |
| | Skewness | 0.0139 |
| | Kurtosis | 2.71 |
| | Coeff. of Variation | 0.1362 |
| | Minimum | 129.8165 |
| | Maximum | 335.4812 |
| | Range Width | 205.6647 |
| | Mean Std. Error | 0.4357 |

*Figure 50: Collection of Crystal Ball output for Expected Time in State 3 (BFILM ± 60%)*

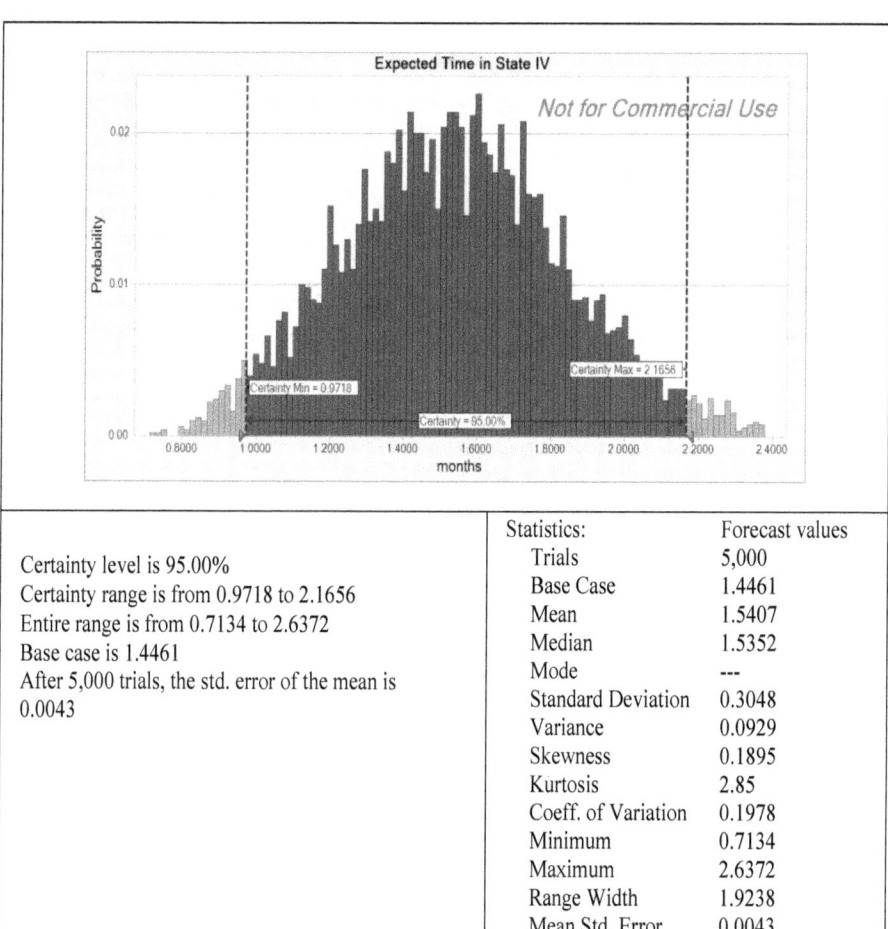

| | | Statistics: | Forecast values |
|---|---|---|---|
| Certainty level is 95.00% | | Trials | 5,000 |
| Certainty range is from 0.9718 to 2.1656 | | Base Case | 1.4461 |
| Entire range is from 0.7134 to 2.6372 | | Mean | 1.5407 |
| Base case is 1.4461 | | Median | 1.5352 |
| After 5,000 trials, the std. error of the mean is 0.0043 | | Mode | --- |
| | | Standard Deviation | 0.3048 |
| | | Variance | 0.0929 |
| | | Skewness | 0.1895 |
| | | Kurtosis | 2.85 |
| | | Coeff. of Variation | 0.1978 |
| | | Minimum | 0.7134 |
| | | Maximum | 2.6372 |
| | | Range Width | 1.9238 |
| | | Mean Std. Error | 0.0043 |

*Figure 51: Collection of Crystal Ball output for Expected Time in State 4 (BFILM ± 60%)*

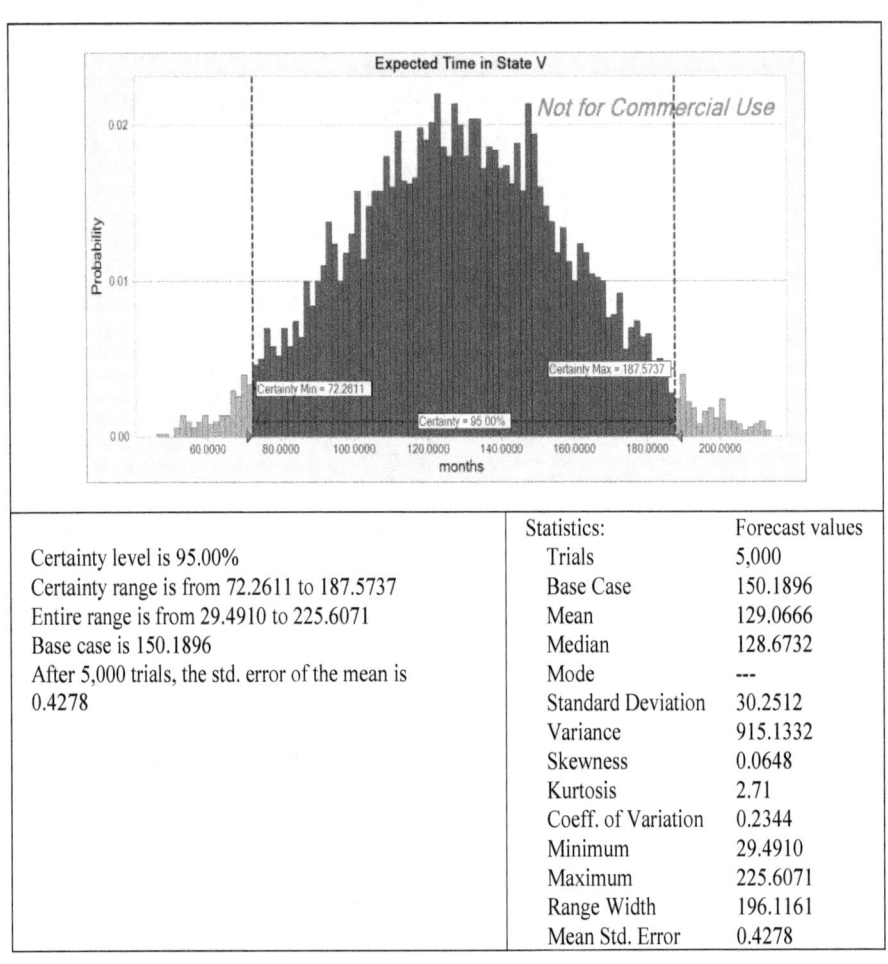

*Figure 52: Collection of Crystal Ball output for Expected Time in State 5 (BFILM + 60%)*

The previous output for States 1, 3, and 5, namely the states of most interest in this research due to relative duration of lifetime, is combined into a stacked bar chart in Figure 53. While overlap exists with variability applied, there is a distinct separation between the expected time in each of the three states. In the majority case, Expected Time in State 1 is less than the Expected Time in State 5 which is less than the Expected Time in State 3.

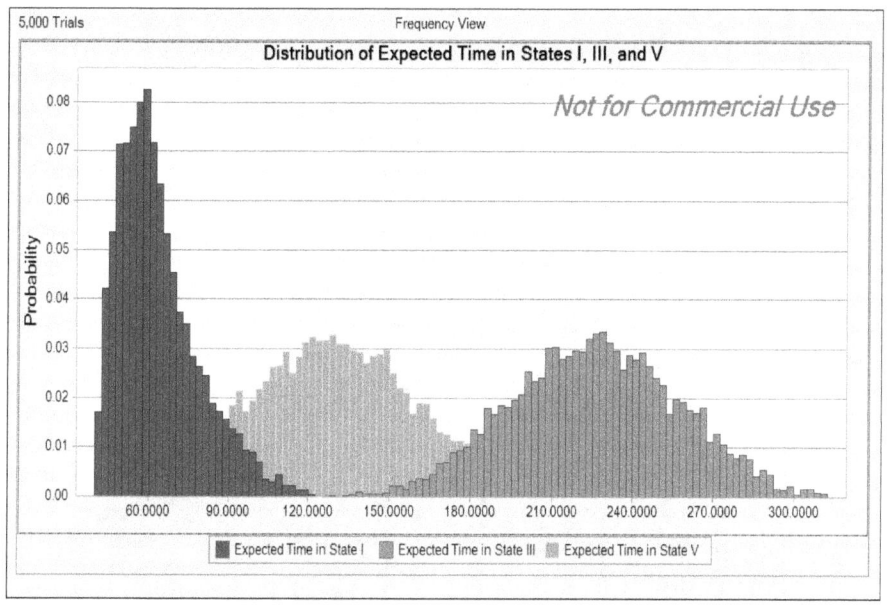

*Figure 53: Stacked Bar Chart of Results for Expected Time in States 1, 3, and 5 (BFILM ± 60%)*

Maximum Probability in n-Steps

To continue with evaluation of the impact of the introduced variability within the select transition probabilities on parameters of interest, Figure 54 and Figure 55 display the results for the Maximum Probability in n-Steps during Lifetime for States 3 and 5, respectively.

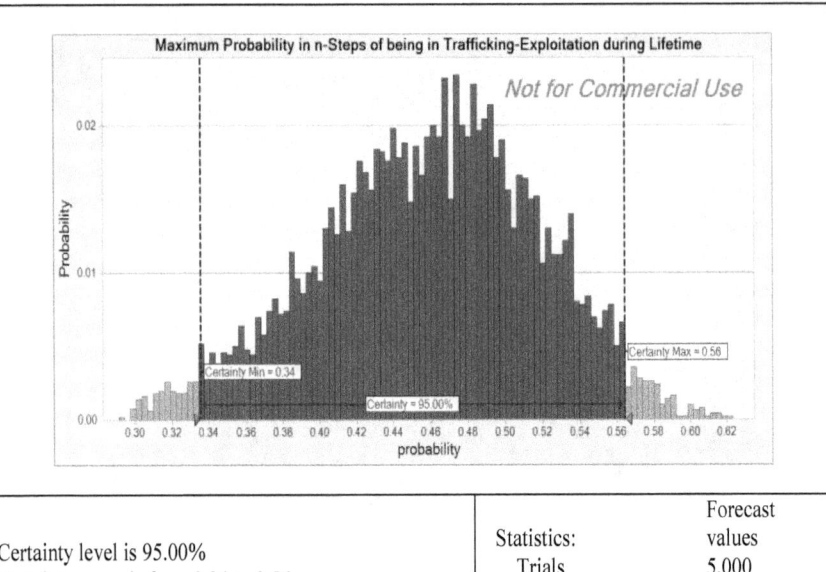

| | | Forecast values |
|---|---|---|
| Certainty level is 95.00% | Statistics: | |
| Certainty range is from 0.34 to 0.56 | Trials | 5,000 |
| Entire range is from 0.26 to 0.65 | Base Case | 0.44 |
| Base case is 0.44 | Mean | 0.46 |
| After 5,000 trials, the std. error of the mean is 0.00 | Median | 0.46 |
| | Mode | --- |
| | Standard Deviation | 0.06 |
| | Variance | 0.00 |
| | Skewness | -0.2334 |
| | Kurtosis | 2.76 |
| | Coeff. of Variation | 0.1303 |
| | Minimum | 0.26 |
| | Maximum | 0.65 |
| | Range Width | 0.39 |
| | Mean Std. Error | 0.00 |

*Figure 54: Collection of Crystal Ball output for Maximum Probability being in State 3 (BFILM ± 60%)*

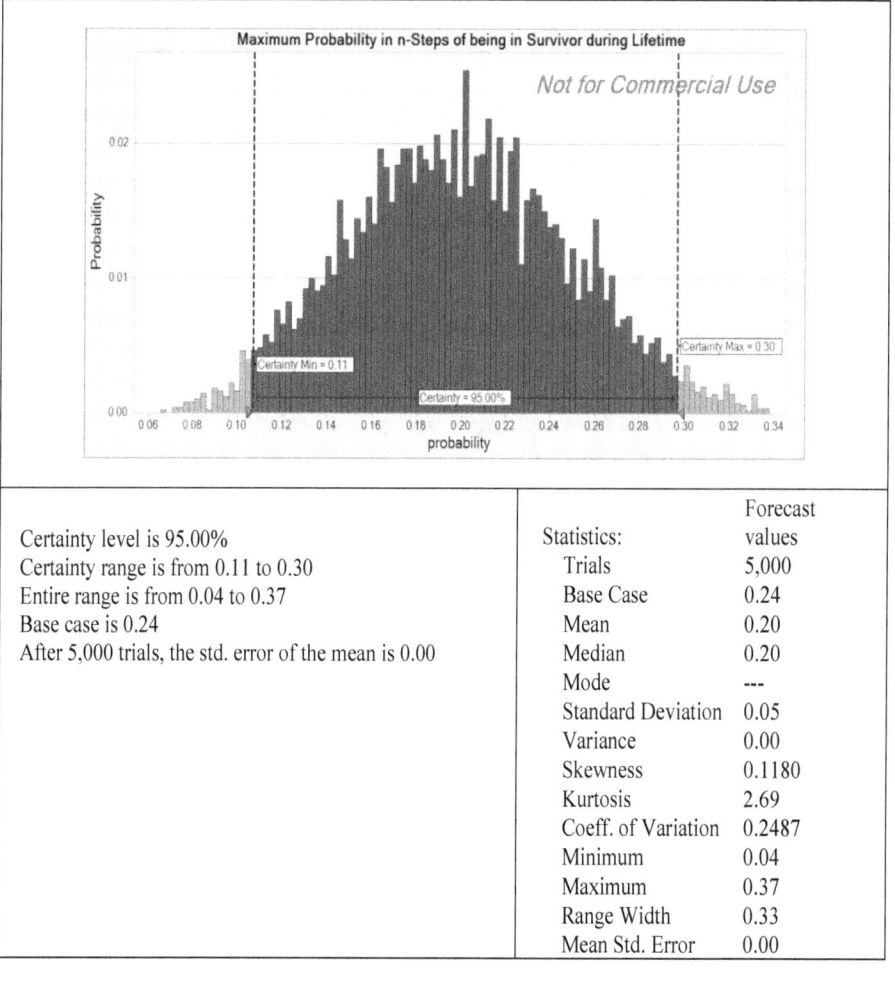

| | | | Forecast |
|---|---|---|---|
| Certainty level is 95.00% | | Statistics: | values |
| Certainty range is from 0.11 to 0.30 | | Trials | 5,000 |
| Entire range is from 0.04 to 0.37 | | Base Case | 0.24 |
| Base case is 0.24 | | Mean | 0.20 |
| After 5,000 trials, the std. error of the mean is 0.00 | | Median | 0.20 |
| | | Mode | --- |
| | | Standard Deviation | 0.05 |
| | | Variance | 0.00 |
| | | Skewness | 0.1180 |
| | | Kurtosis | 2.69 |
| | | Coeff. of Variation | 0.2487 |
| | | Minimum | 0.04 |
| | | Maximum | 0.37 |
| | | Range Width | 0.33 |
| | | Mean Std. Error | 0.00 |

*Figure 55: Collection of Crystal Ball output for Maximum Probability being in State 5 (BFILM ± 60%)*

Crystal Ball Sensitivity Output

Refer to Figure 56 through Figure 62. Sensitivity results for the percent of variability attributable to each select transition probability on the parameters tested are summarized in Table 37. Variability in transition probability B has the maximum and largest average impact on the tested parameters, followed by transition probability I.

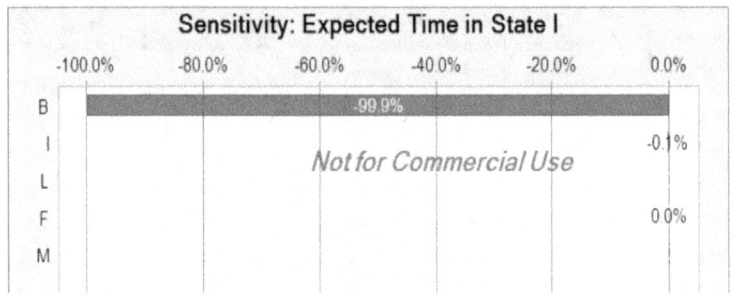

*Figure 56: Crystal Ball sensitivity output for Expected Time in State 1 (BFILM ± 60%)*

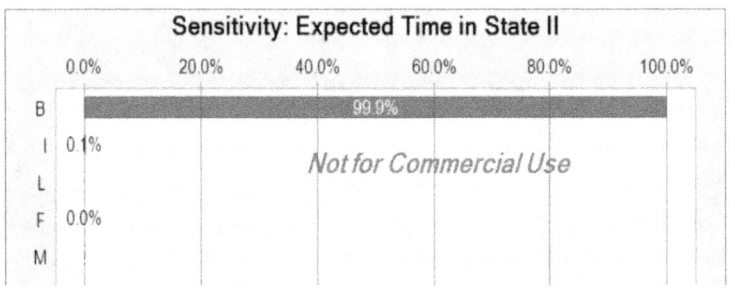

*Figure 57: Crystal Ball sensitivity output for Expected Time in State 2 (BFILM ± 60%)*

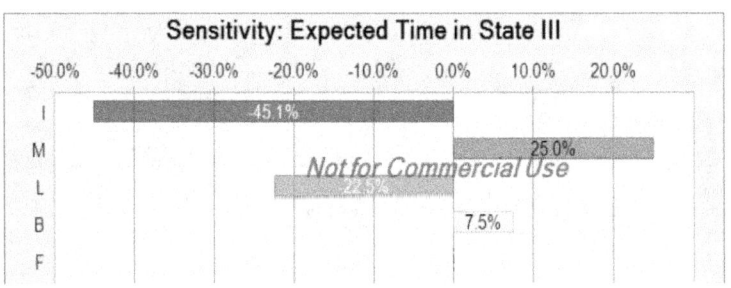

*Figure 58: Crystal Ball sensitivity output for Expected Time in State 3 (BFILM ± 60%)*

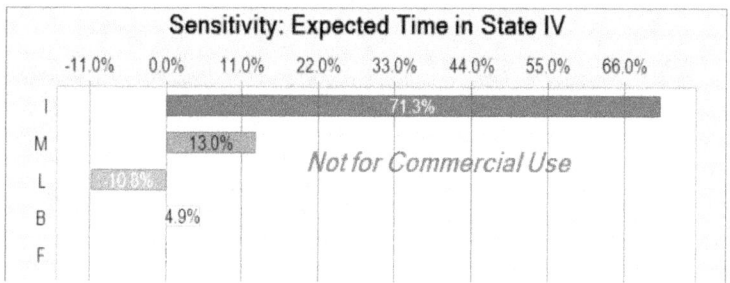

*Figure 59: Crystal Ball sensitivity output for Expected Time in State 4 (BFILM ± 60%)*

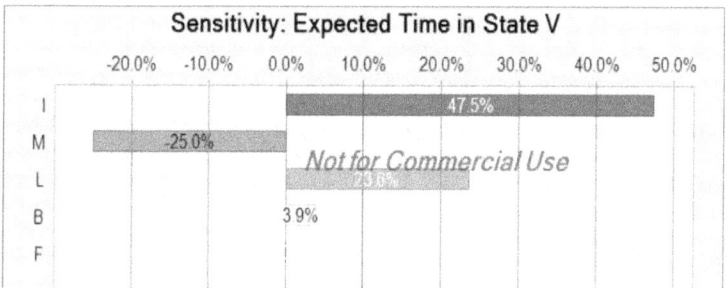

*Figure 60: Crystal Ball sensitivity output for Expected Time in State 5 (BFILM ± 60%)*

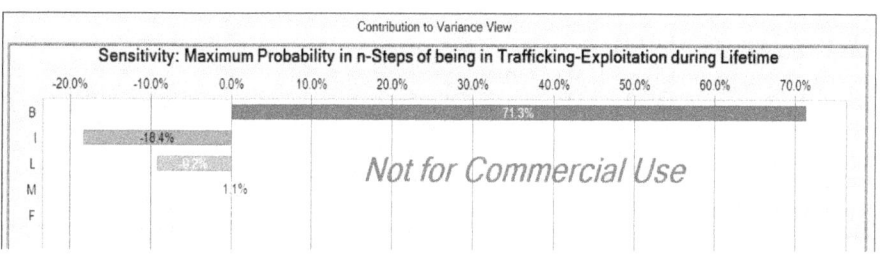

*Figure 61: Crystal Ball sensitivity output for Maximum Probability of being in State 3 (BFILM ± 60%)*

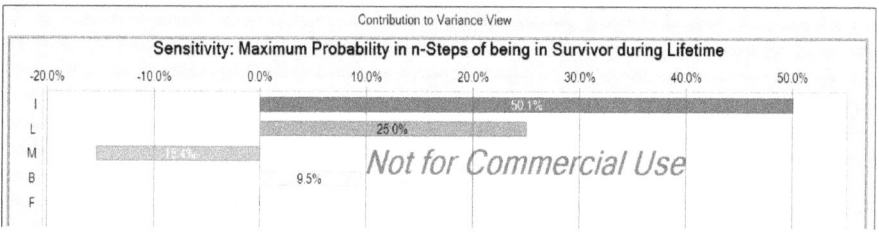

*Figure 62: Crystal Ball sensitivity output for Maximum Probability of being in State 5 (BFILM ± 60%)*

*Table 37: Summary of Figure 56 through Figure 62 Sensitivity Results (BFILM ± 60%)*

|  | % Variability is Due to: | | | | |
|---|---|---|---|---|---|
|  | B | F | I | L | M |
| Expected Time in State 1 | 99.9 | 0.0 | 0.1 | 0.0 | 0.0 |
| Expected Time in State 2 | 99.9 | 0.0 | 0.1 | 0.0 | 0.0 |
| Expected Time in State 3 | 7.5 | 0.0 | 45.1 | 22.5 | 25.0 |
| Expected Time in State 4 | 4.9 | 0.0 | 71.3 | 10.8 | 13.0 |
| Expected Time in State 5 | 3.9 | 0.0 | 47.5 | 23.6 | 25.0 |
| Max Prob in State 3 | 71.3 | 0.0 | 18.4 | 9.2 | 1.1 |
| Max Prob in State 5 | 9.5 | 0.0 | 50.1 | 25.0 | 15.4 |
| Average % of Variability: | 42.4 | 0.0 | 33.2 | 13.0 | 11.36 |

This concludes the observations for sensitivity analysis with Crystal Ball Monte Carlo simulation for Approach 3 that applied ± 60% bounds for select transition probabilities defined as Triangular distributions. In the next section, Approach 4 is discussed where instead of 60% spread of bounds, the bounds span ± 0.0006.

### 4.6.6 Sensitivity Analysis – Approach 4 (±0.0006 Variability)

Expected Time in Each State

In Sensitivity Analysis Approach 4, each of the select transition probabilities were permitted to range by up to a total of 0.0012, again, respecting the reality of probability bounds. In

Figure 63 – Figure 67, the results for expected time in each state are displayed for when subjected to variability in the select transition probabilities. Metrics of output and observations are included with each figure.

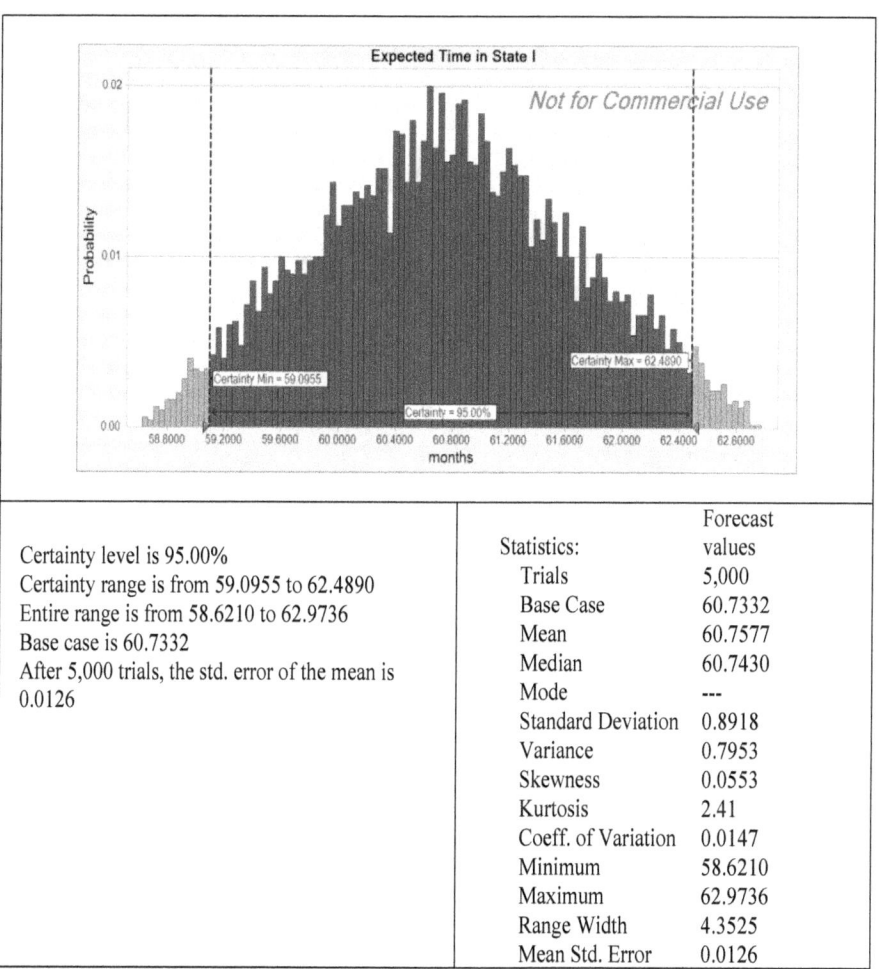

| | Statistics: | Forecast values |
|---|---|---|
| Certainty level is 95.00% | Trials | 5,000 |
| Certainty range is from 59.0955 to 62.4890 | Base Case | 60.7332 |
| Entire range is from 58.6210 to 62.9736 | Mean | 60.7577 |
| Base case is 60.7332 | Median | 60.7430 |
| After 5,000 trials, the std. error of the mean is 0.0126 | Mode | --- |
| | Standard Deviation | 0.8918 |
| | Variance | 0.7953 |
| | Skewness | 0.0553 |
| | Kurtosis | 2.41 |
| | Coeff. of Variation | 0.0147 |
| | Minimum | 58.6210 |
| | Maximum | 62.9736 |
| | Range Width | 4.3525 |
| | Mean Std. Error | 0.0126 |

*Figure 63: Collection of Crystal Ball output for Expected Time in State 1 (BFILM ± 0.0006)*

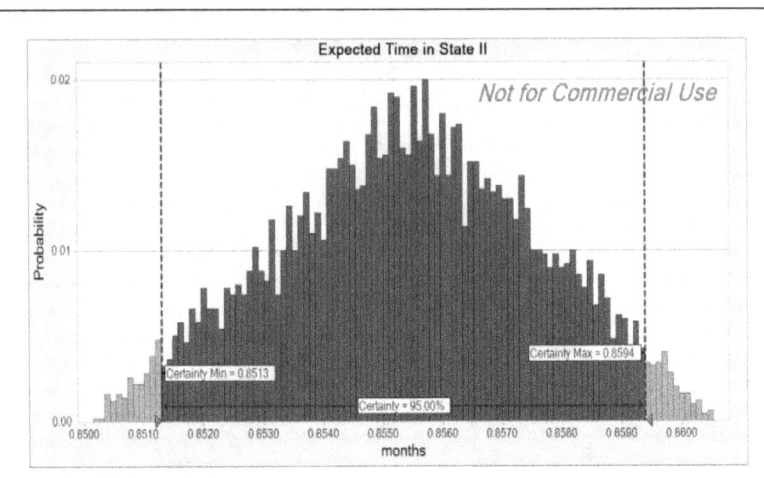

| | Statistics: | Forecast values |
|---|---|---|
| Certainty level is 95.00% | Trials | 5,000 |
| Certainty range is from 0.8513 to 0.8594 | Base Case | 0.8555 |
| Entire range is from 0.8501 to 0.8605 | Mean | 0.8554 |
| Base case is 0.8555 | Median | 0.8555 |
| After 5,000 trials, the std. error of the mean is 0.0000 | Mode | --- |
| | Standard Deviation | 0.0021 |
| | Variance | 0.0000 |
| | Skewness | -0.0553 |
| | Kurtosis | 2.41 |
| | Coeff. of Variation | 0.0025 |
| | Minimum | 0.8501 |
| | Maximum | 0.8605 |
| | Range Width | 0.0104 |
| | Mean Std. Error | 0.0000 |

*Figure 64: Collection of Crystal Ball output for Expected Time in State 2 (BFILM ± 0.0006)*

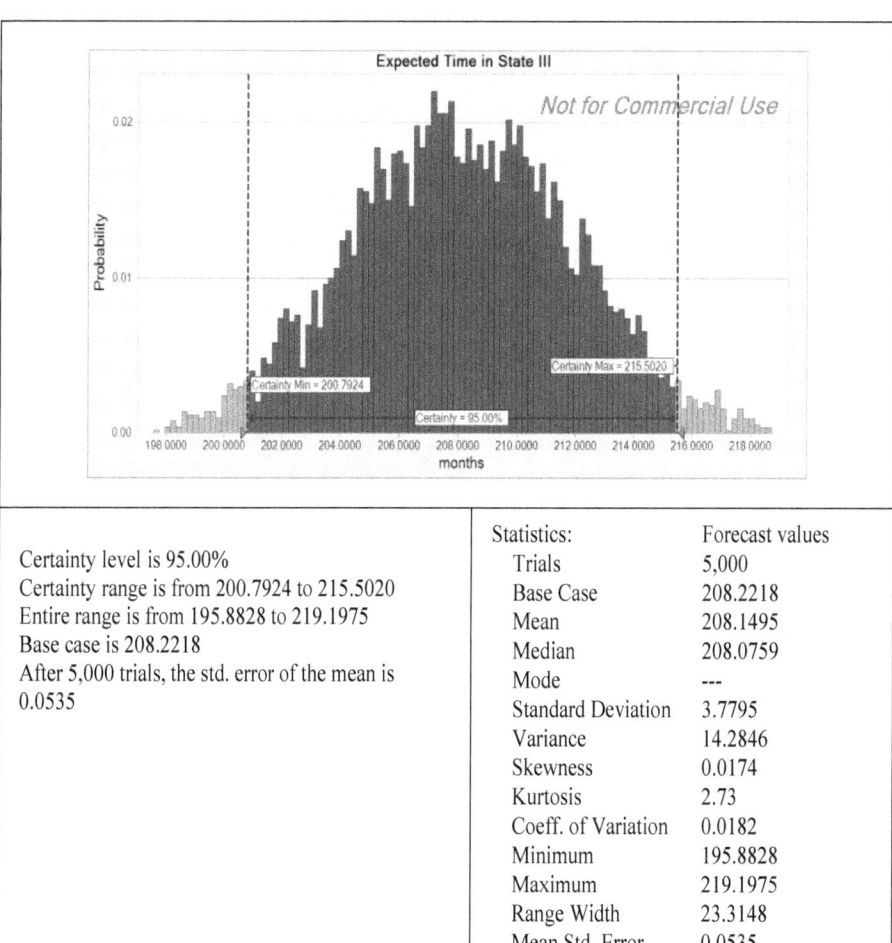

| | Statistics: | Forecast values |
|---|---|---|
| Certainty level is 95.00% | Trials | 5,000 |
| Certainty range is from 200.7924 to 215.5020 | Base Case | 208.2218 |
| Entire range is from 195.8828 to 219.1975 | Mean | 208.1495 |
| Base case is 208.2218 | Median | 208.0759 |
| After 5,000 trials, the std. error of the mean is 0.0535 | Mode | --- |
| | Standard Deviation | 3.7795 |
| | Variance | 14.2846 |
| | Skewness | 0.0174 |
| | Kurtosis | 2.73 |
| | Coeff. of Variation | 0.0182 |
| | Minimum | 195.8828 |
| | Maximum | 219.1975 |
| | Range Width | 23.3148 |
| | Mean Std. Error | 0.0535 |

*Figure 65: Collection of Crystal Ball output for Expected Time in State 3 (BFILM ± 0.0006)*

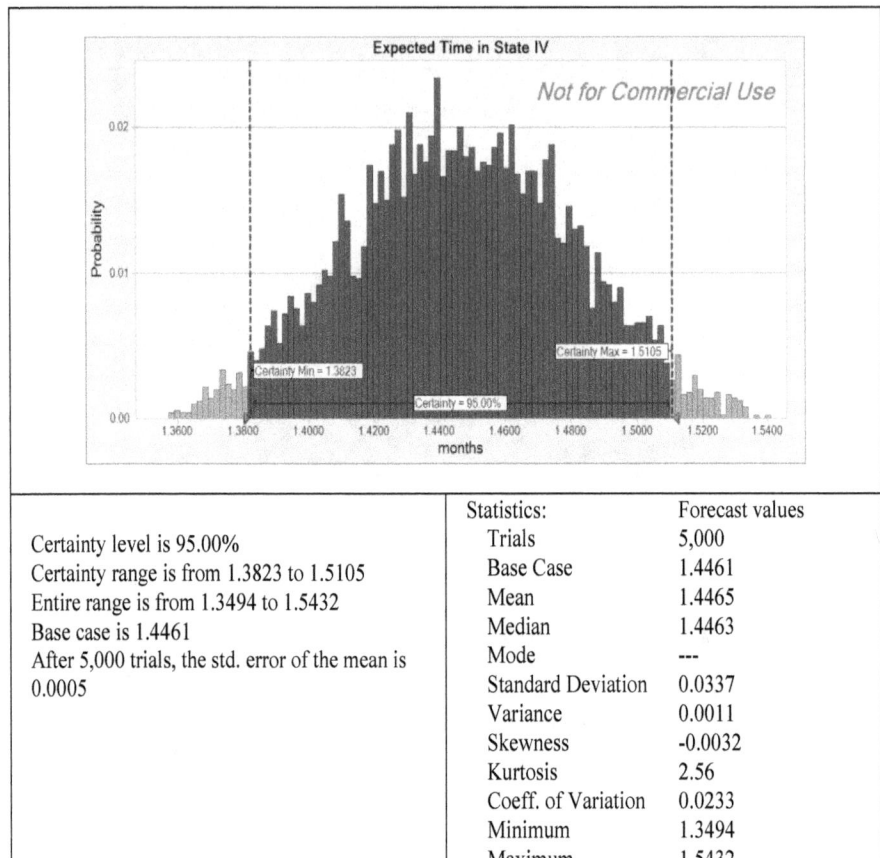

| | Statistics: | Forecast values |
|---|---|---|
| Certainty level is 95.00% | Trials | 5,000 |
| Certainty range is from 1.3823 to 1.5105 | Base Case | 1.4461 |
| Entire range is from 1.3494 to 1.5432 | Mean | 1.4465 |
| Base case is 1.4461 | Median | 1.4463 |
| After 5,000 trials, the std. error of the mean is 0.0005 | Mode | --- |
| | Standard Deviation | 0.0337 |
| | Variance | 0.0011 |
| | Skewness | -0.0032 |
| | Kurtosis | 2.56 |
| | Coeff. of Variation | 0.0233 |
| | Minimum | 1.3494 |
| | Maximum | 1.5432 |
| | Range Width | 0.1938 |
| | Mean Std. Error | 0.0005 |

*Figure 66: Collection of Crystal Ball output for Expected Time in State 4 (BFILM ± 0.0006)*

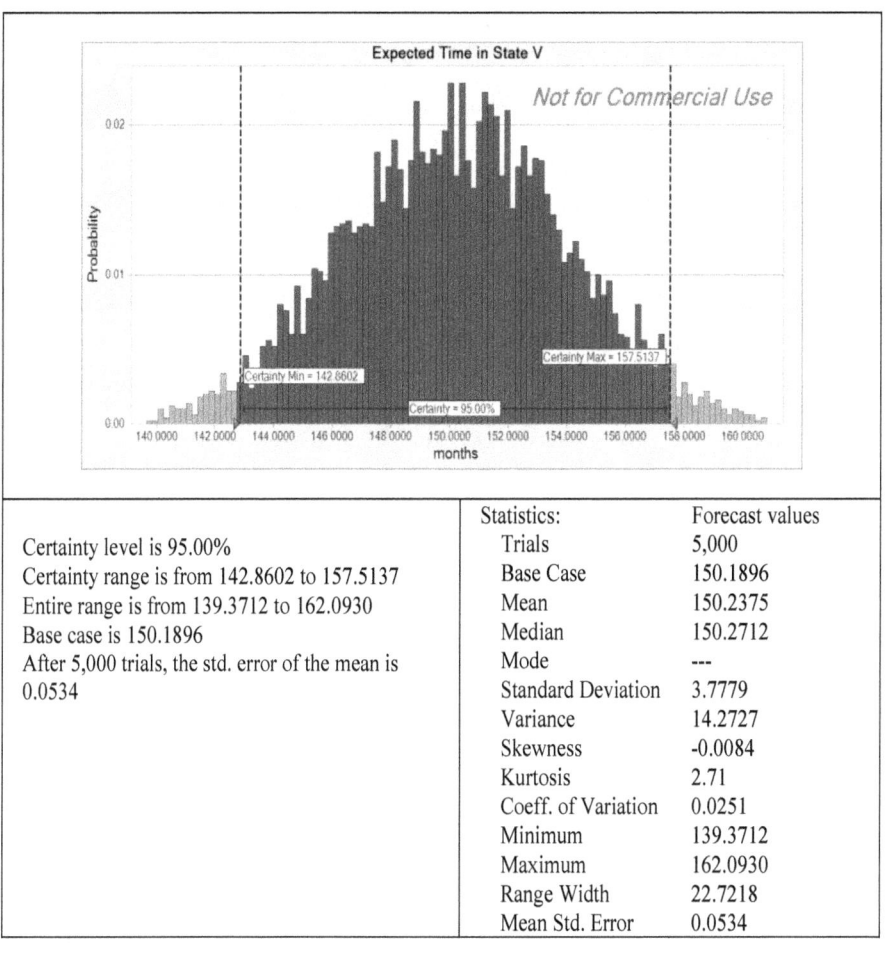

| | | Statistics: | Forecast values |
|---|---|---|---|
| Certainty level is 95.00% | | Trials | 5,000 |
| Certainty range is from 142.8602 to 157.5137 | | Base Case | 150.1896 |
| Entire range is from 139.3712 to 162.0930 | | Mean | 150.2375 |
| Base case is 150.1896 | | Median | 150.2712 |
| After 5,000 trials, the std. error of the mean is 0.0534 | | Mode | --- |
| | | Standard Deviation | 3.7779 |
| | | Variance | 14.2727 |
| | | Skewness | -0.0084 |
| | | Kurtosis | 2.71 |
| | | Coeff. of Variation | 0.0251 |
| | | Minimum | 139.3712 |
| | | Maximum | 162.0930 |
| | | Range Width | 22.7218 |
| | | Mean Std. Error | 0.0534 |

*Figure 67: Collection of Crystal Ball output for Expected Time in State 5 (BFILM ± 0.0006)*

Expected Time in States 1, 3, and 5 are again combined for consideration in Figure 68. In Approach 3, there was notable overlap in the results. In this Approach 4, there is no notable overlap. A distinction between the three states is apparent, with ascending expected time spent in State 1, 5, and 3, respectively.

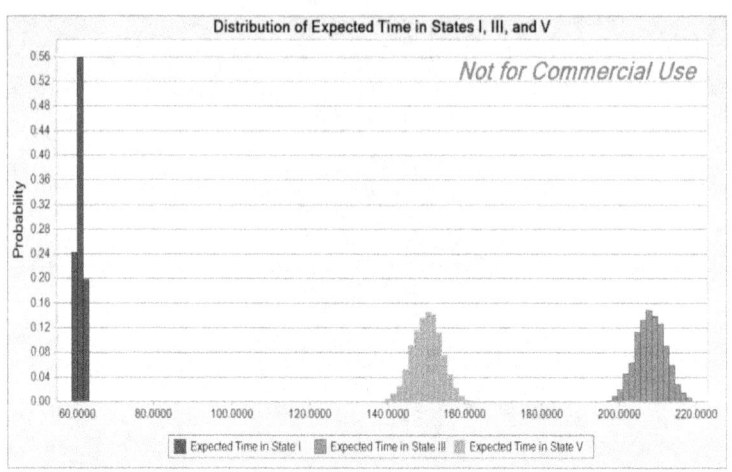

*Figure 68: Stacked Bar Chart of Results for Expected Time in States 1, 3, and 5 (BFILM ± 0.0006)*

Maximum Probability in n-Steps

To the discussion of maximums, Figure 69 and Figure 70 display the results for maximum probabilities of being in States 3 and 5, respectively, in n-steps. The ranges in probability are small relative to Approach 3 results.

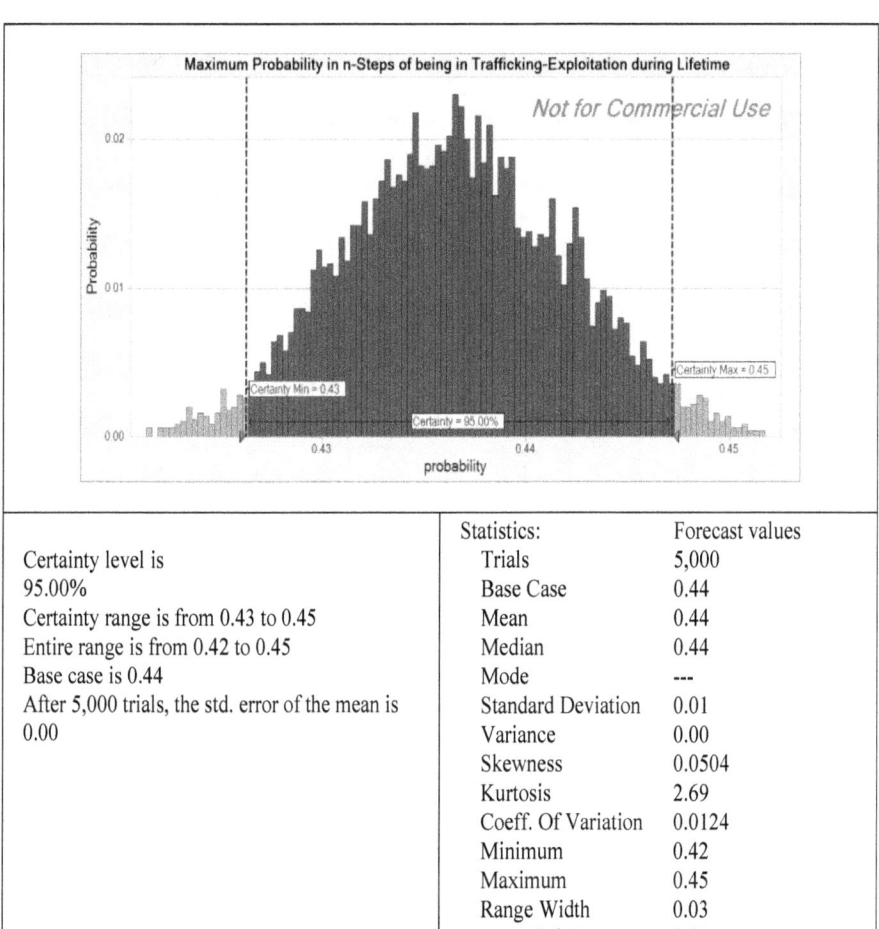

| | Statistics: | Forecast values |
|---|---|---|
| Certainty level is 95.00% | Trials | 5,000 |
| | Base Case | 0.44 |
| Certainty range is from 0.43 to 0.45 | Mean | 0.44 |
| Entire range is from 0.42 to 0.45 | Median | 0.44 |
| Base case is 0.44 | Mode | --- |
| After 5,000 trials, the std. error of the mean is 0.00 | Standard Deviation | 0.01 |
| | Variance | 0.00 |
| | Skewness | 0.0504 |
| | Kurtosis | 2.69 |
| | Coeff. Of Variation | 0.0124 |
| | Minimum | 0.42 |
| | Maximum | 0.45 |
| | Range Width | 0.03 |
| | Mean Std. Error | 0.00 |

*Figure 69: Collection of Crystal Ball output for Maximum Probability being in State 3 (BFILM ± 0.0006)*

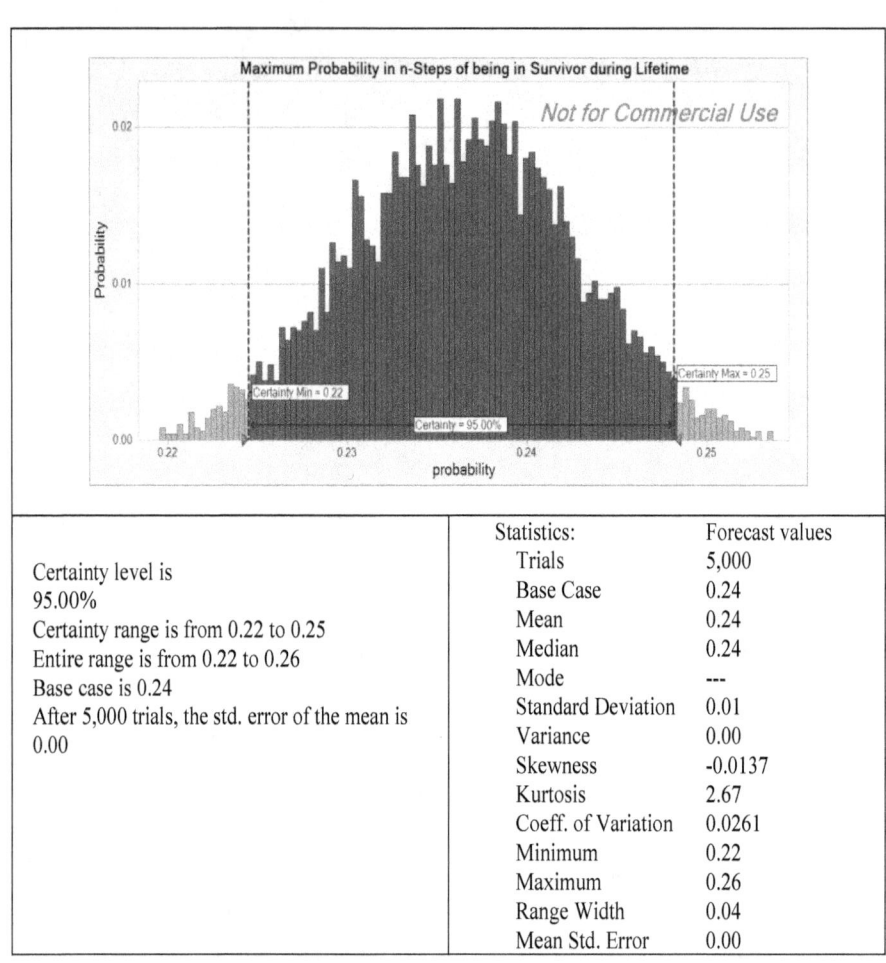

*Figure 70: Collection of Crystal Ball output for Maximum Probability being in State 5 (BFILM ± 0.0006)*

Crystal Ball Sensitivity Output

Sensitivity results for the tested parameters (Figure 71 through Figure 77) are summarized in Table 38. While transition probability B makes an impact on the variability observed in all tested parameters, the largest average percent of variability is due to transition probability I. Transition probability M has a smaller but notable contribution to the variability in the tested parameters.

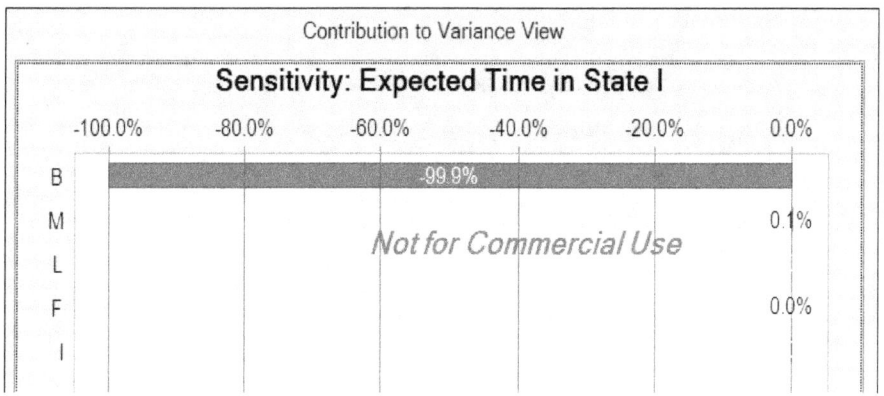

*Figure 71: Crystal Ball sensitivity output for Expected Time in State 1 (BFILM ± 0.0006)*

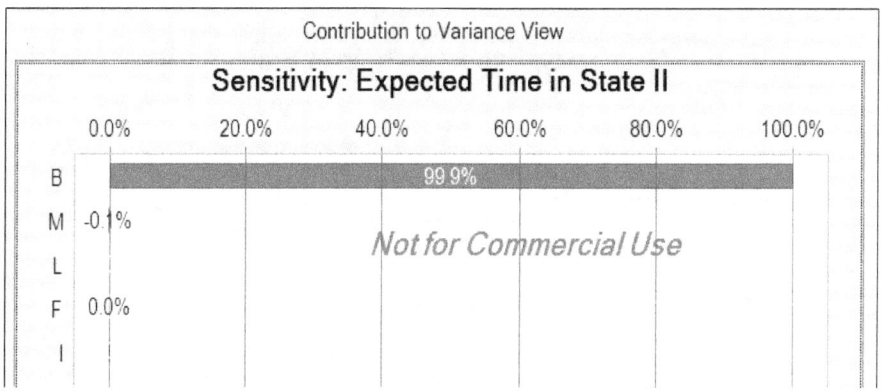

*Figure 72: Crystal Ball sensitivity output for Expected Time in State 2 (BFILM ± 0.0006)*

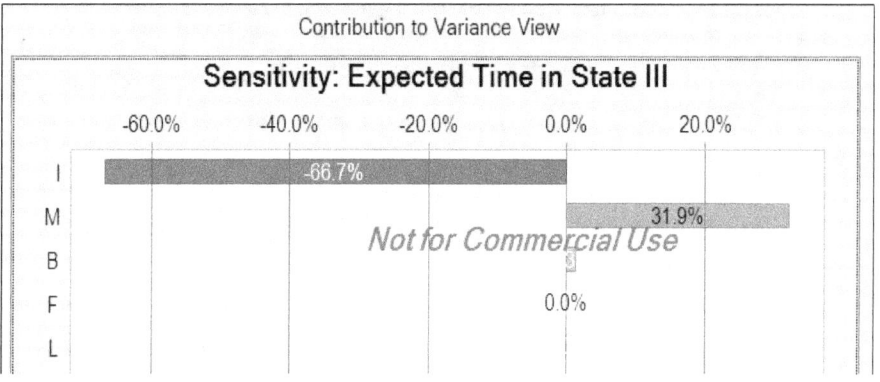

*Figure 73: Crystal Ball sensitivity output for Expected Time in State 3 (BFILM ± 0.0006)*

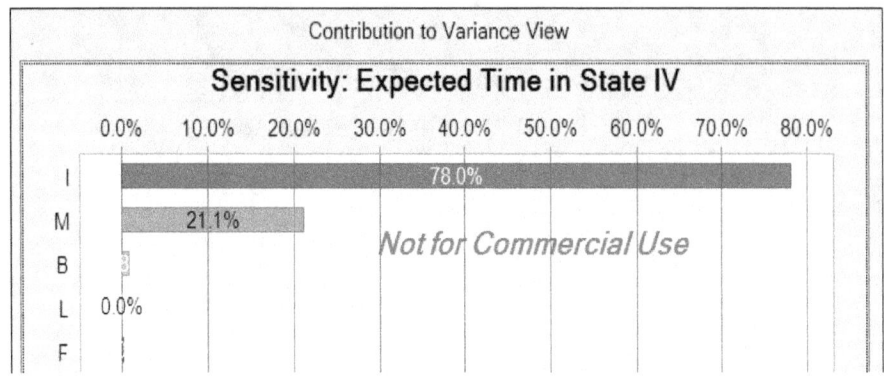

*Figure 74: Crystal Ball sensitivity output for Expected Time in State 4 (BFILM ± 0.0006)*

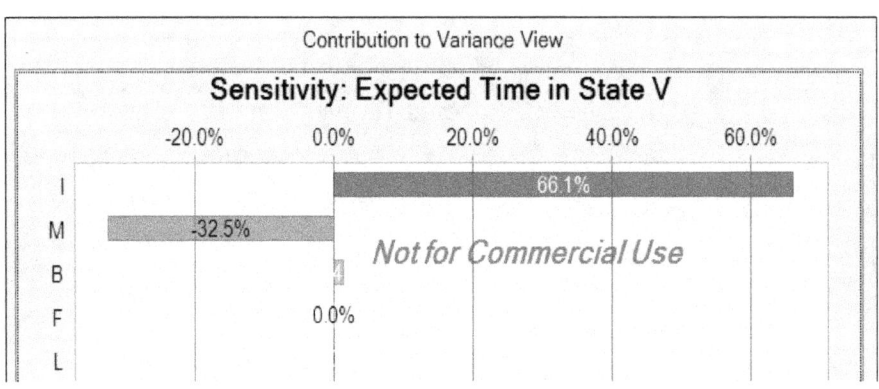

*Figure 75: Crystal Ball sensitivity output for Expected Time in State 5 (BFILM ± 0.0006)*

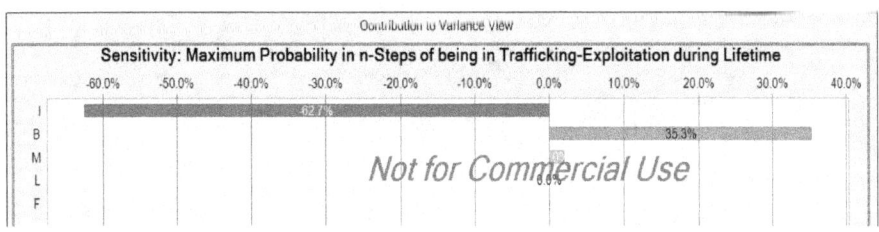

*Figure 76: Crystal Ball sensitivity output for Maximum Probability of being in State 3 (BFILM ± 0.0006)*

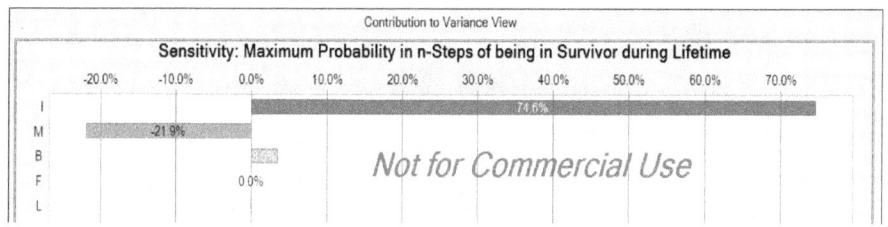

*Figure 77: Crystal Ball sensitivity output for Maximum Probability of being in State 5 (BFILM ± 0.0006)*

*Table 38: Summary of Figure 71 through Figure 77 Sensitivity Results (BFILM ± 0.0006)*

|  | % Variability is Due to: | | | | |
|---|---|---|---|---|---|
|  | B | F | I | L | M |
| Expected Time in State 1 | 99.9 | 0.0 | 0.0 | 0.0 | 0.1 |
| Expected Time in State 2 | 99.9 | 0.0 | 0.0 | 0.0 | 0.1 |
| Expected Time in State 3 | 1.2 | 0.0 | 66.7 | 0.0 | 31.9 |
| Expected Time in State 4 | 0.9 | 0.0 | 78.0 | 0.0 | 21.1 |
| Expected Time in State 5 | 1.4 | 0.0 | 66.1 | 0.0 | 32.5 |
| Max Prob in State 3 | 35.3 | 0.0 | 62.7 | 0.0 | 2.0 |
| Max Prob in State 5 | 3.5 | 0.0 | 74.6 | 0.0 | 21.9 |
| Average % of Variability: | 34.6 | 0.0 | 49.7 | 0.0 | 15.7 |

### 4.7 Implications of Analysis for Anti-Trafficking Interests

Recall the previous definitions and discussion of the 4P Paradigm (as defined in Table 10) (Konrad et al., 2017). This research approached and tested what happens to changes in select transition probabilities B, F, I, L, and M (Note: Table 14). With respect to the 4P Paradigm, the following connects the select transition probabilities with the strongest-related elements of the 4P Paradigm. Note, there may be multiple ties among the 4Ps and only the strongest-related element is the categorization criteria.

- Prevention
    - B – Initial Victimization Risk
    
    Efforts taken to prevent initial victimization.

- o  M – Revictimization Risk

  Efforts taken to <u>prevent</u> revictimization.

- Protection

  - o  F – Intervention Rate (from Recruitment)

  Efforts taken to <u>protect</u> victims identified who are currently in Recruitment state.

  - o  I – Intervention Rate (from Exploitation)

  Efforts taken to <u>protect</u> victims identified who are currently in Exploitation state.

- Partnership

  - o  L – Intervention Success Rate
  - o  Efforts taken to <u>partner</u> resources to improve rate of success for interventions.

- Prosecution

  - o  Prosecution has the potential to impact victim lifetime towards both good and bad outcomes. However, Prosecution is not considered the strongest-related element of the paradigm for any of the select transition probabilities.

While the discussion and interpretation of this research model in terms of the '4P Paradigm' merits extensive future research, general observations from this research in terms of the 4Ps are summarized in Table 39. The observations are intended to inform the decision-maker, tasked with determining the associated value within each resource allocation scheme available.

*Table 39: General policy-related observations from current research*

| Prevention (B, M) |
|---|
| B has substantial impact |
| M has notable impact |
| **Protection (F, I)** |
| F has no impact |
| I has substantial impact |
| **Partnership (L)** |
| Approach 1 & 3 - L has notable impact |
| Approach 2 & 4 - L has no impact |

From the observations, the anti-trafficking decision-maker may notice that the biggest impact on an individual's lifetime in terms of sex trafficking victimization is seen in efforts of Prevention (i.e. transition probability B), as well as in efforts of Protection (i.e. transition probability I).

### 4.8 Decision Support System (DSS)

*4.8.1 Background*

O'Sullivan (1985) defines Decision Support Systems (DSS) as, "automated information systems designed to aid administrative decision making." An effective DSS equips decision-makers with a methodical approach for evaluating available decision input(s) through the scope of one or many parameter outputs. Upon review of existing DSS literature, the applications of these systems are diverse in context area (e.g., banking, policymaking) and vary in specificity.

Anthony (1965) defined three categories of organizational decisions: operational, management, and strategic. The types of DSS includes data-driven, model-driven, knowledge-driven, document-driven, and communication-driven (Power, 2002). In 1985, O'Sullivan reviewed the academic and industrial foundation of DSS for the first two decades of DSS observation. A more recent review work was completed by Power (2007). Many researchers have explored DSS development with Markov models as well (e.g., Leu and Wahyu Adi, 2011). More recently, even work on DSS for trafficking and related policy-guidance exists (e.g., Haas and Ferreira, 2018; Unertl, Walsh, and Clayton, 2020).

The DSS of this research is both model-driven and knowledge-driven due to the need for expertise in determining accurate inputs. The expected user of the model includes both researchers and practitioners. The practitioners are likely experienced anti-trafficking and policy analysts and leadership who may test a variety of scenarios or policies to better understand the net effect during the lifetime of an individual at risk of sex trafficking victimization.

### 4.8.2 *Research DSS*

Two types of DSSs have been developed in this research. The first DSS is an Excel Tool that consists of a dynamic workbook of calculations and analysis output (previously discussed). It was instrumental to running the analysis of this research. To increase usability and accessibility features, a second, open-source DSS has been developed. The intention of the second system is to support ease of use and increased accessibility to the communities who may benefit from it, namely researchers and analysts. Figure 78 and Figure 79 consists of sequential screenshots of the platform, available at http://siddharthc30.pythonanywhere.com/.

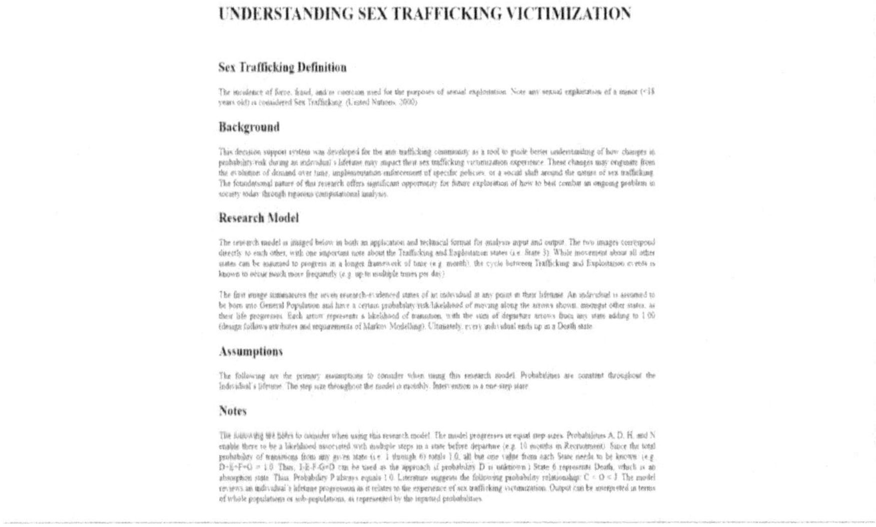

UNDERSTANDING SEX TRAFFICKING VICTIMIZATION

**Sex Trafficking Definition**

The incidence of force, fraud, and/or coercion used for the purposes of sexual exploitation. Note any sexual exploitation of a minor (<18 years old) is considered Sex Trafficking. (United Nations, 2000)

**Background**

This decision support system was developed for the anti-trafficking community as a tool to guide better understanding of how changes in probability/risk during an individual's lifetime may impact their sex trafficking victimization experience. These changes may originate from the evolution of demand over time, implementation/enforcement of specific policies, or a social shift around the nature of sex trafficking. The foundational nature of this research offers significant opportunity for future exploration of how to best combat an ongoing problem in society today through rigorous computational analysis.

**Research Model**

The research model is imaged below in both an application and technical format for analysis input and output. The two images correspond directly to each other, with one important note about the Trafficking and Exploitation states (i.e. State 3). While movement about all other states can be assumed to progress in a longer framework of time (e.g. month), the cycle between Trafficking and Exploitation events is known to occur much more frequently (e.g. up to multiple times per day).

The first image summarizes the seven research-evidenced states of an individual at any point in their lifetime. An individual is assumed to be born into General Population and have a certain probability/risk/likelihood of moving along the arrows shown, amongst other states, as their life progresses. Each arrow represents a likelihood of transition, with the sum of departure arrows from any state adding to 1.00 (design follows attributes and requirements of Markov Modelling). Ultimately, every individual ends up in a Death state.

**Assumptions**

The following are the primary assumptions to consider when using this research model. Probabilities are constant throughout the individual's lifetime. The step size throughout the model is monthly. Intervention is a one-step state.

**Notes**

The following are notes to consider when using this research model. The model progresses in equal step sizes. Probabilities A, D, H, and N enable there to be a likelihood associated with multiple steps in a state before departure (e.g. 10 months in Recruitment). Since the total probability of transitions from any given state (i.e. 1 through 6) totals 1.0, all but one value from each State needs to be known (e.g. D+E+F+G = 1.0. Thus, 1-E-F-G=D can be used as the approach if probability D is unknown.) State 6 represents Death, which is an absorption state. Thus, Probability P always equals 1.0. Literature suggests the following probability relationship: C < O < J. The model reviews an individual's lifetime progression as it relates to the experience of sex trafficking victimization. Output can be interpreted in terms of whole populations or sub-populations, as represented by the inputted probabilities.

***Figure 78: Screenshot of Website Input Page (http://siddharthc30.pythonanywhere.com/)***

**Inputs to assess Sex Trafficking Victimization Experience during Lifetime**

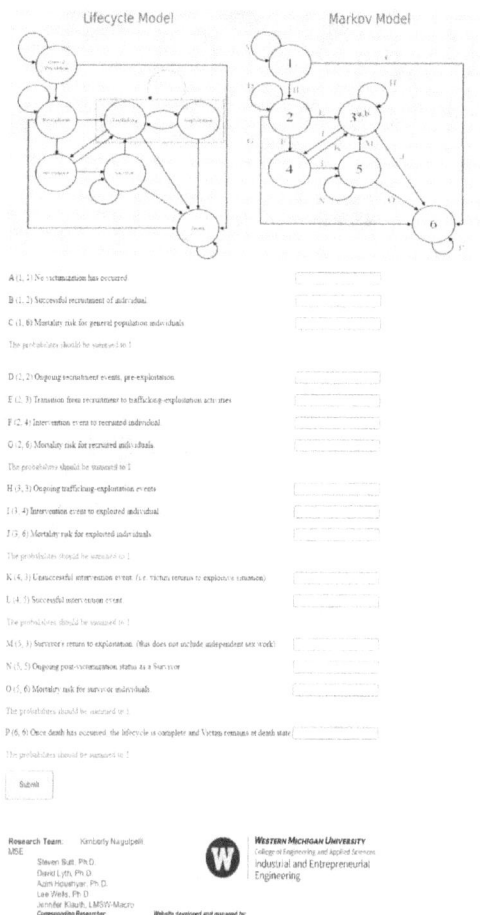

*Figure 79: Screenshot of Website Input Page (http://siddharthc30.pythonanywhere.com/)*

After pressing the "Submit" button, the key parameters of this research are displayed in graphical form (see Figure 80). Not visible in this figure is the ability on this screen to hover over each bar of output and get the detailed calculation results.

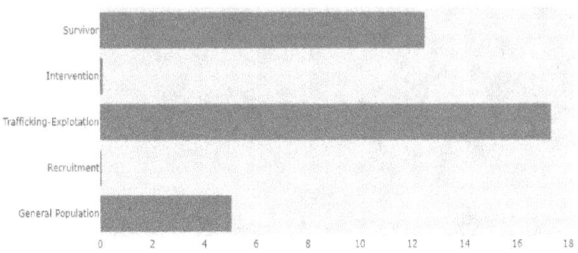

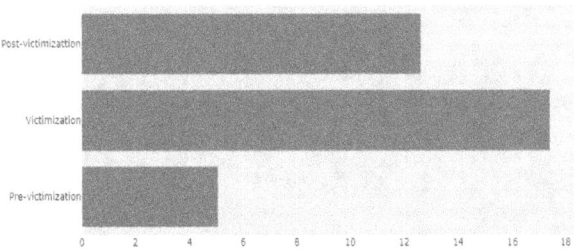

*Figure 80: Screenshot of Website Output Page (http://siddharthc30.pythonanywhere.com/)*

The website has full-functionality, is free to use, and delivers valuable results to users across the world from the A-P collection of inputs. Future work can extend and expand the website experience to include more information as well as improved data visuals to support ease of interpretation.

*4.8.3   Research User Guide*

To aid the user of either DSS, or of this research in general, a User Guide is presented in Appendix C. The model, necessary research background, and key calculations are summarized in a three-page handout format. The guide serves as a helpful reference for users as well as support accurate application of the model.

# CHAPTER 5

# CONCLUSIONS AND FUTURE RESEARCH

Research was driven to deliver valuable methodologies and results surrounding three research objectives. These objectives, first outlined at the beginning of the work, were:

*Objective 1: To determine a method for analyzing the impact of the sex trafficking victimization experience during a human lifetime.*

*Objective 2: To analyze the impact of general, variable-form policy changes on the Sex Trafficking Victim's individual lifetime experiences.*

*Objective 3: To develop an open-source tool to support anti-trafficking activities and initiatives.*

In what follows are the most significant conclusions surrounding these three objectives. Thereafter, implications from this work are identified for the anti-trafficking and policy-making communities. This chapter finishes by outlining the most notable calls for future research that are the next extension or beyond the scope of this work.

## 5.1 Conclusions for Objective 1

Review of existing literature identified the lack of a comprehensive, interconnected model for the sex trafficking victimization experiences an individual may face throughout their lifetime. Thus, extensive work was completed in this research to define a model to fill the void in literature. The elements to build the model were individually, or in subset, well-defined in literature.

The resulting model can be considered from both a "macro" or "micro" view. From a "macro" perspective, an individual begins in a 'Pre-Victimization' stage that may or may not lead into a 'Victimization' stage during their lifetime. Those reaching 'Victimization' may or may not continue beyond the stage into 'Post-Victimization' before death occurs. Through a more detailed, "micro" perspective, there are specific states an individual may transition among during their lifetime relative to sex trafficking victimization experiences. All individuals are assumed to begin in a 'General Population' state and end in a 'Death' state. If victimization occurs, an individual traverses a subset or all of 'Recruitment', 'Trafficking', 'Exploitation', 'Intervention', and 'Survivor' states. All stages/states are interconnected based on literature-defined occurrences to form a model, each connection representing the potential likelihood of a specific transition occurring.

While the model by itself serves a vast value to future research efforts in the anti-trafficking and policy-making disciplines, this research work took a direct analytical approach to further define the established model as a discrete-time Markov Chain (DTMC). Theoretical preparation was completed for analyzing the events during an individual's lifetime through a variety of parameters for durations and probabilities.

## 5.2 Conclusions for Objective 2

In addition to the theoretical preparation of variable-form solutions, a documented case study was used as the basis for demonstrating model analysis. The dataset itself is one example, but the value of this work's output is in both the defined model and the methodology of analysis. While any aspect of the model is candidate for analysis, five transition probabilities were selected as the focus of analysis for the anti-trafficking and policy-making communities. Specific consideration was maintained throughout this research work to analyze and discuss with respect to the '4P Paradigm' (Konrad et al., 2017).

Four scenarios were defined surrounding the case study dataset. Evaluated parameters were expected time in each state, life expectancy, maximum probabilities during lifetime of being in Trafficking-Exploitation (i.e., State 3) and Survivor (i.e., State 5), as well as a plotted result of n-step transition probabilities over an assessment period of 600 months (50 years). The Base Case dataset is shown in Table 40.

Thereafter, four approaches of sensitivity analysis were completed, focused on the effects of changes to the select transition probabilities. One pair of approaches focused on desirable and undesirable impacts of individual, incremental changes in the select transition probabilities. The second pair of approaches implemented simultaneous variability via a Monte Carlo simulation to observe how variability in the select transition probabilities would impact the key research parameters. Notable findings were recorded throughout the analysis chapter.

One of the key findings of the case study analysis was that among the select transition probabilities, the initial victimization risk (i.e. transition probability B) and the intervention rate from Trafficking-Exploitation (i.e. transition probability I) were the most impactful probabilities to target for achieving change. This insight offers valuable direction for anti-trafficking and policy-making decision-makers of how to allocate resources, anticipate policy impacts, and better understand the lived experiences of individuals at risk of sex trafficking victimization.

*Table 40: Case Study Base Case Results for Expected Time, Maximum Probability, and n-Step Transition Probabilities*

| Expected Time | |
|---|---|
| State 1 | 60.7332 |
| State 2 | .8555 |
| State 3 | 208.2218 |
| State 4 | 1.4461 |
| State 5 | 150.1896 |
| Life Expectancy | 421.4461 |

| Maximum n-Step Probability for State 3, State 5 | |
|---|---|
| Max Prob of being in State 3 | 0.4367 |
| When max prob of being in State 3 (month) | 94 |
| Max Prob of being in State 5 | 0.2364 |
| When max prob of being in State 5 (month) | 222 |

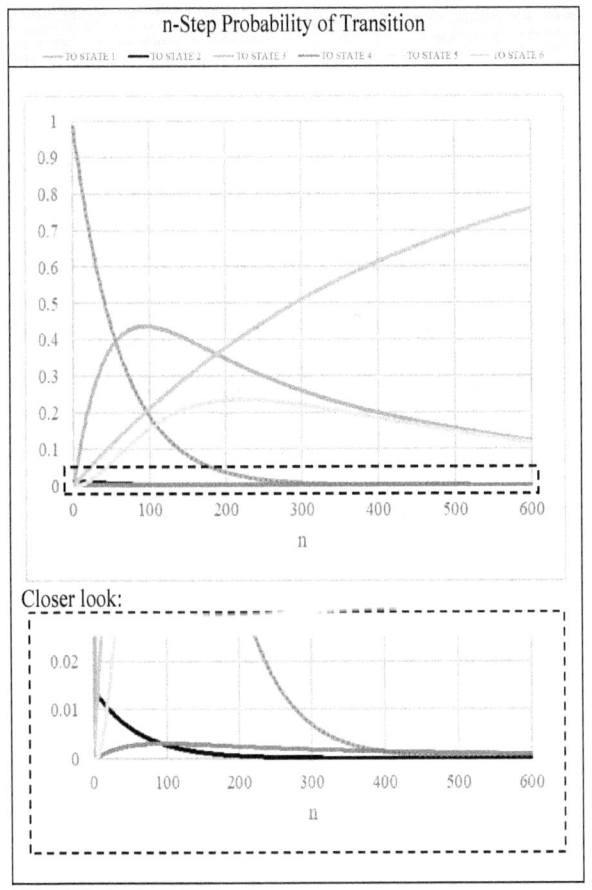

182

## 5.3 Conclusions for Objective 3

Developing and exercising the model are concluded so far. The third, integrated element of research was to make the output of this research accessible for the communities who may benefit from this work. The developed Microsoft Excel® Workbook tool enables the interested analyst or researcher to efficiently process calculations. Microsoft Excel® has strong computational power, more than sufficient for the calculations of this research work, as well as being abundantly accessible as a low-cost software package.

For the more general audience, an open-source DSS website has been developed as part of this research work. Visit http://siddharthc30.pythonanywhere.com/ to access. The website offers a general review of content necessary to use the site, as well as an input area to generate various output calculations.

The combination of a Microsoft Excel® tool and website tool enables assessment within the scope of this research's work, as well as lays the foundation for future work. These tools, along with all modeling and analysis approaches, support continued development towards practical solutions to better equip those battling the social dilemma of sex trafficking victimization.

## 5.4 Conclusions for Anti-Trafficking & Policy-Making Communities

The significant deliverable of this research to the anti-trafficking and policy-making communities is a seven-state, fully interconnected model of the lifetime experience of sex trafficking victimization. This model is the foundation for this research's investigation into application as a DTMC and offers the potential to serve various other research interests in the future. To summarize the results from the case study analysis, resources should be allocated to intervening in the trafficking-exploitation cycle (i.e. Protection from 4P Paradigm), as well as reducing the likelihood of initial recruitment (i.e. Prevention from 4P Paradigm) to have the most notable impact on Expected Time in Each State, Probability of Transition in n-Steps, and Maximum Likelihood of Being in States 3 and 5. Tools have been created as a part of this work to support accessibility and ease of analysis for various community members involved with the social dilemma of sex trafficking victimization.

### 5.5 Future Work

Many opportunities have been identified throughout this work for future research. In this section, the most important and notable opportunities are summarized.

- Policy: Significant value would be gained from policy expert interaction with, and continued development of, the model. An intriguing observation are the parallels between the well-known 'Nordic' model for policy and the results of this research. While this research found that the intervention rate and the initial victimization risk were of highest impact on the experiences within the lifetime of sex trafficking victimization, the 'Nordic' model emphasizes the importance of both increasing intervention success and reducing demand. The logical connection can be observed of tying demand together with initial risk of victimization. Therefore, there appears to be a tremendous opportunity to execute comparative analysis among the finding of this research and the 'Nordic' model.
- Data: The emphasis of this work has not been to draw conclusions from a specific dataset. Instead, it has been to define the foundation and regimen for analyzing datasets of experts in their respective communities. Whether data is defined to analyze an individual, population subset, or an entire population, the approach of analysis is a standard process to follow. Future work would be advisable in the space of defining high-quality datasets for analysis to draw conclusions about the entities whom the dataset represents.

- Assumptions: Various assumptions were defined to complete this analysis. Relaxing or varying these assumptions poses future research to gather new, additional observations beyond the insights gained in this work. A strong assumption made was that the transition probabilities do not change during an individual's lifetime (i.e. a requirement of the DTMC structure). The scarcity of data makes this necessary at this time, but a valuable future work would be to define a dataset that reflects the evolution of transition probabilities according to an individual's age or attributes at the time.

- Parameters: Foundational parameters for assessment were reviewed in this research. There may be more or different parameters of interest to context experts in the anti-trafficking and policy-making communities. Therefore, a readily available extension of this work would be to define and assess additional parameters per the needs of the communities positioned to benefit from their assessment.

- Non-Linear Results: Many instances of output in this work were noted to have non-linear characteristics. Evaluating the distributions that result, especially as they relate to the input parameters, would be a valuable analytical contribution to modeling.

- Tools: The DSS needs to be helpful to the user. A review of the two tools effectiveness to support the user would guide future DSS development and improvement efforts.

- Resources: A very detail review of risks of transition within the model is merited. For example, the types and effectiveness of different types of interventions should be considered. Inspired by this consideration, a question to consider would be if there is any difference in the likelihood and success of an intervention by a law enforcement officer as compared to a social worker? Intervention events have a likelihood of happening, but they also have a likelihood of success tied to the type of intervention exercised.

- Other Uses: There are various opportunities to use the model in ways other than those of this discussion.

    For example, the model could be evaluated for an individual/group at an existing age (i.e. evaluating a portion of a lifetime, not an entire lifetime). This negates the assumption of being born into General Population and could represent instances of starting at a specified age in a different initial state. This can be an approach to relax the assumption of static transition probabilities during a whole lifetime by focusing analysis for only the span of time that the transition probabilities are representative.

    Another example, and as a form of reverse engineering, the model could be used to verify or heuristically identify transition probabilities of concern, based on known output information.

    This work established an original research approach to support anti-trafficking and policy-making communities. As a result of this research, there are many opportunities identified to develop the work further in future efforts. Future work is not limited to operations research audiences and would benefit greatly from multi-discipline involvement (i.e. Partnership from the 4P Paradigm). With the contributions of this and future research, the social dilemma of sex trafficking victimization is better understood.

www.ingramcontent.com/pod-product-compliance
Lightning Source LLC
LaVergne TN
LVHW021236080526
838199LV00088B/4534